On Directing

Other Books by Harold Clurman

THE FERVENT YEARS

LIES LIKE TRUTH

THE NAKED IMAGE

Harold Clurman

On Directing

COLLIER BOOKS
Macmillan Publishing Company
NEW YORK
COLLIER MACMILLAN PUBLISHERS
LONDON

Macmillan Publishing Company
866 Third Avenue, New York, N.Y. 10022
Collier Macmillan Canada, Inc.

Library of Congress Catalog Card Number: 72-77648

First Collier Books Edition 1974

20   19   18   17

ISBN 0-02-013350-2

Macmillan books are available at special discounts for bulk purchases for sales promotions, premiums, fund-raising, or educational use. For details, contact:

> Special Sales Director
> Macmillan Publishing Company
> 866 Third Avenue
> New York, New York 10022

Printed in the United States of America

To Robert Whitehead

"In the theatre, the work of the author does not exist any longer."

—LUIGI PIRANDELLO

"The theatre is a body politic and the art of it a single art, though the contributors to each display of it must be many."

—HARLEY GRANVILLE-BARKER

"Artists build theories on what they would like to do, but do what they can."

—ANDRÉ MALRAUX

Contents

PART III

PART IV

Introduction

THERE ARE several reasons for the presumptuous title of this book. I do not call it "The Art of Directing" because, to begin with, such a title might be taken to mean that there is only one art of directing, one method, one correct way.

The slightest experience in the theatre teaches us that this is not so. Many English and several American directors, for example, require actors to commit their lines to memory before rehearsals have begun. To other directors such a practice is sinful! Many directors see little value in having the cast sit together for more than one or two sessions reading the play. They wish to have the cast on its feet—in movement—from the very first day of rehearsal. So distinguished a director as the late Jean Vilar, for many years the head of the state-subsidized Théâtre National Populaire of France, writes that the cast should spend one-third of the rehearsal time "script in hand with buttocks on the chair." This particular injunction may be ascribed to the fact that, in general, the French theatrical tradition places so much emphasis on the written and spoken word.

Every director makes his own "law," depending not only on his own temperament or artistic inclination, but on the circumstances of production. Since this is so, I cannot in good conscience write a "how to" book. This book is not intended to teach anyone how to direct a play. Though there are several manuals of stage direction that are said to have proved useful to students, I doubt that any director of distinction has learned his job through such reading. And very few people have learned to direct by constantly reading and seeing plays. (Peter Brook asserts that this was his chief source of instruction.)

Most directors acquire their technique by having first worked in the theatre as actor, stage manager, scene designer, producer or playwright. The great Russian director Vakhtangov, according to his pupil Nikolai Gorchakov, "believed that directors should be trained at a theatre, learning as they went along. He affirmed that a director-to-be should accumulate experience at every rehearsal and work out his own laws of directing."

What I propose is to set down my thoughts on the theatre in general as they have formed themselves through my own work as a director. This, then, is the statement of a person who has occupied a central position in the *making* of theatre. It is addressed not simply to the prospective director, the student or the already practicing theatre worker with that profession in mind, but perhaps even more to enthusiastic playgoers, to the important audience whose interest in the theatre is something more than casual.

I shall be dogmatic only to the extent of my own convictions; and not even all of these, I trust, are altogether and permanently established with me. James Gelb, a stage manager who has often worked with me, tells a story about how he came to choose the theatre as a career. He had wandered into an open discussion of stage problems in which a large number of professionals were engaged. One person after another rose to hold forth and each one prefaced his remarks with the phrase "In my opinion—." "Ah," Gelb thought, "if this business is only a matter of opinion, it's just the thing for me!"

Still, I do not wish my readers to suppose that the open-mindedness or subjectivity of my approach to the matters to be dealt with means that I take them to be mere matters of opinion. There is such a thing as knowledge. Ignorance of craft—not at all uncommon in the profession—is what I hope this book will in some measure serve to reduce. If there are principles, or, at any rate, guidelines, it behooves us for the better conduct, proficiency and enjoyment of the work to seek them out and to enunciate them as clearly as possible. Common sense, which entails a grain of humorous skepticism, should not be excluded from the quest.

The direction this book deals with assumes the existence of a written text, a drama, what most stage folk call a "script." For the past ten years or more, however, productions have come into being in which, to begin with, little or no script existed. Plays are based on a theme or a rough scenario on which the actors, guided by a director, improvise movement, gesture and visual and auditory effects together with occasional spoken lines. The verbal text is shaped in its final form by the director in frequent collaboration with the author of the scenario. Speech, the use of words (*literature*), is employed as a prop to the overall theatrical concept and structure, the enacted play.

This tendency, much in vogue today, is often dubbed "new theatre." Actually, it marks a return to the theatre's origins. Words did not constitute the core of the rituals and tribal celebrations of primitive communities. Even in the classic Japanese theatre the dramatist or "playwright" was considered a minor figure. The acting or performance was the crucial factor.

Theatre precedes drama. This historical fact has immense

aesthetic impòrtance. But in our traditional modern theatre we reverse the process: we convert or "translate" drama into theatre. This creates a confusion from which theatre criticism and theatre practice have both suffered. To quote Ellen Terry, "The Drama is the child of the theatre. It goes to my heart that the child should be brought up to despise its parent." Subsequent chapters (especially the one on "The Audience") may help resolve the apparent conflict.

There are two reasons for bringing this matter up here. Since this book deals largely with my own experience and beliefs, stage direction is discussed in a manner more or less typical of the contemporary theatre. I do not preclude the possibility of a book on a technique of direction for the "new theatre"—some have already been attempted—but that is not the objective of this one.

I do not, however, mean that what I have to say here applies to only one type of production. New principles of direction are rare; they are usually only variations on the old. Though Peter Brook, for example, has learned much from the exponents of the "new theatre," his productions of *King Lear* and *A Midsummer Night's Dream* follow the "rules of the game" observed by directors for at least the past hundred years. What is new in the Brook productions (Grotowski's may be another matter) is the idiom of action, the unusually free approach to texts which were formerly interpreted in an entirely different vein. The difference is mainly one of feeling, content, style. But these are different with every director of stature: each has his own artistic bent.

Part I

CHAPTER 1

"The Director's Theatre"

IT HAS BEEN a commonplace (I first heard the formulation some years ago from Peter Ustinov) that while the French is a playwright's theatre, the English an actor's theatre, the American is a director's theatre.

This contains as much truth as most such dicta do. Considered aesthetically, it is a total falsehood. The theatre cannot live through any single organ of its being. The theatre as an art is indivisible. The finest text is often seriously damaged or destroyed by an inadequate cast or improper direction, occasionally by inept physical (scenic) treatment or even by the wrong playhouse.

Excellent acting has been known to compensate, that is, to lend value and meaning to wretched literary material. But the ablest direction will sometimes fail with the best of actors when the dramatist's contribution is basically empty or dull.

On the other hand, we have all seen brilliant performances —viewed as independent factors—rob meritorious dramas of their significance *as theatre*.

Anouilh's *The Waltz of the Toreadors*—one of his most scintillating plays—failed in Paris because, as Anouilh once admitted, he chose to direct it himself. With better casts and two different directors the play was successful in both London and New York.

Before proceeding any further a decisive distinction, crucial to my "argument," must be made. There is a certain ambiguity in theatrical terminology which ultimately leads to critical confusion. We speak of "the play," by which we mean the written text (or script). The play signifies *drama*, a form of literature. On stage it becomes a production. The play does not exist in the theatre as a written text; it has been absorbed in the process of production. Drama is "translated" or transformed into the person of the actor—"the body of the art of the theatre," as Stark Young put it. But the actor does not exist in isolation on the stage. His physical being—appearance, voice, movement, manner of address—is seen in a specific environment. Architectural and scenic elements mediate through color, illumination, costume, music, etc. All these materially alter or enhance the quality of the original script. This new phenomenon born from the fact of production is the Play.

That is what Pirandello meant when he said, "In the theatre the work of the author does not exist any longer," and what Stark Young with less precision suggested when he wrote, "Drama is not literature but literature in terms of the theatre." Granville-Barker put it another way. "The playwright," he said, "is essentially a collaborator, even though he be the creative beginning of the collaboration."

All these apothegms need further explanation and qualification, to which we shall repeatedly return. To begin with, I shall simply assert that the theatre is not an art of separate elements arithmetically cumulative but an art which might be seen to form a single organism. One or several members of this organism may make the whole function, that is, come to life. To make an analogy from another art we might say that while a painting may be discussed in terms of color, drawing and composition, it is a *picture* that we look at. The "heart" of the theatre is not situated in one of its organs, though certain of these may nourish and quicken the others.

The director is important certainly, but he is not all-important. Though without the actor the theatre is almost inconceivable, not even he contains the art. This may be said also of the playwright himself. No part is the whole!

Certain actors have infused life into texts held to be faulty or threadbare. Shaw, in an essay which is one of the masterpieces of theatre criticism, speaks of Duse's artistic superiority to Sudermann, the author of "Magda" (*Heimat*). *La Dame aux Camélias* may be said to have endured by virtue of extraordinary embodiments of the title role. But perhaps there is more to *La Dame* than we commonly suppose. The great Russian director Meyerhold thought so.

It is also true that gifted directors with the collaboration of responsive casts have occasionally made lively theatre out of feeble scripts. Some texts, on the other hand, are themselves so vital that they have sustained our interest in rather indifferent performances. We can all remember the painful occasions when Shakespeare on the stage has not only been rendered dull but nearly unintelligible through productions in which the flaw was not merely a matter of muffled, incorrect or inaudible speech.

The question of the director's importance is not as simple as it might appear because, to begin with, due to the theatre's nature, it is not the director alone who gives the play its direction. This is something which the neophyte director, for his own efficiency and well-being, should constantly bear in mind. The director has an independent function but, like everyone in the theatre, he must depend on his collaborators.

The direction of a play is to a certain extent implicit in its script. The playwright as playwright is in part a director. If he is truly a man of the theatre (some playwrights only suffer the theatre but do not feel they belong to it) the playwright "sees" the play on the stage as he writes. His dialogue as well as his notations of stage behavior suggest movement and part of the total physical life that the script is to acquire when it is produced.

If this thought should depress a would-be director he may rejoice in the correlated axiom that the director, as we shall discover, contributes in more ways than one to the making of the play.

In passing we may recall Gordon Craig's injunction to the dramatist that he refrain from setting down any remarks at all about the direction or performance of his text. But Craig always went too far, in the manner of the poet he was, to emphasize a new and extremely valuable way of thinking about the theatre.

Actors also contribute to and partially shape direction. I am not referring to the actor's possible insistence on having his own way in interpreting a role—and hence the play. This is a hazard that we shall discuss in a later chapter. The actor willy-nilly contributes to the direction of a play through his natural temperament, intuition, imagination and skill. Indeed, the good director will stimulate the actor to make such a contribution. Too great a dependence on the director is unhealthy for both actor and play.

I saw an interesting production of Tennessee Williams' *The Glass Menagerie* in Paris in which the very meaning of the play was considerably altered because the actress playing Amanda had very little of the substance of Laurette Taylor's genius. This may have been due to miscasting (a directorial blemish) or possibly to a misinterpretation or even to the director's having a different interpretation from the one I supposed was justified.

This is a subtle matter, involving both critical judgment and, if you will, theatre aesthetics. It must be broached at another point. Let us remind ourselves at this juncture that one of the agonies and wonders of the theatre is that the play is always a *new* thing with each production, indeed with almost every performance. This thought so distressed Craig that he went so far as to maintain with his usual bent toward paradox that acting was no art at all. Still, at another time he devoted a whole volume to extolling the art of Henry Irving!

Significant bits of byplay ("business" in stage parlance) are often introduced by actors through spontaneous invention. Only an obtuse director refuses to take advantage of such enrichment of the play's fabric. Still, he has the right and duty to veto what he considers inappropriate or misleading. The director may therefore be forgiven when he takes credit for some of the actors' improvisations and accepts compliments for them!

The play's scenic arrangement (the floor plan, architectural form, visual style, etc.), for which the director is responsible even when he has had little to do with their actual design, is another contribution to the shaping of a play's meaning. Boris Aronson's sets added special lustre to such musicals as *Cabaret, Company* and *Follies,* but by his own admission his setting of Odets' *Paradise Lost* (which I directed) detracted from what he had felt about the play when he saw it acted on the bare stage. But in such cases, as we have already implied, the director rather than the designer must be held to account.

Even the audience may affect the direction of a play. An extreme instance of this was *Arsenic and Old Lace,* which legend has it was directed as a thriller but which, because of the opening-night audience's reaction, was transformed into an uproariously approved farce. It was played as such from that moment to the end of its long run.

In what sense then can the term "the director's theatre" be justified? The director, as we think of him today, is a recent phenomenon in theatre history. In my early days as a playgoer —in the "teens"—hardly any director except David Belasco enjoyed program credit. This does not mean that the play had not been directed in one fashion or another.

The director has to some degree always been present. The

playwright sometimes served in that capacity. Aeschylus is said to have directed his plays, as we know Molière did his. The *Choregus* (leader of the Chorus) in the Greek theatre was in effect a director. In other instances, the director was the producer, the leading actor or the actor manager. Even if it is conceivable for a theatrical performance to be produced without anyone officially in charge, it is clear that someone, through force of nerve, prestige, talent or power, will give the performance some sort of coherence.

The director as we know him today is a product of the nineteenth-century theatre. For convenience' sake (I will not dispute the accuracy of this statement with scholar or historian), let us say that modern direction began in 1866 with the Duke of Saxe-Meiningen, who was chiefly a painter and a stage designer. The actual staging of his productions was done by Ludwig Kronek but the Duke himself was the founder and moving force of the Meiningen Players. It is also worth noting that Otto Brahm, the creator in 1889 of the famous German Free Theatre who introduced Gerhardt Hauptmann and other of the new realists to the playgoing public, was first a critic and never actually staged his productions. But like the Duke of Meiningen, Brahm set the tone and the style, and placed the stamp of his personality on his company.

What Meiningen did was to establish the idea of *ensemble* playing, the coordination of the various components of an acting company so that a unified impression might be created —the total performance summing up to a Play. This coordination included not only the main actors, but bit players and the so-called extras or supernumeraries as well. Meiningen, moreover, was much concerned with historical authenticity in costuming, furnishings and all those objects used on the stage which come under the heading of "props" (or "properties"). Beyond their historicity he wished them to be tasteful and set in a theatrically helpful arrangement.

The Meiningen Players influenced not only Stanislavsky, the famous Russian director (in discussing them the famous Russian director emphasizes Kronek rather than the Duke), but also André Antoine, who *circa* 1887 introduced naturalism to French theatregoers. Henry Irving, too, fell under the Meiningen spell.

What crystallized the concept of stage direction as we understand it today may be gathered from the writings, beginning in 1905, of Gordon Craig. The mainspring of the Craig doctrine is his insistence on unity. A Play, Craig insisted, is not a text on which actors, setting, music, etc., are superimposed, but a single body of which all the separate elements are parts. This precept, from which I derive my own "credo," has manifold consequences.

In the early nineteenth century in England—to go no further back and to confine ourselves to theatre of our own language—the texts of plays were hardly respected and perhaps as a result were barely respectable. What was then called Shakespeare on the stage was nothing Shakespeare would have acknowledged or even recognized. Shakespeare and most other dramatists were treated as mere scenarists. Their characters and plots were employed as vehicles for the exhibition of actors' talents.

Costumes and props were not only a matter of the actor's (or theatre lessee's) choice, but were generally what the theatre had in stock and were rarely relevant to a particular period or a definite style. "Scenery" was conventionalized without regard to period, place, mood or specific use. The companies were composed of stars—some of them magnificent actors—supported by routine players who often were accorded no more than two or three rehearsals with the guest star. The star dictated stage positions (he himself usually occupied stage center), movement and business, to which the other actors had to accommodate themselves. That was the "staging." People came to see the great man do his stuff.

There could be very little differentiation in lighting except between the bright and the dark. Means of illumination were primitive and not readily controllable. Interpretation was implicit chiefly in the star's performance.

With the renewal of interest in the literary or artistic aspects of a play and the increased technical methods for the projection of a play's significance on the stage a leader became a necessity. If all the elements of production were to be made into one theatre work—a true Play—then there had to be someone to conduct them to that end. Hence the emergence of the contemporary stage director.

In America today the author is contractually the pivot of the organized production. His consent must be obtained as to choice of cast, director and general interpretation. But, to quote Boris Aronson, "The theatre is a collective art in which the strongest man rules."

The playwright very rarely exercises his legal right either because he is timid or more frequently because he is intelligent enough to realize his incapacity. Beyond his own writing he is seldom a practiced theatre craftsman. He is usually uncertain as to the means which most suitably serve to embody his text. There are playwrights who are effective directors of their own and sometimes other people's scripts, but the talent for writing and the talent for directing are infrequently to be found in the same person. So at this point we need not dwell on the playwright, who only partially understands the significance of what he has written or appreciates the theatrical potentialities of his script.

The actor is (hopefully) a creator. Samuel Johnson said that the actor only *recites:* but no living playwright is happy if his actors do no more than that. As a creator the actor has an artistic weight of his own—not to speak of the other kinds of influence he may unadvisedly exert. How the actor is to be dealt with so that he not only will be "effective" for himself and his admirers but also for the entire "team" responsible for the play is one of the chief problems of direction.

We are now better prepared to understand why the term "the director's theatre" has come into use. That fine American actor Louis Calhern once declared, "The reason why the director has become so powerful is that there are no more great actors." If we pursue this line of argument we might conclude that the reason why the director up until very recently has been less important in England than in America is that there are still so many splendid actors or, at any rate, stars there. It is a fact that on the whole English actors of note prefer directors who "interfere" as little as possible, though there has been a change in this regard in the past twenty-five years.

Such actors wish the director to be utterly precise in "blocking" (or staging) a play—that is, in assigning the placement of actors on the boards and indicating crosses from one position to another—but they are wary about being *directed*—that is, helped in the creation of their parts. The assumption is that there must be a conflict between director and actor or that where the actor is a truly creative person (and what star thinks of himself as anything less?) he needs little or no "outside" assistance.

The assumption is mistaken. It is based on the practice of the two artistically least organized theatres of the Western world: the English and the American. Even the value of ensemble playing was regarded with skepticism by the playwright-critic St. John Ervine on the grounds that actors of eminent stature through personal artistic bias must of necessity rebel against the "totalitarianism" of the ensemble idea. Even the Meiningen Players, where the director, Kronek, according to Stanislavsky, was very much the dictator, numbered among their members such a fine artist as Albert Basserman who throughout his career worked with directors of first-rate calibre: Otto Brahm and Max Reinhardt.

Reinhardt's various companies were always composed of magnificent actors. The original Moscow Art Theatre, the prime example in the early twentieth century of the ensemble ideal, boasted a company in which at least six members possessed star radiance. Though contrary evidence may be adduced from the examples of such productions as Peter Brook's *Marat/Sade* or Tyrone Guthrie's *The House of Atreus* (cast with good companies without "star names"), I should like to make it axiomatic that the finer an acting company is, the greater the need for a masterly director. This may ensure that what is presented are plays rather than exhibitions.

Meyerhold's theatre in the Soviet Union (till his career was stamped out by state interdiction and the ukase on "socialist realism") and Brecht's Berliner Ensemble—perhaps, too, Joan Littlewood's first company at Stratford East in London—might be dubbed "director's theatres." These theatres, and others like them (Grotowski's Laboratory Theatre, for example), are theatres in which the director is a true leader, that is, an educator, a person with a special aesthetic and technique who trains his company accordingly. Still, even Meyerhold leaned heavily on two or three brilliant actors, just as Brecht's Berliner Ensemble profited greatly by the presence of Weigel, Schall and Ernst Busch.

Toward the end of his career Max Reinhardt was inclined to believe that our industrial age of mass production was not conducive to the formation of outstanding actors. (He might perhaps have cited our American theatre as an example.)

There is something in this. The disarray of the American theatre economy at present makes the development of major actors extremely difficult. There is not sufficiently sustained employment. Of gifted young people there are enough to establish as many permanent troupes as there are anywhere else. But even the so-called successful actor in America is usually confined to a limited range of parts. He seeks a fat role in a hit show, lest he diminish his market value. He fears for his status as a desirable performer. A good many very able actors in America today are more often active in scene classes (or "studios") than on the stage. They supplement these "workouts" with appearances in summer stock and guest performances in regional theatres, films and on television. The young actor perforce remains an amateur.

One of the worst effects of this situation is the actor's loss of confidence in his profession and in himself. Psychologically the American actor under fifty is nearly always a "beginner." By the time he is fifty he is either out of the theatre or a warped person.

Who can encourage, inspire, renew the faith of the actor in

this condition? Why, the new medicine man, the well-known, the much-touted director! A superstition surrounds this character. (Superstition, even if only in the form of publicity, is always a sign of a sick state of affairs. Where nothing is secure, magic must work its wonders.) The director, the actor trusts and prays, will sustain him, make him a star. The director as fetish is a symptom; "the director's theatre" is very often little better than a commercial tag.

Capable direction is no doubt a vital factor in the making of a sound production. There is certainly a distinction to be made between the abilities of one director and those of another. But if we list the plays which have been highly successful on Broadway we may well arrive at the conclusion that any number of efficient directors might have returned box-office hits from their scripts. The quality of each production would have been different with each director, but it is rarely the quality of direction which is perceived by the audience, whose spokesman is the run-of-the-mill critic, but rather the degree of monetary success the production may achieve. No matter: when a director has turned out two or three hits, supernatural powers are attributed to him; he is regarded as a "genius," the cause of everyone's prosperity and joy.

Signs of this peculiar syndrome may be observed at early rehearsals of a new Broadway show. Except where a star actor is involved (in which case he has been consulted as to the desirability of a particular director or is aware of the director's prestige) many actors—especially the younger ones—sit in a state of quasi-cataleptic expectancy. They are waiting to be electrified, exalted, transfigured. They seem to have converted themselves into so many vessels into which they hope the director will pour the elixir of his greatness.

At one time I might have agreed with Granville-Barker who said, "The art of the theatre is the art of acting or it is nothing." But this is only a partial truth, though it is always worth keeping in mind. Later I arrived at what I believed was a happy formulation: "The director is the author of the stage play," a generalization of which I am now somewhat skeptical. It is deceptive; a good measure of conceit is concealed in it. It may lead to disappointment and trouble for all concerned. The art of the theatre is contained in the entity of production in which the director may play a crucial role.

Direction is a job, a craft, a profession, and at best, an art. The director must be an organizer, a teacher, a politician, a psychic detective, a lay analyst, a technician, a creative being. Ideally, he should know literature (drama), acting, the psychology of the actor, the visual arts, music, history, and above all, he must understand people. He must inspire confidence. All of which means he must be a "great lover."

CHAPTER 2

Choosing the Script

If we think of a director in terms of Broadway only, there is little to say about the choice of a script. The director chooses what he can find. In "dry" seasons when, as is quite common at present, there is a dearth of new script material, a director may feel as Joshua Logan did when he said, "If I discover a script I can finish reading, I'll do it."

Joshua Logan is an eminently successful director. Why should he have any difficulty choosing a script? The answer is that with the latter-day shrinkage of production (a condition which dates back to the depression of the thirties) and the consequent lack of theatrically competent writing the competition for scripts has become hectic.

There are perhaps no more than a half-dozen "hot" directors on Broadway; every producer and playwright has his own favorite. If Tennessee Williams, Arthur Miller, Edward Albee or Neil Simon (or their agents) prefer one particular director, the others will not even be offered the opportunity to read the new play. The pattern remains the same with inexperienced producers and playwrights: they habitually turn to the "surefire," the "hit directors."

Every season brings forth one or two "geniuses" among directors. This means that when a young director not yet tagged as one of the "top" men is fortunate enough to have staged a "smash," he will immediately be showered with offers. One might say that this should be regarded as altogether normal. True—if producers and playwrights judged the newly acclaimed director solely on his merits as a director. But very few producers or playwrights are capable of judging a director's intrinsic abilities. The box office is their barometer. That is why so often after his initial success the director's subsequent failure usually meets with sharp disfavor as ignorant as the praise previously accorded him. This is the law of the jungle—I mean the Broadway theatre.

The European director is not in the same case. (Nor possibly is the director of a regional theatre in the United States.) When an English director finds himself without a new script he will choose to direct a play by Shakespeare or Ibsen or Shaw or Congreve. Tyrone Guthrie directed very few new plays—and most of them were in America. A German director is not only in a position to choose among the classics or among plays of the contemporary continental and American output, but very often he will seek to do a play produced in one of the theatres in Berlin, or Munich, or Vienna, or in another of the fine theatres in such cities as Cologne, Hamburg, Frankfurt, *et al.* His production will be entirely his own, not a replica of the original one. This is true in the Soviet Union and other of the East European countries as well. When I visited Moscow in 1934 I saw two utterly dissimilar productions of Gorky's *Yegor Bulitchev* during the same week—one at the Moscow Art and the other at the Vakhtangov Theatre.

The American director is limited in his choice of scripts

not only by the economic straits in which the Broadway theatre is bound, but also by our lack of repertory companies
(which rarely undertake to produce new scripts) and by the
commercial inadvisability of reviving old plays. Off-Broadway has profited by this situation: such plays as Williams'
Summer and Smoke and O'Neill's *The Iceman Cometh* and
Long Day's Journey into Night have had their life renewed
and been "redeemed" off-Broadway.*

Because of the high cost of production (Odets' *Awake and
Sing* in 1935 cost $6,000; it would cost $100,000 today) and
the restricted audiences who can afford the resultant high
price of tickets, Broadway managers must think of the script's
chances of success. This has always been a dominant factor in
the selection of scripts—even though no one has ever been
able to determine exactly what will be "commercial"! One of
my own box-office hits was Carson McCullers' *The Member
of the Wedding*, so commercially dubious that only one theatre owner would consent to house it.

Directors have artistic or temperamental dispositions. To
the degree that they have some freedom of choice they exercise it according to their taste and what they deem to be their
specific talent: what they not only like but feel they can do
best. I myself have hesitated to do certain plays of which I
approved critically but which I judged might be more satisfactorily treated by other directors.

This was perhaps a mistake. The director often extends his
capacities by undertaking assignments which he may at first
consider outside his "line." Typecasting of directors is almost as habitual with producers as it is of actors.

When my direction of *Awake and Sing* met with approval a
great many scripts about depressed middle-class families were
sent to me. When I was complimented for my direction of

---

* The shortage of new plays has brought about a change: the successful
revivals of *You Can't Take It with You*, *The Show-Off*, *The Front Page*, and
Harvey are beginning to turn producers' thoughts to the prospect of prosperity in such ventures.

Odets' *Golden· Boy* I found myself inundated with scripts about toughs of the race track, jazz bands and kindred rackets. (I had never seen a prizefight before the production of *Golden Boy.*) When I did *The Member of the Wedding* I was hailed as a specialist in plays about children! But it is not only the producer or the playwright who may hold a narrow view of a director's gifts but the director himself.

Ask a director what sort of script he would like to stage and he will probably answer, "A good one"—which is no answer at all. When the question was put to me years ago I usually replied, "I prefer a well-written script with a theme of contemporary relevance couched in theatrically poetic terms." To be somewhat more specific about "contemporary relevance" I went on to say that I sought a "realistic" core in every play, a reflection of some immediate issue. I was not referring to *topicality* nor did I care for scripts which might be classified as reportage or stage journalism. By "theatrically poetic" I meant the scripts had to "sing" their themes, to be written in eloquent language, to be possessed of vivid characterization, color, a degree of glamor and intensity.

I was also and still am attracted by scripts which offer "juicy" parts for actors, parts which demand flair and virtuosity. I had decided that I was, among other things, an "actor's director."

Since then I have done plays of a rather different nature than those of the thirties and forties: Giraudoux's *Tiger at the Gates,* Anouilh's *The Waltz of the Toreadors,* O'Neill's *Desire Under the Elms* and *A Touch of the Poet,* Shaw's *Heartbreak House,* Chekhov's *Uncle Vanya,* all of which may be thought of as having broadened the scope and redefined the earlier canon.

None of these examples nor any personal declaration of intention, however, is truly pertinent to the question we have to deal with here. It would still not be to the point if I extended my list to indicate the scripts I would have liked to have done but was not asked to do. What the question, broadly speaking, comes to is this: Is there any criterion, apart from excellence and personal inclination, that may serve to guide a director in his choice of scripts?

A question the director may put to himself is this: To what audience do I hope the projected play will appeal? I am not alluding to "audience appeal" in general, for this is a term which, when employed without regard to specific circumstances, begs the question. Strindberg's *The Ghost Sonata* and *Dream Play** are almost everywhere deemed important as dramatic literature. They have audience appeal in Sweden and in most mid-European theatres. Short of amazing productions I would judge that they would have very little appeal on Broadway. But an excellent production off-Broadway, or in a "club" theatre or at a university theatre of "advanced" tastes might lend these scripts audience appeal.

It was perhaps ill-advised to do Sartre's *No Exit* or Beckett's *Waiting for Godot* on Broadway. But I do not mean that such plays should never be done there: there must always be producers and directors who will engage in enterprises of artistic merit deemed commercially foolhardy. (Producer Robert Whitehead persuaded me to risk *The Member of the Wedding* on Broadway.)

Before 1930 the leading producers presented four plays a season, of which at least two, they surmised, would fail (at no great financial loss), but at present even such a "popular" piece as the Brecht-Weill *Threepenny Opera* would not, I believe, prosper on Broadway any more than it did when it was first presented there in 1933.

If what I am suggesting here seems crassly commercial it is worth noting that Goethe, as theatre director at Weimar, said that he would not produce a play no matter how much he admired it if he were certain that it had no chance of pleasing his audience. Of course he, too, may have been wrong since there can be no certainty in these matters.

---

* *Dream Play* was a success at the Comédie Française in 1970, but the Comédie Française is a nationally subsidized repertory theatre.

Audiences differ in different places and under different conditions. It is not being "artistic" to be unconcerned about audience reactions. To discount the nature of one's audience is to be anti-theatre. The audience is the theatre's prime factor and chief "actor." In the deepest sense it is the audience —the community or a particular segment of it—which produces the play.

In former times—in ancient Greece, in the Middle Ages, in seventeenth-century France, in other words, in more or less homogeneous societies—the audience's composition was known; it could be taken for granted. The "artists" were very much part of their audience; artists and audience were, to a large degree, one. In heterogeneous societies such as ours, audiences are bewilderingly varied. It is natural to expect a receptive audience for Jack Gelber's *The Connection* or Barbara Garson's *MacBird!* in small Greenwich Village playhouses but it would surely be quixotic to suppose that the same is true at theatres on West Forty-fifth Street.

Ambitious directors from New York appointed to regional theatres often insist on selecting plays they like simply because they believe them to be good ones. This is praiseworthy; it may also prove disastrous. One must know what one's audience is prepared for, what its disposition is. But on the other hand, recent experiences in Washington, San Francisco and Minneapolis indicate that theatres (often subsidized) in such centers attract audiences far more catholic in their tastes than those who attend the Broadway theatre.

It is certainly possible to educate an audience, but can one imagine something like *Who's Afraid of Virginia Woolf?* being produced on Broadway in 1917? The Theatre Guild itself was amazed—as were all the professional wiseacres—when Molnar's *Liliom* and Andreyev's *He Who Gets Slapped* became hits in the early twenties. But the directors of the Theatre Guild were hardly aware of the change which had come about in the New York audience between 1915 and 1920 even though they were themselves representative of that new audience. Even as late as 1928 they thought they were flying in the face of destiny (that is, the theatregoing public) when they produced O'Neill's *Strange Interlude*—one of their greatest box-office successes.

There is an element of hazard (beyond the monetary) in all theatrical production and it is part of the theatre's challenge that it should exist. It is a serious fault to be overfearful of failure. Many an artist has been crippled by it. Still, a director who neglects to consider certain aspects of a script's prospective life in the theatre doesn't know his business. Historical timing itself may be something to consider. The English were said to resent John van Druten's agreeably innocuous comedy *The Voice of the Turtle*—intrinsically unrelated to any war situation—when it was produced in London shortly after the end of hostilities in 1945. The dalliance of an American army man in New York at the time of the blitz in London did not amuse the West End.

Just as a true Theatre, that is, a permanent producing unit, because it looks toward its ideal public, in time develops its loyally attentive audience, so also it fosters its own playwrights. Clifford Odets emerged from the 1931–41 Group Theatre's acting company to be hailed as the dramatic spokesman of the decade. Hauptmann attached himself at first to Otto Brahm's German Free Theatre. Chekhov was encouraged to write all his plays after *Ivanov* and *The Seagull* flopped for the Moscow Art Theatre. Shakespeare wrote for the company of which he was a member, designing parts for particular actors on its roster.

Some directors—rarely in recent times, though as we know from the example of the *commedia dell'arte* not uncommon in the past—begin with a theme, a skeletal plot or a scenic notion and through improvisation develop scripts with the cooperation of a writer. The results are sometimes strikingly pertinent and lively. Recent examples in the American theatre are the productions of Joseph Chaikin and Jean-Claude van Itallie's *America, Hurrah!* and *The Serpent* for the Open Theatre. Their relevance to the theatre in general has already been mentioned in my introduction.

Years ago when I spoke to the governing board of the
Theatre Guild about the possibility of developing dramatists
for the company which was to become the Group Theatre, I
suggested that we make young writers part of the organization
—even assign them jobs. The response was something like
outrage. "You mean you want dramatists to write with your
actors in mind?!" I pointed out that Edmond Rostand had
written *Cyrano de Bergerac* for Coquelin with a by no means
deplorable outcome. I might have even more pedantically
mentioned that Shakespeare and Molière had written certain
roles with particular actors of their permanent companies in
mind.

This leads to another phase of our topic. I have sometimes
undertaken to stage a script about which, solely as a piece of
writing, I was rather indifferent when I learned that I could
cast a particular actor who I felt would give it special interest,
a new dimension. On the other hand, I have admired certain
scripts which I hesitated or refused to direct because at the
moment I found no actor (or company) available that I believed capable of doing these scripts justice. For, I cannot too
often repeat, a script cannot do all the "work" as a play; it
does not play itself.

This is not merely a personal view. When some years ago I
asked Helene Weigel, then the managing director and leading
actress of the Berliner Ensemble, why it had not produced
Brecht's *Schweik in the Second World War* which had been
done in Paris and many other cities both in Germany and
elsewhere, her reply was, "We haven't the right actor for it."

Perhaps a director of a community or university theatre
need not be so scrupulous or severe. Still, one has to bear in
mind what a particular audience will accept in the way of acting. I have also seen quite respectable companies in community playhouses strain their actors' capacities with results
which were entirely unacceptable and unequivocally detrimental to the comprehension of the dramatist's intention.

CHAPTER 3

Reading the Script

THE DIRECTOR has chosen a script with enthusiasm or a considerable degree of trembling. (His trembling diminishes sensibly if the script is one which is well tried and generally admired.) His work is about to begin. It begins by reading the script—in a new way. For now he is no longer thinking of the script's "possibilities": it has become a task, a reality with which he has to contend.

Bernard Shaw in a little essay, "Rules for Directors," has some excellent things to say. The very first is: "The director, having considered the play and decided to undertake the job of directing it, has no further concern with its literary merits or its doctrine (if any)." An extraordinary statement! The script's literary merits will have played some part in the director's choice. He may have been attracted by its writing. But good writing (fine dialogue) in itself is only one facet of a script's interest. There is also its theme, which must involve the audience and serve as a tie that binds the stage artisans (the director, the actors, the designer *et al.*) together.

The director reads the script. He reads it again and again and again. He need not read it in consecutive daily sessions. In fact, he would do well, if time permits, to set it aside for a while after each reading and check on what he remembers of it. He might even try to forget it. He should let it work on him before he works on it. First impressions—and he must regard the first two or three preliminary readings as first impressions—are often deceiving, that is, conventional. To begin with, even experienced directors may see little more in a script than an intelligent theatregoer would. Like him, the director will be amused, laugh or cry, shudder or thrill. These reactions are not without value; they may even prove important. (Stanislavsky thought them *very* important.) But they do not suffice as guides to the directorial problem, which, I repeat, is to translate the script's words into the language of the stage where men and women of flesh and blood who move in three dimensions among real objects are to replace description. The theatre is a new medium. If the director is not careful he may find to his dismay that the lines which seemed to soar on the page sound flat and dull when actors begin to speak them and the audience is called on to hear and "see" them.

The director will undoubtedly be stimulated by new insights as his acquaintance with the script grows more intimate. He will take note of them in his mind or, better still, on paper. Among my early notes for an (unsuccessful) play by Clifford Odets, *Night Music,* I find such things as "there is a constant sense of *impermanence* and insecurity in the people and in the town. . . . When Steve [the central character] cries out for a 'better world' he means a 'secure' world." Another note further on, without apparent connection with the first: "Steve's toughness is a kind of lovemaking. If he were soft, he feels he might be scoffed. Harsh, he always gets a response!"

Or again: "Everyone carries a little suitcase. The characters seem to have no other possessions except those they carry in their little suitcases." I find isolated quotations from the play's dialogue: clues to character or to mood such as "Steve speaks of 'punching around in the dark.'" Still another note reads "All the characters are romantic dreamers."

Such disparate impressions, the images which form themselves higgledy-piggledy in the director's mind, should not be rejected because they appear disorganized or "impractical." They may at first seem "mystical," too imprecise for definite use. When I read Odets' *Awake and Sing* it made me think (perhaps irrelevantly and certainly inaccurately) of the "chaos" in cubist paintings. (Good cubist paintings are not at all chaotic.) And when I read the same author's *Paradise Lost* (his second play) I imagined seeing lights refracted through a multicolored prism. I was not at all certain what these reactions denoted or how they might serve my purpose. Yet they finally did enter into my calculations and produced definite results.

As the readings progress and a great number of "stray" thoughts accumulate, a general production scheme begins to shape itself in the director's mind. After the director has read the play, let us say, a dozen times, he must put some questions to himself to which he must find specific answers.

Before stating the nature of these questions and the kind of answers they require I should make it clear that my reference to a dozen readings is an arbitrary one. I have already said that these readings may occupy a month or more during which the director may allow time for his mind to turn away from the script. During these hiatuses the script will still be exercising a "secret" effect on him.

Meyerhold once said that with the ordinary script he had to deal with—a new Soviet piece, for example—he found six to eight weeks a sufficient time to prepare and rehearse the production. But, he added, he had been thinking about certain plays such as Gogol's *The Inspector General* for years, during which he set down notes, drew sketches, read commentaries and dreamed about the project. The same, he said, was true of his plan to direct *Othello*. (He never did.) The project, he remarked, occupied his thoughts for even a longer time than the Gogol play—for one does not improvise Shakespeare! Not, at any rate, in "respectful" interpretations.

My notes—production ideas, thoughts on the visual aspects of the play, remarks about the characterization of the various roles—are all put down in writing, helter-skelter to begin with, in ever more formal order as rehearsal time approaches. There is nothing obligatory about the *writing* of notes: it is a matter of personal preference. I am not sure I know what I really think until I am able to articulate my intuitions and reflections in this way.

In questioning other directors I have learned that this practice of writing one's general and then one's specific instructions (*to oneself*) is more common than I had supposed. Reinhardt did it brilliantly; Jean Vilar recommended it. Directors developed in the Group Theatre—Elia Kazan, Robert Lewis—also follow this procedure.

Whether or not directors set their thoughts down on paper, the general process I have described goes on in their minds. It is this mental process I would stress rather than the "literary" activity. On the other hand, in *teaching* direction (wherever such a dubious course is hazarded) I suggest that the teachers insist on having the students state in writing all that they propose for themselves and their collaborators— actors, designers, etc.—in the planning of a production. General notions or a nebulous inspiration may delude the student.

Vilar in his essay on direction says, "The work of production should include a written analysis of the play. The director must not despise this thankless job. The drafting of such an analysis compels the director to a clear and exhaustive knowledge of the play."

Such an analysis is more or less what I have been describing. I say "more or less" because in itself the word "analysis" is ambiguous. Analysis may mean no more than a statement of the play's theme, its "message," its language or literary quality. Analysis is "less" than what I have been discussing, for what the director should be thinking about are the *means* whereby theme, message, etc., are to be *embodied.*

The process is a progression from the general to the particular. After careful perusal of the script the director becomes clear about its theme. But the theme of a play, roughly stated, is not what the director seeks in reading. Any intelligent reader will know that Chekhov's *The Cherry Orchard* dramatizes the decline of the gentry in czarist Russia and the rise of the industrial middle class, and that *Hamlet* is about the dangers of indecision—or similar platitudes. Such knowledge is of little use to the director.

Certain dramatists deny the presence of any "theme" at all in their plays. "I do not write plays with themes," a well-known playwright said to me once. "I write about people." The gentleman had a point but was assigning too narrow a definition to the word "theme."

The theme of a play may consist of a mood, an attitude, a general sentiment—the abstract essence of a play's inspiration. Thus I have heard *Twelfth Night* spoken of as "a game, a toying with life." In the purely intellectual construction of the term, not every play has a theme, but in the broader sense of an overall "feeling," which is present even in the purest form of dance or non-representational painting, every play does possess a theme.

What the director should establish for himself is the script's content in *dramatic* terms. He may begin by asking himself what the audience is to feel and enjoy in seeing the play. Still, even this is not sufficiently basic groundwork. To begin active direction a formulation in the simplest terms must be found to state what general action motivates the play, of what fundamental drama or conflict the script's plot and people are the instruments. What behavioral strug-

gle or effort is being represented? It is best, though perhaps
not altogether essential, that the answer should be expressed
as an *active verb:* for drama (and acting) are based on doing,
on action. (Do not tell the actor "You are in love" but "You
love," that is, "You pay attention to" or "You take care of,"
"You help," etc.)

Richard Boleslavsky, my first formal instructor in theatre
(after Jacques Copeau, who influenced rather than taught
me), called the answer to the questions I have just put the
play's *spine*. It is a term Boleslavsky probably inherited from
his work at the Moscow Art Theatre where he was trained.
(The term must have suggested itself because the body's spine
holds the vertebrae in place, and these might be compared to
all the smaller actions and dramatic divisions in the play.) In
An Actor Prepares Stanislavsky calls the "spine" the play's
main or through action which leads to what he calls the
"super-problem"—the dramatist's basic motivation in writing
the play.

Many things are contained in O'Neill's *Desire Under the
Elms*: passion, Oedipal impulses, confessions of unhappiness
and hate, guilt feelings, paternal harshness, filial vindictiveness, retribution. But what holds all these ingredients together, what makes a complete meaning, a single specific
drama of them all, is the play's spine. As director, I determined that the play's spine, or, if you will, its "main action,"
was a struggle for the Farm, abbreviated into the bare "to
possess the Farm."

With this as both starting point and interpretive goal I
was able to make a dramatic whole from the various strands
in the script. The older brothers, learning that they will
never possess the Farm, give up their share of it, abandon it
to their younger brother and go off to seek material satisfaction in California. The young wife seduces her stepson because she has been promised the Farm if she gives birth to a
boy, and her dreams of bearing a child may be more easily realized through the stepson than through the boy's father,

whom she has married for the sake of goods and security. The young man is attracted to his stepmother, but in taking her yields not only to his desire but to an impulse to avenge himself against his father who dominates him. When the acquisitive drive gives way to desire and becomes transformed into love, the conflict is joined on a higher plane. The play ends with the sheriff coming to arrest the guilty couple for murder of their child; his final words—the last lines of the play— are "It's a jim-dandy farm. . . . Wished I owned it!" In short, even the subsidiary characters of the play must in some way be related to its spine.*

Gordon Craig thought *Hamlet* a quest for Truth which he (Hamlet) discovers by means of the Play wherein he will catch the conscience of the King. The quest for Truth ("to seek the Truth") was the spine, the dramatic seed, main action or super-problem of Craig's *Hamlet*. Hamlet seeks for Truth everywhere—among his friends, his beloved, his mother. Everywhere, with the single exception of Horatio, he finds little but lust, deceit, conventionality, corruption, chicanery, frivolity and foolishness. Everyone is blemished by the kingdom's gilded world, the rotten state of Denmark.

If the reader should find himself protesting that this is too narrow or distorted an interpretation of *Hamlet,* the point to be remembered is not that I consider Craig's interpretation correct but that his direction of the play sprang from the dramatic premise—or spine—I have cited. He drew from it all the consequences of his production: its sets and costumes, his instruction to the actors. To cite only one detail: Everyone was wrapped in gold tissue, except Hamlet, who was clothed in black; Ophelia, too, was contaminated by the court atmosphere.

Hamlet has been interpreted in countless ways. (Often it is not interpreted at all, merely staged.) According to Jan Kott, a Polish production some years ago made *Hamlet* a political

---

* Further examples of the use of the spine will be found in my **Production Notes**, pp. 179-266.

play in a world of universal suspicion with everyone spying on one another as in Nazi Germany or in Stalin's Russia. What is in question here is not the "true" interpretation but how the interpretation of any script is arrived at and then fulfilled through the stuff of stage life.

The director chooses the spine of the play, the key or springboard of his interpretation, according to his own lights, not to mention the actors he has at his disposal, the audience he wishes to reach and the hoped-for effect on that audience, for he and his audience in a very critical sense are part of the play. It is no accident that the production of *Hamlet* mentioned by Jan Kott was devised in Poland.

But what of the author? Has he no say in the matter? We shall return to this most pertinent query further on. We must continue now with the next step in the director's preparation for the production as he studies the script. Defining the spine, the function of which is intended to *guide himself* in all his other tasks, is the first artistically inescapable step. Where a director has not determined on a spine for his production, it will tend to be formless. Each scene follows the next without necessarily adding up to a total dramatic "statement."

The second step—intimately correlated with the first—is to find the manner in which the spine is to be articulated. It is conceivable that the spine a director has fixed in his mind and *named* might serve any number of different productions with a similar intention. Thus to say that the spine of *Desire Under the Elms* may be summed up as "to possess the Farm" does not necessarily lead to the detailed and practical uses to which it was put. By itself, it presents no "picture." One critic spoke of my production of *Desire* as grandiose, almost operatic. This critic supposed the play's personages to be humbler than the larger-than-life figures I endeavored (and apparently succeeded) to depict. The distinction is not one of "content," in the sense of an intellectual statement or idea, but of *style*—the particular tone, mood, atmosphere, emphasis and "dimension" in which the idea is conveyed.

Style in the abstract may not be difficult to define for literary purposes, although there is something elusive about all aesthetic distinctions. (The reason is that the manner in which something is said is in itself part of its content; indeed one is usually inseparable from the other.) Style is related to the artist's—in this case, the dramatist's—particular way of seeing and feeling things, his spiritual vocabulary, his personal or temperamental stress, his "face" and individuality which make him himself and no one else.

Shaw's *Heartbreak House,* for example, might be described thematically as a picture of the educated middle class in the limbo of their waning power and effectiveness in England. But the same with the exception of locale might be said of *The Cherry Orchard.* My spine for *Heartbreak House,* that which sets all the characters in motion, is the desire, as one character puts it, "to get the hell out of this place"—the place being the condition of a particular social group.

So far, so good! But such a spine might be treated sombrely, lyrically, naturalistically, or, as some critics, taking Shaw at what appeared to be his word, in a Chekhovian key. What struck me, however, in reading *Heartbreak House* was its extravagance, a manner very close to comic opera! In intellectual purpose the text is entirely serious but in its body or mode it is akin to what the French call *vaudeville.* As a stage piece it is a lark and almost as remote from Chekhovian realism as Gilbert and Sullivan. Therefore in its stage treatment, I believed, it had to be made as playful and gay as if it were a fashionable bit of camp.

Apart from the parallel with Chekhov which Shaw mentions in his preface to *Heartbreak House,* it may be worth considering how he envisioned his plays on the stage. There is a strong indication in his letters to Granville-Barker, his managerial partner and frequent interpreter as actor-director, that Shaw's theatre taste inclined to the theatrical rather than to any of the modified forms of naturalism which the work of Ibsen, Galsworthy and Granville-Barker himself called for. In a letter to Granville-Barker Shaw wrote, "When will you understand that what has ruined you as a manager is your love for people who are 'a little weak, perhaps, but [have] just the right tone.' The right tone is never a little weak perhaps; it is always devastatingly strong. Keep your worm for your own plays; and leave me the drunken, stagey, brass-bowelled barnstormers my plays are written for. . . ." And again to Barker, "You hate the thing [barnstormers' acting] because it is so blatant and unreal . . . my plays are built to stand that sort of thing."

In one of his little essays Shaw said, "I went back to the classical style and wrote long rhetorical speeches like operatic solos, regarding my plays as musical performances. . . . As a producer [the English theatre word for our director] I went back to the forgotten heroic stage business and the exciting or impressive declamation I had learned from the old-timers."

In the same piece Shaw tells of an actor playing Burgess in Candida "who after rehearsing the first act in a funereal mute, solemnly put up his hand as I vengefully approached him, and said 'Mr. Shaw: I know what you are going to say. But you may depend on me. In the intellectual drama I never clown.' And it was some time before I could persuade him to clown for all he was worth." In my production of *Heartbreak House* there was a considerable amount of "clowning."

Judging from photographs of the original London production under Shaw's supervision I would say there was much less clowning. Was I then falsifying Shaw? I doubt it. I was doing the play—a dismal failure in 1919—for an American audience in 1960. My audience would accept a frolicsome interpretation of the material more readily than the English audience immediately after the First World War, and understand its serious implications.

This is not a defense of my production of *Heartbreak House*—ancient history as such things go in our theatre. I am addressing myself to the problem frequently raised by students as to the director's prerogatives in the treatment of a script—particularly a "classic."

There is perhaps an analogy with performances of music. We do not hear Bach or Mozart precisely as they were rendered in their day. Our audiences would probably not enjoy them if we did. But such an argument would be an evasion: the analogy will not hold. The director discerns a script's style—the production method best suited to convey its quality and meaning—not through the stage directions set down in the script or through discussion with the author himself, but by what the author has actually written: his plot line and his dialogue. The director then translates his understanding of the material into stage language. When Louis Jouvet was told that his Tartuffe was not Molière's, the actor retorted, "Do you have his telephone number?"

I am not suggesting that a director make a play "modern" by indulging in arbitrary tricks with it, though on occasion this may have some interest and value. Generally speaking, I do not approve of fanciful "stylization" as a display of directorial ingenuity. A production should be all of a piece; it should reveal no discrepancy between the text the audience hears and what it sees. It should strike the audience as being in every way self-consistent.

The actor who chose to play Shaw's Burgess solemnly was obtuse because he misread the part, which had little to do with traditional realism, even though Shaw in his early years claimed to be a follower of Ibsen.

Realism, by the way, is itself a style—a comparatively new one in theatre history. And there are various sorts of realism. Hardly any two notable playwrights have exactly the same style; for example, Chekhov's realism is not Ibsen's. All theatre must be real, but not all theatre is "realistic." And "stylization," an extremely vague term which covers a multitude of sins, is in itself no style at all. Those who "stylize" a script through caprice are dilettantes.

Let us be somewhat more exact about our terminology. All plays worthy of the name have a style. "Stylization" has come to designate any style which markedly departs from the "realistic." When actors paint their faces to resemble masks, when furniture and props stand askew on the stage, we speak of "stylization." This is a shorthand indication that conventional realism has been eschewed. But stylization is of many kinds; only a method of presentation particular to each play may be spoken of as a style.

We read of the Greek, the Elizabethan, the Renaissance, the neo-classic styles. Such nomenclature is more historic than aesthetic. It rarely leads the director to a specific solution of his task. Many designers dealing with a text of a bygone era consult illustrations (plates) from the period for architectural shapes, costumes and stage settings. The results —except when the designer is stimulated to his own concepts through such investigation—are closer to archaeology than to creative activity.

One source of a play's style may be related to its national or racial roots. An American, English or French cast, for example, will not duplicate the exact tone of a Chekhov play. Perhaps it shouldn't try! But within their own limitations every director and his company should study the salient traits of alien behavior patterns, "psychology" and environment which they wish to approximate. They may serve as clues to some aspects of a play's style.

It may be helpful at times to study the actual "soil" from which a dramatist's work has emerged. A trip to our Southland may throw some light in preparation for some of Tennessee Williams' plays. Books relating to costumes, manners, morals and everyday practices, and other literature—verse, novels, chronicles and diaries—as well as the folk music of a particular people and time may also prove invaluable in the quest for a convincing style. My long residence in Paris probably influenced my direction of Anouilh's *Colombe* and *The Waltz of the Toreadors*. In doing *Golden Boy* I received a considerable education through visits to the haunts of the boxing world and through many meetings with its personnel.

It is important to remember that style in the theatre is not chiefly a matter of décor, costumes and the like, but of acting.

The most basic actions—ways of speaking, sitting, walking, smiling, eating, expressing love—are affected. Have you never seen an actress in elaborate court costume of the sixteenth or seventeenth century cross the stage as if she were on her way to a tennis match?

Jules Feiffer's play *Little Murders*, a London success and a failure in its first New York production, offers a striking example of stylistic confusion in the direction of acting. The play was a cartoon of contemporary American mores. Everything said and done was outrageously caricatured. The constant sounds of shooting to kill on an ordinary city street were more or less taken for granted as normal. The effect was properly comic. At the end of the second act the sympathetic ingenue of the play, while talking to her lover in her home, is shot and killed by an unseen triggerman from the street. The production was ruined: the fun was over.

Such a "death scene" might have been rendered as funny as the rest of the play without sacrificing any of its satiric bite. The actress's fall should have been made as hideously grotesque as horrible catastrophes and brutalities are made in movie cartoons.

In one production of *Macbeth* the director's announced intention was to stage the play as a savage epic. Macbeth's first appearance struck the keynote: he looked like a hairy beast. But in the scene in which Lady Macduff teases and fondles her little son what we were shown was a genteel young woman being as charmingly maternal as she might be in a commonplace domestic comedy. If the production had been true to the proposed style, all of the acting would have been physically primitive.

I can make my last assertion clearer by another example in a production of a play about Jacob and Rachel I saw many years ago in Paris. The director conceived the characters as creatures barely past the neolithic stage of civilization. Makeup, clothes and vocal timbres corresponded to this conception. Nothing was so memorable for me as the moment when Jacob, to flatter his prospective father-in-law took to tickling Laban's feet, to which the older man reacted with something like animal "giggles" and movements to show how much he appreciated the compliment.

What is wrong with most "traditional" productions of Shakespeare (this usually means nothing but the nineteenth-century English manner) is that they have little relation to the nature of Shakespeare's writing. The same is true of Molière. I once saw a Molière play done by youngsters in Greenwich Village which a reviewer condemned as a distortion. All he meant was that the play was not being staged as it was in Paris. But the rowdy Village show was far closer to Molière's high jinks than the "conservatory" recitation of Molière so frequently seen at the Comédie Française, the "House of Molière."

The conflict between director and playwright is a common subject of controversy. We have all read about Chekhov's complaint that Stanislavsky had turned his characters into "crybabies." With authors long dead the issue is certainly a legitimate aesthetic and literary subject for critical dispute. But we may arrive at a firmer grasp of this ticklish problem if we cite instances of our common experience among contemporary playwrights and directors.

Clifford Odets set *Golden Boy* in such places as an Italian fruit vendor's home, a gymnasium and a prizefighter's dressing room. He set *Rocket to the Moon* in a dentist's office in mid-Manhattan. Most of the sets I had Mordecai Gorelik design for these plays had very little resemblance to the designated locales. The reason for this is that in reading the two scripts I did not feel that either of the texts was primarily concerned with a depiction of the stated environments or with the business of boxing or dentistry. Audiences accepted the settings—rather free abstractions—as "characteristic," i.e. realistic!

I envisioned one of the characters in *Golden Boy,* Fuselli, an Italian gangster, as a sort of "Renaissance prince." He seemed to me to possess a certain elegance, there was something almost "aristocratic" about him. He would be as meticulous about his dress as a courtier; his gait and address would strike the unaware observer as particularly poised and polished. Elia Kazan played the role in accordance with this aim.

When Odets saw a complete run-through of the play during the third week of rehearsal he protested that I had made Fuselli into an utterly unbelievable figure not at all like the New York gangster he had imagined. I knew little about gangsters, and those I had encountered had no similarity to Kazan's Fuselli. But I insisted that the personage that we had set on the stage was the very image of *what Odets had written*; with some vehemence I maintained that I had "invented" nothing. Odets allowed Kazan and me to go ahead with our interpretation as much for the sake of peace as from conviction.

After the play's opening when Thomas Dewey (then New York's District Attorney) and J. Edgar Hoover had, on different occasions, seen the play they complimented Odets for having so keen a perception of the true nature of gangsters. His intuition as a writer was greater than his visual stage sense.

I have often thought that the productions of Edward Albee's plays—particularly *A Delicate Balance* and *Tiny Alice*—might have been rendered truer to his texts and probably more convincing to their audiences if his director, Alan Schneider, had not followed the auctorial instructions so faithfully. The realistic or semi-realistic settings did those plays a disservice.

Jean Vilar, a director who scrupulously adhered to the dramatist's text with a minimum of scenic elaboration or embellishment, asked, "How many playwrights would be capable of giving one a precise analysis of their play or even of their plots!" Chekhov never tried to explain any of his plays to his director or actors—though he would complain when he found something "wrong." Stanislavsky wasn't wearing the right clothes as Trigorin in *The Seagull,* for example. When asked to be more specific Chekhov would only say, "But it's in the play. Read the play." There were no references to the characters' apparel in any part of the text.

This does not mean that the playwright does not "understand" his script. In a very real sense he thinks in another medium than the director: in words—speeches, story line, situations, characters. The director's medium is the behavior of living men and women, physical shapes, lights, color, movement. When a director controverts the playwright he does so only to arrive at a result more congruous with what the playwright has conceived than that which the playwright *believes* he has written.

The director may, of course, be mistaken. The playwright is often converted. The text has been absorbed in the production. The audience or the critic may serve as the final judges. The issue may always hang in the balance, with no final "verdict." That is part of the theatre's incalculability. It explains why there can be so many different productions of the same play. As a critic, I did not altogether approve of the Peter Brook-Paul Scofield *King Lear* but I found it far more interesting than any other production I have seen in which the director assumed the humble position of the dramatist's lackey. Gorky was wise or simply shrewd when he assured both directors of *Yegor Bulitchev*—one at the Moscow Art Theatre, the other at the Vakhtangov Theatre—that each had done the play in exactly the right way, though the two productions were so dissimilar that they looked as if they had been based on two different scripts.

To sum up: A particular rather than a generic style is what the director must achieve for each play. Generic styles only befit academe.

Another way of viewing the moot subject of new productions of revered drama considered to be too "far out" or distortions was astutely put by Grotowski when his treatment of Calderón's *The Constant Prince* was challenged as a desecration.

Grotowski extended the issue beyond the individual case. He was well advised to do so because those who protested could not be sure how much Grotowski's adaptation had retained of the original, for they had no Polish. Nor has it been determined whether those familiar with the language could understand what they heard: Grotowski's company speaks (or shrieks) the lines at an extremely rapid pace.

The Polish director held that every theatre piece represents the thought and feeling of the company which produces it. It is their work as much as the dramatist's. Though Chekhov may have been justified in claiming that the Moscow Art Theatre (or Stanislavsky's) *Cherry Orchard* was not presented as he (Chekhov) had conceived it, the staged play was theirs. If it had substance and valid meaning, then their *Cherry Orchard* was as much a creation as Chekhov's writing. The audience which saw Stanislavsky's *Cherry Orchard,* sprung from Chekhov's text, had been moved, indeed transported, by it.

We never see Shakespeare's *Hamlet* on the stage, only that of Walter Hampden, John Barrymore, John Gielgud, Nicol Williamson and so on and on. Shakespeare's *Hamlet* exists solely in the book. A vast literary fraternity has argued for centuries as to what it connotes.

The issue about which students are constantly questioning their teachers is not resolved by so simple an example as the Stanislavsky-Chekhov "controversy." Grotowski also pointed out that Meyerhold's *The Inspector General* was decidedly the creation of that master director. He had cut the text, rearranged some of the scenes and added new material. Yet many respected Russian critics found Meyerhold's production closer to Gogol's genius than any of the "faithful" productions they had seen.

I have never consciously "tampered" with a masterpiece. My view as a critic, however, is that a director may choose his own interpretation of any text if the result gives pleasure and has creative value. But text and theatrical body must be rendered compatible with each other, and carry conviction as coherent theatre pieces. Dramatists from Shakespeare to Giraudoux have done no less, revising old plays from which they wrought their own original work.

A difficulty arises when a production which takes "liberties" with an honored text is not intelligible or aesthetically satisfying on its own account, that is, when one's enjoyment depends on previous knowledge of the work from which it derives. Richard Schechner's *Dionysus in 69,* part translation of, part improvisation on Euripides' *The Bacchae,* was effective and meaningful, while his *Makbeth* project, which employed no other lines than a portion of Shakespeare's, was not. There was entertainment in Joseph Papp's *Hamlet* experiment but it did not constitute a self-sustaining play. André Gregory's ingenious and well-performed *Alice in Wonderland,* which retained much of the book, also had its bright moments, but it, too, failed to be independently valid.

The director (if permitted) has the right to do what he pleases with a script provided what results is persuasive, enriching and consistently intelligible in itself. My complaint against William Ball's production of *The Three Sisters* was not that he had played fast and loose with Chekhov but that the results were trivial. The same director's *Six Characters in Search of an Author,* in which the acting company of Pirandello's script was presented as juvenilely American, possessed imaginative impact.

My personal preference is for *complete* plays, by which I mean original texts created in view of or as parts of specific productions. The work of Bertolt Brecht provides the best contemporary example. When I asked Brecht if he felt that his plays had to be staged exactly as he had done them, he answered, "Certainly not." Yet I have seen very few productions of his plays produced in a different mode which did not diminish them.

CHAPTER 4

Script Work
with the Playwright

ONLY CRITICS, scholars, students and assiduous playgoers of
literary inclination complain about the liberties Tyrone
Guthrie, Peter Brook or (in France) Roger Planchon take
with the "classics." Shakespeare and Molière have neither
immediate heirs nor telephone numbers. But living playwrights are present not only on the telephone but in person.
One of the director's duties is to deal with them. With only
four exceptions the playwrights whose scripts I have staged
were very much alive. I have had very little difficulty with
any of them during the time of production; dissatisfaction, if
any, came later!

To direct with the playwright attending every rehearsal in
the early days of staging may prove as disturbing to a director
as having an editor look over his shoulder while he is engaged in writing his first draft would be to a novelist. I must

confess gratitude for a playwright's absence for at least half
the rehearsal period. Many playwrights of their own accord
stay away for this duration, since their continuous presence
may not only bore them but may dim their judgment.

Rehearsals of a play constitute a *creative process* as delicate and arduous as the writing of the script itself. The process is not helped, it is impeded, by nervous impatience or the
insistence on immediately convincing results. These are the
fruits of gestation. While this is going on, what we see is
rarely pleasing as "performance." Only the late stages of rehearsal provide testimony as to the progress made.

Under ordinary circumstances the playwright's script is the
core and basis of the theatrical event. To begin with, the
playwright is the director's closest collaborator. The script,
once chosen, is to be respected as are all the people—actors,
scene designer, costumer, musicians and, ultimately, the audience—who compose the Play.

The playwright confirms or initiates the choice of the
director. He is presumed to have confidence in the person to
whom his script has been entrusted. The director, likewise,
has supposedly elected to stage the script because he admires
it. As with marriage, there is often an element of uncertainty
on both sides. A playwright may have been persuaded to accept a director by the producer or by the star. Directors have
been known to undertake an assignment because they believed the producer even more astute than themselves or because of their esteem for a particular actor or quite simply
because they needed employment.

The playwright may have checked with his professional
friends to ascertain whether the recommended director is
the "right man" for his particular play. "Yes," the writer may
have said, "X did a fine job with that play about those New
York toughs but will he know how to handle my play about
polite society?" or "So-and-so is great with heavy drama, but
my play is a scintillating comedy," etc., etc., *ad nauseum.*

"There is a genuine impulse in this script, and some fine

dialogue," the director may have mused, "but the plot is somewhat predictable, the construction a little feeble. Will the author realize the need for correcting these flaws? And even if he is ready to do so, is he capable of it?"

Under normal conditions—if conditions in our theatre can ever be thought of as normal—mutual regard exists on both sides. Once the director has conveyed his enthusiasm for the script (and he had better do so as playwrights are even more touchy than actors), the playwright is prepared to listen to his opinion and advice on matters of cast, setting, etc.

Ideally the director should have no other function than to direct. It is a great relief to a director, unless he is an inordinate egotist, to come upon a script which requires little or no revision. One occasionally encounters such scripts. Cutting is often necessary, but experienced writers readily concur with suggestions which entail certain minor changes. Eugene O'Neill, extremely attentive to the integrity of his texts, agreed, at his director's suggestion, to extensive cuts in *Strange Interlude.*

Bernard Shaw never permitted his scripts to be cut. Having watched many productions of his plays (I myself have directed three), I venture to believe him to have been mistaken. An early uncut, though excellent, production of *Misalliance* was a failure in New York, while some years later an inferior one with judicious cuts proved far more effective. Europeans, I have observed, tolerate *longueurs* in a play far more patiently than Americans.

Neophyte playwrights frequently offer their scripts to directors with the assurance that "though the script needs further work, I am sure I can do it satisfactorily with your help." This may show a commendable modesty, but it betrays an amateur attitude. Some directors encourage it—it flatters them—and some have been known to profit financially from the practice of contributing to the "rewrite."

This is not to deny that many scripts have been greatly strengthened by the guiding hand of a sympathetic and per-

ceptive director. A knowledge of play structure and dramatic
writing, a combination of artistic sensibility and stage acu-
men, are therefore important, possibly indispensable, qualifi-
cations for the direction of a new play. (In Europe—particularly in Germany—the director often performs the auctorial
service with the assistance of the theatre's *Dramaturg*, literary
manager or "play doctor.") But as Elia Kazan once said, "If
you aren't willing to go ahead with the direction of a script in
its unrevised and perhaps still imperfect state then you had
best not do it at all." This may be overstating the case but it
is sufficiently astute to be given serious consideration.

The first order of business, then, in preparing for a production should be a series of director-dramatist consultations.
They ought to discuss (and agree on) the operative content
of the script. Sometimes the director is sufficiently eloquent
and cogent (to the playwright's surprise and delight) to add
to or alter the playwright's material. New lines or scenes may
be suggested to clarify the script's theme or story points.
There may be divergent opinions on any of these matters but
the responsibility for any changes ultimately rests with the
writer.

Stanislavsky did not direct the Hebrew production of *The
Dybbuk* (Vakhtangov did) but it is said that he suggested the
symbolic character of the Stranger to the author. In the preliminary outline of Odets' *Golden Boy* Joe Bonaparte's father
was a musician. I argued that he should be a much humbler
figure. Odets finally made him a fruit vendor.

In an early draft of the same play one of the characters
was Joe Bonaparte's older brother, a fellow who sold score
cards at the ball park. Though minor, he was a well-drawn
figure. Odets' purpose in introducing him was thematically
irrelevant. The spine of the play, as I had adduced it, was "to
win in the *fight* of life." Odets meant his play to show a person who "fought" the wrong way—one damaging to human
personality.

I asked for a "fighter" whose struggle contrasted with that

of the misguided protagonist. Odets then made the older brother a labor organizer—a familiar ("committed") type in the thirties. As this character was usually in the "field" away from home, he could exercise little influence on Joe, but it was clear that he also "fought" and was not doing so for "fame and fortune."

Playwrights have from time to time blamed me (after the fact) for not having insisted on more drastic cutting or for having made suggestions detrimental to the play's effectiveness. After the opening of *Rocket to the Moon* Odets himself decided to eliminate a character and an eight-minute scene which he had come to consider redundant. The Group Theatre, under whose auspices the play was produced, rarely tried out its plays in pre-Broadway tours.

When Arthur Miller's *Death of a Salesman* was being readied for rehearsal, its director, Elia Kazan, made several suggestions meant to clarify the play's plot. Miller complied. When the revised script was read, doubt was expressed as to the efficacy of the changes. Asked his opinion, Walter Fried, the play's co-producer, ventured, "The play is clearer now, but less interesting." The script was put into rehearsal as originally written.

In the controversies over the revision of Tennessee Williams' *Cat on a Hot Tin Roof* the author intimated that he yielded to Kazan's reasoning on the issue. I was not present at the conferences. For purposes of illustration, however, I shall describe ("allegorically") what may have happened. The director voices his criticism of Williams' ending; the playwright demurs. This goes on for hours, perhaps for days. The director becomes ever more convinced that his criticism is sound; the playwright maintains his position with decreasing resolution. The director finally says, "Please try my ending. If it doesn't work during the tryout we will go back to the original version. But I'm sure I'm right artistically. I'm on even surer ground as to the audience reaction. The change may make the difference between a hit and a flop." The playwright yields. The new third act is written and tried. The play is a hit; the director is vindicated.

In the backlash of later criticism from friends and professional commentators the ending urged by the director is denounced as a compromise. The author, it is objected, is bidding for sympathy, he has gone soft, etc., etc. The playwright then ruefully explains that the ending was not altogether his idea. As testimony, he has both endings published.

Whatever our personal judgment in the matter may be, the author evinces bad faith if he defends himself with the excuse of pressure from the director. The director has no jurisdiction over the play's verbal text. The audience judges the Play as a whole—what it sees and hears—and need not concern itself with what role each of the collaborators in its making has performed. That is a special consideration within the province of criticism, though the critic is rare who is able to distinguish between a script and its direction.

The question of assigning blame for failure or credit for success, about which we often hear talk (it is likely to be empty chatter), brings us to another aspect of the dramatist-director relationship in the preliminary phases of production.

During the tryout period of Dorothy Parker and Armand d'Usseau's play *The Ladies of the Corridor* it became evident that a good portion of the audience was upset by a suicide scene near the end of the play. I asked the authors if in view of this reaction they wished to eliminate it. Their answer was an emphatic "no." I did not insist. The play—admired by George Jean Nathan, who also found the scene undesirable— failed. There were no recriminations. But my forbearance, many thought, was a directorial blemish. Perhaps so. The question remains whether it was that scene alone which caused the play's failure.

The atmosphere of the theatre world is predominantly naive. There is always the all-too-human urge to find a "villain," somebody to reprove for every misadventure. Any excuse will do. But even a good reason—such as the one just mentioned—may not be the true one. And why must failure inevitably be deemed shameful or reprehensible?

Many faults were found with my direction of Tennessee Williams' *Orpheus Descending*—nearly all of them after the play's "mixed" reception. In Philadelphia, immediately before the New York opening, the author assured me that none of his previous plays had been so truly interpreted. With the play's failure he exercised the privilege of changing his mind. (I had exactly the same experience with Clifford Odets in the production of his *Night Music*.) I had permitted a leading character in *Orpheus* to be shot in full view of the audience as set down in the script. We had been warned by Gore Vidal that this was a mistake. When the play closed I had some misgivings on this score. But there were other criticisms: the setting was wrong, the casting was misguided, etc.

I had occasion to see the play again in Paris and then in London. In these productions the killing of the woman was not staged with such brutal directness as in mine. There were also quite different sets. The productions were received exactly as mine had been. The play was a success in Moscow where it was "freely" adapted—no doubt to emphasize the barbarous cruelty of American life!

A learned man of the theatre once asserted that Lillian Hellman's *The Autumn Garden* was not as successful as its writing warranted because its setting was too literal. An interesting sidelight on this is the fact that the set had been designed in consultation with the author before I had been engaged as director—a sign of the artistic disorganization and ignorance of the director's function. I myself agree with my colleague's criticism of the set. I would have asked for something quite different, although I am by no means certain that the author would have accepted the style of set I thought suitable. I am convinced, however, that the play—Miss Hellman's best, I believe—would not have been anything more than a *succès d'estime* if the set had been "ideal." It is one of the misfortunes of the American theatre that if a new play is done on Broadway and is not a "smash," it is almost never seen there again.

Let us now return to the initial director-playwright consultations, which, I repeat, should precede the director's notes on the play's theme: spine, style, etc. The director has asked many questions of the playwright. The playwright sometimes proves reticent or less than explicit in reply. On the other hand, he may say things about the origins of the script: how and why he came to write it; he may make allusions to its characters and milieu, or to its ideologic and social background. These remarks may reveal facets of the script the director did not immediately apprehend. He will often learn as much from what he discerns through such personal contact with the playwright's attitudes as he has from the playwright's specific explanations. His observation of the playwright's general cast of thought may possibly become a factor in the eventual treatment of the script.

More useful results will ensue from director-playwright colloquies when they actually get down to cases. This occurs when rewriting is to be done, or during the sessions devoted to the choice of actors and in the joint examination of set and costume designs. Most important will be the playwright's observations and criticisms at rehearsals.

Should the director at the outset be uncertain as to what script revisions are needed he had best leave well enough alone. The rehearsal period itself will prove a most instructive time for both director and playwright. The director can only be persuasive if he is sure of his ground. He must constantly assume when dealing with a practiced dramatist that the latter has given more thought to the writing and construction of his play than anyone else.

Years ago that shrewd showman David Belasco remarked that "plays aren't written, they are made," i.e., revamped. This was generally true on the Broadway of Belasco's time and still holds true of musicals, farces and melodramas. It is far less true of drama today. The theatre now is increasingly devoted to writing which aspires to the status of literature; the good playwright is a literary artist. The director must be aware of what the literary sensibility entails.

I recall my experience with Carson McCullers' *The Member of the Wedding*. A novelist, she had had almost no previous contact with the stage. Someone was chosen to dramatize her book. He tried to make a "regular play" of it. I never read that dramatization but I was informed not only that Mrs. McCullers had rejected it but that it had rendered her seriously ill. She was then persuaded to undertake the dramatization herself.

The first directors who read her dramatization thought it theatrically hopeless. They maintained that it had to be drastically revised for it to be a viable stage piece. When called in to direct it I was asked what revisions I would demand. "None," I replied to the consternation of certain people who had Mrs. McCullers' success very much at heart. What, not to "fix" a script so awkward, repetitious, undramatic!

I did nevertheless suggest a few additional lines to sharpen certain situations and representative ideas. When Mrs. McCullers tried her hand at following my suggestions I realized at once that she was incapable of doing more than she had done to begin with. With all its faults her script was a complete expression of what she had to say. "Fixing" it to satisfy some arbitrary notion of professional dramaturgy would ruin it. (A play's form cannot be imposed by technical rules. A play's form rises out of its own organic nature.) Two scenes were cut at the out-of-town tryout. They had been entertaining and revealing episodes in the novel but destroyed the play's unity on the stage. Some minor cuts were made. The play was presented in New York very much as Mrs. McCullers had written it. It worked.

Another instance of artistic discretion, indeed wisdom, concerns a brief exchange between Lillian Hellman and myself in regard to her play *The Autumn Garden*. During rehearsals Miss Hellman agreed to some suggested cuts. She

herself was dissatisfied with the final scene. She rewrote it
several times. One day before the rehearsal period had begun
she asked me if I had any fundamental criticism of her script.
With some diffidence I told her that while the whole tenor of
her play was an ironical presentation of its characters, she had
not made them as "forgivable" as they might be. I pointed
out that though Chekhov's characters were often foolish and
feckless, one ended by loving them. "True," was Miss Hellman's immediate response, "but I'm not as good as Chekhov."
I had nothing further to say. My criticism had been "just"—
and futile.

The director should not be sanguine about the writer's
ability to exceed his limitations. Nor, generally speaking,
should he be too hopeful of compensating for a script's inherent weaknesses by further writing. If there is to be an extension of the playwright's scope—or an attenuation of his faults
—it must be accomplished through direction. I once heard a
producer exclaim about a comedy he had bought, "If only
the dialogue was as deft as Maugham's!" Understandable as
sentiment, it was silly as project. There is a kind of criticism
in the theatre which no matter how justified in the absolute
is practically speaking not only idle but harmful.

During rehearsals (or sometimes during the lapse of time
between the writing of a play and its first rehearsal) playwrights themselves often discover passages, scenes, even
whole acts which demand alteration. When I read *Awake and
Sing* for the first time I realized that its second act was a brilliant achievement but I was reluctant to accept the play as a
whole. I could hardly explain my reservations. I spoke of its
"cramped atmosphere." This was not a reference to the environment in which the play's action took place but to something in the writer's outlook. This left Odets thoroughly
puzzled. One day, however, he announced that he had cut the
script's first twenty pages and after discussion with me had
rewritten the last act. I hadn't realized (this was my first independent venture as a director) that the script's major de-

fects could be remedied by protracted study and effort by both dramatist and director.

When I read the first draft of William Inge's *The Dark at the Top of the Stairs* I was uncertain as to what troubled me about it. But its initial deficiency was immediately discerned by Elia Kazan, who directed it. Inge revised it along the lines indicated by that director. Inge, like the early O'Neill, is one of those playwrights whose work acquires a body on the stage not always apparent in the "book."

The theatrical impact of Sidney Kingsley's *Men in White* was barely evident to more than a handful of people before it reached the final moments of production under Lee Strasberg's beautiful direction.

In the long haul of a play's production the writer himself may begin to find fault with his script. A week before the opening of *Golden Boy* Clifford Odets felt certain that its last act did not follow logically from the premise of its second. He was at fault, he admitted, and had to rewrite the entire act. It took all my dialectic powers to prevent his making the change.

I conclude: Most sound craftsmen—directors and dramatists—work well together with little friction. Unpleasantness usually arises when the director makes demands on the playwright without regard to their initial understanding on the script's essential form and meaning. A playwright doesn't want his play "improved" if the improvement leads to making a different play than his own. He wants *his* voice to be heard, unless he thinks of himself as a journeyman prepared to provide a commodity which might somehow prove profitable. But not many playwrights think of themselves in that light.

CHAPTER 5

Settings

THIS BOOK is arranged in segments; production does not advance in such orderly steps. Two, three or more activities are engaged in at almost the same time. The director, playwright and producer—the usual trio of American practice—may have begun casting during discussions of the script. After having decided the nature of the play—its spine and style—the director goes on to a more detailed study which entails the drafting of a scene-by-scene production plan. To be efficient in this he holds advisory consultations with the production designer.

There are variations in this procedure. On and off Broadway, where rehearsal time for a "straight" play, as differentiated from a musical, is three and a half weeks before previews, the designer must undertake his job six weeks, at the very least, before rehearsals commence. While permanent companies abroad and certain of our regional theatres build their sets and sew costumes in addition to fashioning and gathering such accessories as furniture, drapes and hand properties within the theatre's premises, all this preparation in our professional theatre is delegated to separate and independent companies. These are located at some distance from the theatre. At the same time, in the same shops, other productions for different managements are usually being readied to meet other opening-night deadlines. This makes for haste.

In some European theatres—the Berliner Ensemble, for example—the designer attends nearly all the rehearsals to observe the working out of details of movement and the "business" which has been invented by the director and the actors. The designer is therefore not obliged to fix the ground plan—placement of platforms, set pieces, objects of use, etc.—before he has had the opportunity to attend rehearsals. The ground plan is technically the crucial element in setting. The artist's design in these European theatres is "custom tailored." With us, the actors and director are constrained to fit the setting which has been designed and is already being built prior to the first rehearsal. The actors in my productions (and probably in most others) are always shown a quarter- or half-inch model of the setting before they begin the joint reading of the play. The setting itself is rarely placed on stage till very late in the rehearsal period. But seeing the model helps the actors visualize the play's environment.

The tight rehearsal schedule in our theatre has unfortunate consequences. For one thing, it gives designers an undesirable independence. They frequently take to their drawing boards with insufficient knowledge of what actors are to use their settings, what their physical limitations may be and what they are going to be required to do. Much of a play's movement arises from the stimulation of rehearsal. Since the designer cannot anticipate this, the actors' spontaneity in the invention of stage business may be limited by the setting.

Not long ago a designer devised a very fine set for a new

musical. It consisted of a series of scaffolds placed high above the stage floor with winding steps descending to the main playing area. But many members of the cast were of a certain age; they found the descent from the top scaffold to the stage floor perilous. Railings, not previously provided because the set was deemed more attractive without them, had to be supplied during the dress rehearsals, which was both time-consuming and costly. A stage setting should be adjusted to the play's action, and not the reverse.

The choice of a designer is part of the director's function. I have already mentioned an occasion when the producer and playwright engaged a designer before a director had been assigned. On seeing the completed sketch of the set, already under construction, the chosen director realized at once that it would be an impediment rather than an aid to him.

The director does not dictate to the designer.* He serves as the designer's guide, critic and, if possible, inspirer. He communicates his vision of the play to the designer and designates the technical problems he foresees. He does not, for instance, order "a setting in blue" or arbitrarily insist on some special mechanical device such as a revolving or a jackknife stage, a particular kind of cyclorama, scenic projections, etc.; he describes the role the set should play in the production's desired effect. He writes the "notes" which the designer is to sound. (This is also the key to the actor-director relationship; but of this, later.) The designer's creative contribution is manifested in his solution of the problems posed.

The director speaks of the play's style: its atmosphere, mood, the kind of impact he would have the play produce. He indicates the sort of movement he will call for, the most important acting areas, the position of entrances and exits, the matter of timing between scenes.

---

* There are always exceptions. For my production of Roblès' *Montserrat* at the Habimah Theatre in Israel, the designer, a noted Israeli painter, was an artist whose work I did not know. I therefore instructed him minutely on every aspect of the set and costumes. They were virtually of my design.

A stage setting is not a picture. Nor is it primarily decoration. Audiences understandably tend to applaud sets which are pretty or imposing. Robert Edmond Jones, a pioneer in his day, thought of sets chiefly in terms of mood, the spiritual ambience in which a play was to be immersed. "A stage setting," he said, "is not a background, it is an environment." His was a reaction against both the conventionalized renderings of living rooms, mansions, outdoor scenes, etc., commonly in use in the late nineteenth century, and the more detailed realism for which David Belasco between 1900 and 1920 was much admired and which in many respects still obtains as the Broadway norm.

What matters most in modern stage design is the proper use of space. Designers today attempt first of all to fulfill the various demands of action and movement. Certain designers have termed settings "machines for actors." Atmosphere, suggestions of place and time, along with decorative elements, need not be neglected on that account.

Though Gordon Craig was Robert Edmond Jones' chief influence in the designing of atmospheric settings Craig did not confine himself, in theory at least, to that one element alone. "No scene that I have worked at," Craig said, "was worked at for its own sake. I thought solely of the movement of the Drama . . . of the actors, of dramatic moments. . . . I saw as I progressed that *things can,* therefore should, play their parts as well as people, that they can combine with the actor and plead with the actor to use them."

For the production of Giraudoux's *Tiger at the Gates,* first produced in London, I chose Louden Sainthill as designer. The author's notation as to setting indicated no more than "a terrace [outside a palace] overlooking other terraces." Sainthill was in England, while I was still in New York. I suggested that he begin work alone without specific instructions from me. He was then to send me a sketch of what he proposed.

I received a beautiful picture, lush in color, baroque in

ornament, elaborate in structure. It was something I would have been pleased to hang in my apartment or enter in an exhibit. It was not at all what I had in mind.

I had not then seen Christian Bérard's setting for the original Paris production. After I had directed the play, I did see a photograph of it and I could not help but admire it. But it was not a setting I would have requested for my production. Bérard's set, though there were a few elevations in it, was largely flat: movement had to be confined to the stage floor. This was no doubt suitable for the French production, but not for mine. The script is markedly rhetorical. Reading it, one would suspect that it consisted of nothing but fine speeches.

The French are endlessly pleased by fine language, beautifully spoken. The English, and more especially Americans (and it was chiefly a New York audience I was thinking of), are bored by "talky" shows: they demand overt action. How was I to create this in a play which required first of all that its verbal splendor be thoroughly appreciated?

I asked Sainthill to eliminate most of the purely decorative elements (even color) and to eschew ordinary furnishings: chairs, tabourets, settees and the like. He was to arrange a setting of asymmetrically ordered planes (or platforms) rapidly descending from about ten feet above floor level, at the height of which Michael Redgrave as Hector was to make his first triumphant entrance. On this stage, every step the actors made would cause them to ascend or descend in space. Thus they were always beheld in movement; without the audience being entirely aware of it, the setting "propelled" the actors— up and down.

The actors had to be surefooted: the stage incline was steep. In his London review of the production Kenneth Tynan wrote that the setting appeared to have been designed for mountain goats! I might have countered that the play's legendary characters were not lambs or that the part of Asia Minor where Troy, the play's locale, was presumed to have stood was mountainous and that I was trying to suggest its topography. But none of this would have been relevant. I was concerned only with devising playing areas which would make every figure stand out boldly and, above all, serve as a "podium" for Giraudoux's sumptuous writing while at the same time enforce movement and induce a sense of physical action. Color was supplied by vivid costumes.

Another detail is worth mentioning. Despite himself the designer clung to considerations of realism. He had the platforms painted an indefinite tan because in the open space of a palace courtyard, he pointed out, the sun would have tarnished the "stone." This gave the set an unpleasantly muddy color. I overlooked the blemish in London but had the steps repainted an "impossible" pearl blue in New York.

It is a mistake to think of a setting as a copy of a real place. What matters is the sort of reality the play aims at. And every play has its own reality. Boris Aronson's room for Arthur Miller's *The Price* was ostensibly realistic. But as Aronson composed it, the apparent mess, a deserted room full of stored furniture, became a sculpted form which bespoke the passage of time, the rich substance of a now abandoned family life, the dissolution of former middle-class comfort. "Real life" milieus are nowadays rendered in ever more markedly abstract designs. But abstraction or stylization must communicate something of a play's essence. Still, a design should not be totally declarative: it should not "say everything." A setting must serve as a contributing factor to a play's "message," not be a thing in itself.

It is occasionally asserted that apart from considerations of economy, the theatre might profit if all "scenery" were eliminated. Nonsense! There is always a setting in the theatre. The audience always sees *something* and what it sees inevitably conveys an idea of some sort and should perform a meaningful function. A bare stage, as Aronson once cannily remarked, is more difficult to design than any other.

A number of Brecht's practices have now become routine.

He never availed himself of the traditional curtain, did not conceal the sources of stage illumination, was frugal in the use of furniture. He used white light only. Settings for his productions were usually given a more or less neutral background. He wished his audience to be aware that they were in a theatre, so that there would be no pretense of naturalistic imitation. Above all, he hoped to make the spectator see the play in objective repose instead of being bemused by what he deemed false glamor. His chief aim, in short, was to direct the audience's attention to what the actors were saying and demonstrating.

Yet his settings (actually Teo Otto's) were both handsome and rich in tonal values. A Parisian critic observed that there were several hundred different shades of brown in the settings for *Mother Courage*. The background throughout his *Galileo,* including exteriors, was covered with bronze foil which recalled the sedate opulence we associate with the Italian Renaissance. Mother Courage's medium of livelihood, her wagon, was tooled with meticulous care to indicate the wear and tear of her long peregrinations through Europe and the vehicle's steady decline, symbolic of her own.

I have said that the director should not dictate to the designer. More emphatically: he should stimulate his powers of invention. Ben Edwards' setting for my production of Eugene O'Neill's *A Touch of the Poet* owed nothing to any instruction from me. O'Neill's stage directions and text were his sole guide. But for my production of Arthur Laurents' *The Time of the Cuckoo* I spoke to Edwards about the tremulous shimmer of the Venetian canals which made the adjacent buildings look as if they were veiled in a watery tissue. The effect was overly conspicuous at first but was later modified. For Anouilh's *The Waltz of the Toreadors* I suggested that Edwards seek inspiration in Cézanne's and Vuillard's colors. When in a similar vein I suggested that Aronson make the set for Inge's *Bus Stop* look like an Edward Hopper painting, his rejoinder was, "Why not like an Aronson?"

To Moredecai Gorelik I spoke of the motorcar sleekness of many offices in which wealthy business executives conduct their affairs, apropos of John Howard Lawson's *Success Story* which Lee Strasberg directed in 1932 for the Group Theatre. (On this occasion Strasberg granted me the privilege of serving as scenic adviser.) A few days later Gorelik showed me a reproduction of a cubist painting by Braque: superimposed planes of black and brown. "Is this what you mean?" Gorelik queried. I confess to having been slightly puzzled at the time, but agreed to have him translate this abstraction into a serviceable locus for the play's action. He did so. The result was like no office I had ever before seen but one which was altogether right for the play; furthermore, one that the audience accepted as "real."

From my hypothesis that Odets' *Golden Boy* had little to do with pugilism but had much to do with winning the battle of the ego he shaped the play on the severe nudity of a boxing ring though the script called for no visible match. Properties required by the action were placed on the bare platform. The homey warmth of the Italian father's household was conveyed by the texture of the woodwork in the scenic frame. Though the text contained references to the city, a gray velour cyclorama served as a backdrop throughout. For a scene in Central Park nothing was visible but an isolated bench against a fragment of stone wall. Two nights prior to the play's opening a friendly playwright confided to Odets that he thought the production had ruined the play (oh, these whisperers in the night!) because cops amble through parks, also dogs, and one hears the seductive hiss of passing limousines—and none of these things were present in the production. When I was told about this I blurted out, "Yes, and why doesn't Hamlet carry an umbrella when called to meet the ghost at the approach of the wet Danish dawn?"

As an instructor in scenic design at various colleges, Gorelik formulated his method by saying that all settings should stem from a basic metaphor, a central image inspired by the play or the director's interpretation of it. A valuable insight. In retrospect I think of a very early Aronson setting for a scene in Hell which he inserted inside the outline of a huge human cranium, as later in *Cabin in the Sky* he set the inferno imagined by poor blacks with an immense refrigerator in the background.

As I am dealing with settings as part of the director's craft I omit references to the minutiae of scenic mechanics. While these may be extremely important in the smooth running and ultimate success of a production, they are rarely of the *first* importance. They chiefly concern the designer, the builder and the stage carpenter. These associated craftsmen may, for example, be obliged to make certain adjustments in design and construction in a production which is to troop extensively through the country where transportation by train or truck is involved. I have been told, for instance, that when Maxwell Anderson's *Anne of the Thousand Days* was being tried out in Philadelphia the actors, clothed in voluminous costumes, were hardly able to get through the spaces provided for making their entrances. The entire setting had to be redone for the New York opening.

The likelihood of such accidents is increased in the Broadway theatre because there are no permanent theatre organizations with their own coordinated technical staffs. Playwrights belong to a guild of their own, loosely related to Equity, the actors' union. The stagehands have their own union, with their own separate interests, the scenic artists theirs, the business managers, directors, box-office personnel and ushers likewise.

It is on this account that Boris Aronson has said he would call his book on the theatre "Organized Calamities." It is a miracle that so much good work is done in our theatre, but as Nemirovitch-Danchenko, co-founder and co-director with Stanislavsky of the Moscow Art Theatre, once remarked on learning that a Theatre Guild production he liked had been rehearsed for only four weeks, "It's a miracle and I don't believe in miracles."

The division, or more precisely, the contention, of labor in our theatre begins with real estate. Very few producers or directors nowadays possess their own theatres. They rent them when they have a play to put on, an eventuality ever more infrequent since the thirties. It is not within the province of this book to expatiate the damage to the theatre as an art caused by this circumstance. But the fact that the buildings in use for our productions are all structured in exactly the same way is unquestionably restricting to freedom in scenic design.

There is nothing absolutely wrong with the old "picture frame" arrangement of the stage as a raised platform cut off from the audience by a proscenium arch within which sets are placed. It developed from the needs of a society in which plays were written to its measure. Plays and theatre architecture have almost always been engendered within a single matrix.

The proscenium stage has long served the theatre and will continue to do so for many years to come. Brecht and other non-realists among playwrights have employed it without artistic embarrassment. But it does not facilitate—it impedes —some types of production. For the presentation of new types of plays today and for the new ways we believe they should "happen," the old playhouses are the wrong instruments.

Solutions by way of new edifices proliferate to the point of fetishism. In many cases they are hasty and arbitrary, a matter of guesswork, often products of architectural fantasy or snobbery. (The lobbies and public facilities—coatrooms, bars, lavatories—are always superb.) Theatres in the round do away with the proscenium arch; they by no means constitute a universal panacea. Nor is the arena theatre with a thrust stage always serviceable. I have found that producing Chekhov in such a theatre leads to awkward staging. The lines of sight anywhere apart from the center of the house make for distortion of vision. These bring about falsifications in stage movement which do not exist in the theatres for which Chekhov's plays and many others were written. Architectural "improvements" or experiments abstracted from the total theatre organism disable it.

It is surely desirable to bring the audience and the playing area in closer contact than the old theatres permit. Having actors enter from the rear of the house and pass through the aisles to the stage is occasionally interesting but sometimes ludicrous. I found it so when the Spanish peasants of Lorca's *Yerma* emerged from the special entrance in the middle of the Vivian Beaumont Theatre auditorium and passed onto the stage in front of the fashionably dressed ladies and gentlemen in Row A. Audiences are generally prepared to play the theatre game in any way directors propose. But that does not mean that all methods are sound.

The use of an empty space which may be adapted to any structure including a variable disposition of the audience for particular occasions might prove of inestimable value. When desired, this allows an easy interpenetration or mingling of actors and spectators. But merely to depart from the so-called peep-show or theatre-of-illusion architecture, which some theorists condemn as "archaic," does not prevent aesthetic fraudulence. When Max Reinhardt, many years ago, had actors rise from the audience to heckle the orators in the convention scene of Büchner's *Danton's Death* the device was a thrilling and justified novelty. But since then I have seen more traditionally staged productions of the play which were equally exciting.

Architectural changes in theatre structure are valid only when they are generated by the intrinsic demands of particular kinds of performance. These in turn depend on social, economic, geographical and historical circumstances. Because necessity dictated the use of factories as the site of certain theatre activities during the early years of the Russian

Revolution, a good many settings were made to simulate industrial environments. What is right in theatre architecture as in setting is that which conforms to the artistic purpose of the stage event and the conditions surrounding it.

The varying structural schemes devised by the Grotowski productions correspond to the intimate communion to which his art aspires. It is no whim or personal eccentricity which reduces his theatre to a seating capacity of no more than a hundred. When his company goes abroad he painstakingly seeks a location which approximates his own workshop theatre in Poland.

The very meaning of Ronconi's *Orlando Furioso,* with its mad riot, street-fair hurly-burly and crowd folly, called for an Italian piazza or such a place as Les Halles in Paris.

A theatre's or a setting's very dimensions affect a play's impact. In a relatively intimate house in Rome *Rugantino* was a charming musical gambol. In the vast expanse of New York's Mark Hellinger Theatre it became feebly exotic. *Waiting for Godot* cannot retain either its comedy or its tension in a large auditorium. While Rouben-ter-Arutunian's set for Edward Albee's *All Over* was an interesting and in many respects a fitting one, it rendered the play remote by its inordinate size in a theatre too large for the play's repressed emotion.

Theatre discussion which fails to consider all the circumstances attendant on the production of plays in particular times and places tends to produce little but hot air. In the commercial theatre where, I repeat, real estate interests control playhouses, producers are often constrained to contract for theatres which cripple their efforts. The system, the system is to blame!

CHAPTER 6

Casting

"CHOOSE A GOOD SCRIPT," I sometimes advise students, "cast good actors—and you'll all be good directors!" There is more than a little truth in the jest. Casting constitutes the first step in the practical interpretation of a play.

Casting possibilities in small permanent companies are limited. The Group Theatre (1931–41) had only twenty-five actors to choose from. The British National Theatre has about seventy, as does the Royal Shakespeare Company; the Moscow Art Theatre had more than a hundred. The larger companies command a sufficient number of good actors to deal satisfactorily with any play they wish to produce.

With time the permanent company develops a common vocabulary of work, an ease and a bold variety of interplay, and above all, a most helpful rapport between actors and director. The director knows his "instruments," the shortcomings and assets of every member of the company. Everyone is responsive to the others. All function smoothly together as a unit.

Seeing the Royal Shakespeare Company in Brook's *Midsummer Night's Dream,* followed immediately after in a production of Maxim Gorky's *Enemies,* a play of quasi-Chekhovian character, afforded me once again a most impressive example of the range of styles a permanent company may be able to encompass. The actors' capacities are extended through membership in a permanent company. It is not talent alone which has made it possible for Laurence Olivier, Maggie Smith, Albert Finney, Peggy Ashcroft, Robert Stephens and many others to achieve their great scope of characterization. Think of the roles these stars have been called upon to play within a relatively short time. Maggie Smith appeared in *The Beaux' Stratagem* and in *Hedda Gabler* during the same season. Laurence Olivier's repertoire in recent years has included Shakespeare, Sheridan, Farquhar, Chekhov, Osborne and O'Neill. We think of such actors as being "able to play anything." While this is not literally true, it is as much a sign of the advantages of permanent company organizations as of their individual gifts.

Although there have been a few attempts to create them, the American theatre has almost no such companies. We proceed on the basis of "piecework": for every new production an entirely new cast must be found—somehow, somewhere. Casting a play in this fashion is an arduous task.

To begin with, the New York director chooses among the actors he has seen and admired in the course of his playgoing or among those with whom he has previously worked and liked.* If among these two groups he finds actors who are available and interested in the plays and parts for which they are summoned, the job of casting is greatly simplified.

* Equity insists that there be a limited number of "open calls" for which any member of the union may apply for a part. I doubt whether many actors have been engaged through this procedure.

We must remember that in casting new plays, the writer, who contractually has the last word in the matter, must sometimes be persuaded that the actor the director wants is the right choice for a particular role. The producer also carries weight in the decision. There are hesitations and debates.

It is customary to seek stars for leading roles. But nowadays stars or "movie names" no longer assure success. In England a weak play may hold the boards for several months if a cherished actor appears in it. Not only is the public there more loyal to its actors than we are, but there is a more steady stream of playgoers and the economics of the theatre are less stringent. Unless a play in New York is found to possess intrinsic interest (and receives favorable notices), it cannot be "saved" by a star. Our theatregoing public is no longer as interested in its actors as it was before 1929.

The "open market" method of casting in our theatre is further complicated by the fact that comparatively few actors nowadays achieve a shining reputation by work on the stage alone. Many of our most promising actors have abandoned the stage for films. (This trend began in the thirties and has continued until very recently. The gradual decline of Hollywood may reverse the tide. But there is still television.) The actors whom films have made famous exercise extreme caution in venturing onto Broadway's treacherous paths. The people engaged in casting are therefore obliged to seek players free of commitments to films, television and advertisement. The problem of casting often reduces itself not to the question of the best actor for a particular part but of "Who can you get?"

The main business of casting is accomplished by means of auditions or readings. Even well-known actors are frequently asked to read, especially at the insistence of the playwrights. Reading for parts is a species of theatrical shopping, usually distasteful or painful to the actor, unless he has little New York experience and is hoping to "break through."

Apart from those few managements which employ a person

capable of making intelligent recommendations to the ruling triumvirate (director, playwright and producer), scripts are sent to agents who arrange for their actor clients to be interviewed by the crucial Three. Those whose appearance and experience make them likely candidates for a role are given the script to look over a day or two before the readings are held.

I have never charted the statistics but I have the impression that at times hundreds of actors have been interviewed for a play which requires a cast of no more than ten in addition to several understudies. I must have heard at least a dozen readings a day for weeks to choose players even for some of the lesser roles. The number of auditions for musicals is astronomical. Whatever the objections to this procedure, directors and actors are obliged to suffer it. It is unavoidable given the ordinary conditions of production.

There are some directors and producers—fortunately very few—who ask actors to read "cold," that is, without time to look through the entire play and to think about the role for which they are expected to indicate their fitness. The practice is stupid and shameful. To avoid the embarrassment and uncertainty involved in the routine of auditions, I have occasionally suggested that the playwright judge an unknown actor by allowing him to play a scene he has acted with satisfaction to himself and others in a previous engagement. But playwrights almost never concur: they want the lines of *their* plays read. This may be a symptom of a deficiency in their understanding of acting.

The candidate for a role reads part of a scene, a whole scene or, in some instances, several scenes. The partner for these readings is the stage manager, who usually "feeds" the actor his cues in a flat, neutral voice. What does the director gather from such readings? He checks the actor's suitability as a physical type. He may already have considered this at the initial interview, but at the reading, which ordinarily takes place in a theatre, the director is in a better position to determine the effect of the actor's presence, his voice and speech.

The actor may also reveal some aspects of his (or her) dramatic sensibility and intelligence. Still, the results are rarely conclusive. Many good actors read badly. This is sometimes due to resentment at having to read at all and sometimes to a reticence about externalizing emotions without sufficiently genuine inner motivation. There are actors (particularly those with extensive radio experience) who read with remarkable facility. During the rehearsal period they often fail to reveal much more than efficiency in reading. Due to these hazards, actors are sometimes requested to read at three or four different auditions. Some of them refuse.

When a choice has been made—the director's judgment is usually preponderant, though it may prove a mistake to "force" it on the playwright—it is the producer's responsibility to negotiate the terms of the actor's engagement. The transaction (contractual details such as billing, salary, etc.) is almost always conducted for the actor by an agent. It is one of the odd and distressing aspects of the system that actors seem to have become entirely dependent on their agents. Many agents request their actor clients not to contact producer or director without their (the agent's) previous advice and consent. The actor has been reduced to a commodity and gradually comes to regard himself in that light. There are, to be sure, agents helpful to actor and producer, but some are a plague.

Having outlined the mechanics of casting as professionally practiced, we reach the heart or the "art" of the matter. What I have said might lead one to suppose that the actor's physical type is the main consideration. It isn't and shouldn't be. Does the actor "look the part"? It is the simplest question to deal with. The director deludes himself who yields to the temptation to believe that an affirmative answer settles the matter. An actor's looks will impress an audience initially but after his first five minutes on stage it becomes aware of what he or she communicates (or fails to communicate) through *acting.* This is even true of conspicuous good looks. The pretty woman, the handsome man, will naturally please an audience at once. But if either of these creatures proves inept or dull, a damaging "backlash" ensues. As a rough working rule, it may be said that for tiny roles without special dramatic bone the correct physical type is especially desirable.

It is recorded that Edmund Kean, who was of small stature, made a great Macbeth. Still, though actors resent the emphasis on "type," there are parts in which the right physical image (along with ability) is very nearly decisive. The credibility of *Uncle Vanya,* for example, is considerably weakened if the audience does not share in both Astrov's and Voinitsky's intense appreciation of Yelena's magnetic attractiveness. On seeing a production of O'Casey's *Cock-a-Doodle-Dandy* in which feminine allure is repeatedly referred to with a mixture of eager appetite and apprehension, I was put off when the ladies presumed to personify devilish charm in no way corresponded to the description.

Before discussing the less superficial phases of the subject, it should be pointed out that the reason for the stress on physical type is due to the brief rehearsal period in our theatre and the consequent panic pressure of time. Casting for type simplifies the director's task in creating characterizations. With type casting, characterizations come "ready made." Some actors (their number is happily in decline) not only acquiesce to this routine, they promote it by the assurance that they've "played this sort of part many times."

There is more to the notion of "type" than the actor's physical attributes. "Type" may be thought of as the quality of an actor's inner disposition, his true self, which may be belied by his outward appearance. An actor I have directed was very nearly ruined because while he looked like the kind of forthright, ruggedly upstanding, dignified American whose counterpart we sometimes see in the U.S. Senate, he always disappointed the audience in such parts. He was actually a person of introverted nature.

Stanislavsky, a strikingly handsome man, confessed that he

was rarely well suited to roles of romantically successful lovers. He was most effective in "character roles"—roles in which
the actor assumes the "mask" of a person markedly different
from himself. Though quite personable, Paul Muni was always best in such parts: in fact, he began his career at an
early age playing old men. Very few producers believed he
could play anything else. To be themselves such actors must
transform themselves. Meskin, a veteran of Israel's Habimah
Theatre, a splendid actor who has never been known to
strike a false note, is virtually incapable of portraying evil: it
is a dimension wholly foreign to his nature.

There are beautiful women without sex appeal and plain
ones aglow with it. Rare indeed is the actor, no matter how
gifted, who can "play anything." That is why Stanislavsky in
My Life in Art says, "The misunderstanding of one's true
ability and calling in art is the strongest obstacle in the further
development of an actor. It is a blind alley in which he
spends dozens of years until he realizes his mistake."

A part may be viewed in many different lights. Have we not
seen Iago played as a fiend, a playboy, a colorlessly blunt
military man and as a "Iago from Chicago"? Is Lear a decrepit
old fool, a heroic patriarch, a nice old papa cursed with nasty
kids or a monster of pristine pride? Many of the so-called interpretations we read about are not interpretations at all, but
accidents of talent and personality. Interpretation may be
said to exist only where a deliberate choice has been made
among the myriad possibilities. The individual role is one
part of the entire play; where a sense of the whole play is lacking, the definition of the theatre as "a collective art in which
the strongest force wins" is inescapable.

In Odets' *Golden Boy* there was a difficult choice to be
made in casting the role of Joe Bonaparte. He is a musically
inclined youth who also happens to be endowed with a physique and skill for boxing. He belongs to an Italian immigrant family and has developed the all-American desire to get

ahead, to become "somebody." So he chooses the fighting game.

There were three members of the Group Theatre's acting company who were capable of playing the role satisfactorily (eventually all did). Odets preferred young John Garfield. But there was also Elia Kazan, strong and fiery. He had given first-rate performances in two of Odets' earlier plays: *Waiting for Lefty* and *Paradise Lost*. The most experienced actor of the three was Luther Adler, somewhat older than the others and not quite so convincingly "in the pink."

The fact that Bonaparte becomes a champion of the ring mattered less to me than that he was a yearning boy with something in him of the potential artist. There had to be in him that fluidity of emotive faculties and the peculiar vulnerability which frequently accompanies ambivalent impulses. There was an honest simplicity in Garfield that resembled callowness. His Joe Bonaparte would not have been as conscious of himself or as articulate as Odets had made him. There is a mounting hysteria in Joe due to his inability to resolve his inner dilemma, a hysteria which leads to his destruction. With Kazan, I surmised (one cannot be *certain* in these matters), Joe's suffering might reveal itself only after the situation had come to its crisis. The audience, I believed, should perceive the immanence of tragedy before its final crystallization. The boy's fate is contained in his character rather than in the logic of circumstances. Luther Adler's fluent and rich sensibility struck me as the right quality for the role. When cast he was trained to "look it" by a hard and prolonged gymnasium workout. In the same play Kazan was superb as the gangster Fuselli; Garfield unforgettable as Siggie, the lovably vulgar hackie.

A director's choice in casting is delicately nuanced and motivated by a variety of considerations. In reading Williams' *Cat on a Hot Tin Roof* one would suppose that the role of Maggie, the "Cat," demanded a strong-willed and slightly embittered personality. Kazan feared that if these were made the girl's salient characteristics, the role might become unsympathetic and her quandary a matter of indifference to the audience. He therefore chose Barbara Bel Geddes, whose natural charm would emphasize Maggie's normal American womanhood.

Because there is no absolute in these matters, there is an endless fascination in seeing the same role transfigured by different interpretations and personalities. In many of the permanent companies in Europe several actors are chosen to alternate in the same role during the play's life in the theatre's repertoire. Roles and plays are human things, not fixed or static. They must forever remain fresh and new. Above all, they must make sense within a specific context. Complete control on the director's part is impossible—is not, in fact, really desirable.

A prime factor in casting, one too often overlooked, is that the process should not concentrate solely on individual parts but on the nature of the company as a whole. One might cast a play with actors, each one individually "right," yet not acceptable in conjunction with the others. This goes beyond the obvious matching of ages, homogeneity in family relationships, the height or weight of actors who play scenes together. An excellent actor may simply not "mix" with others equally proficient. I do not refer to personal incompatibility and the ensuing temperamental clashes, but to the requirement for unity of texture which a production must possess if it is to signify more than a disparate assemblage of talents.

The unity I speak of has to do with social and cultural background, the ways in which the actors have been trained, their techniques and artistic ideals. Combining actors, even when all are qualified for their particular assignments, without their possessing something in common in all these respects may have the same disquieting effect as a real tree placed on the stage among painted ones: it becomes difficult to ascertain which causes the greater disharmony, the real or the artificial.

To sum up: Any choice in casting becomes pointless unless one has determined how each of the characters is connected with the play's spine and style. To understand that connection better we must return to the study of the script, which has continued from the first day the director has agreed to undertake his assignment.

CHAPTER 7

The Director's Work Script

HAVING READ the script six or more times and decided what the play's main action or spine is, the director would then do well to study the play in still another way. He should read all the parts separately *as if he himself were going to act each of them*. This will help him find the *spines or the chief motivating action for each character*. The character's spine must be conceived as emerging from the play's main action. Where such a relation is not evident or non-existent, the character performs no function in the play. There is no basis for a true characterization unless the character's prime motivation or spine is found.

The chief motivation or spine for each character must be conceived and stated from the character's own viewpoint. The audience, usually given to moralistic judgments—favorable or otherwise—will draw its own conclusions. Thus Iago is a villain, Lady Macbeth a fiend, Gertrude a bitch, Horatio a pure soul, Polonius a fool, James Tyrone in O'Neill's *Long Day's Journey into Night* a bad father. But the actors who play these roles must think of them in positive terms. A director might conceivably tell the actor playing the part that Iago wants "to right an injustice done him by Othello." Didn't Othello neglect to appoint him to the office he deserved! James Tyrone has contributed to the ruin of his wife and sons. He is a "stingy bastard," etc. But the spine I assigned for the actor playing the role was "to maintain the family." The fact that his efforts in this direction result in disaster is the play's drama.

Very few people who behave badly consider themselves "wicked." They justify themselves, and the director who plans their theatrical embodiment must "justify" them too. The actor who plays a villain as such (with negative intent) is usually a bad actor: obvious, stagey and often involuntarily laughable.

In speaking of these hypothetical characters I have repeatedly used the words "doing" and "action." Drama signifies action and the characters in all plays must be viewed chiefly in terms of what the fundamental pattern of their behavior is. Every character has his own spine, his own main action. And this, I repeat, is always to be considered as a function of the play's spine.

No one is constant in the nature of his behavior. The peaceful man may lash out fiercely. The ardent revolutionary will at times act mildly, the kindly teacher may take to the whip. But in every case these changes of behavior must be judged to have their origin in the character's prime motivation. It is a good rule for directors and actors to find those moments in a play where the bad guy behaves like a good guy and the decent fellow turns savage.

Not all people similarly motivated are alike. Not only may the reasons for particular types of action have different causes, but every character is marked by special traits, individual *characteristics.* Thus, two aspects of a role must be jointly considered: the basic character and its external characteristics. The fiery leader may stammer. The stammer may be a symptom of some inner disturbance, the consequence of overzealousness or an attempt at control. Or it may be a strikingly accidental trait, as is sometimes associated with Hotspur in *Henry IV.* The inner and outer characteristics constitute a *characterization.* The two aspects of the characterization, as just noted, are often but not always interrelated. Certain actors stress a character's outer features to the neglect if not altogether to the exclusion of everything else because these are most readily communicated to an audience and therefore most stagily effective. Every theatregoer recalls some performance in which an actor's peculiar accent or an idiosyncrasy of gait, facial expression, voice, costume or makeup rendered it memorable.

A more specific example in the study of character in drama is furnished by references to Odets' *Golden Boy.* The spine chosen for the play was "to win the fight of life." (Naming the spine is a personal aid to the director: in itself it has no other merit. Its importance, I repeat, is that it helps clarify the director's thinking.) The spine of *Golden Boy* is most directly applicable to the central character, Joe Bonaparte. Joe's father enacts the play's spine by encouraging what is best in his family and friends. This may be clarified by defining his spine as "to preserve the integrity of those about him." (As I have lost the original notebook I am no longer certain of how I actually designated the spines of this play.) Joe's brother-in-law Siggie's ego is sustained by the acquisition of that symbol of well-being which for him is a splendid cab of his own. His spine is "to enjoy the attributes of comfort and position due his estate." The gangster Fuselli satisfies his ego by his determination to bend everything to his own will. His spine is "to possess." The character called "Tokyo," Joe's trainer, wants to do his job well, "to work honestly."*

* Further examples of spines for other plays will be found in the series of Director's Notes on pp. 179–266.

Joe was outwardly characterized as somewhat adolescent in manner: his "poetic" speeches were not spoken pompously but gropingly like a kid trying to articulate what he feels but does not altogether comprehend. Soft at the core, he is fresh with youthful bluffness. His father was depicted as a lusty, smiling, immovably moral person in love with the world in its humblest aspects. Tokyo spoke softly, an intrepid worker given to few words. Fuselli had the fierce gravity, the muted power and the sleek grace of a master of men. His suave manner boded trouble. There was a faint hint of the homosexual in his masculinity.

Such notations describe the "flesh" overlaying the spines; they are "colors" immanent in what the dramatist has written. The descriptions and explanations for these "colors" in the director's notebook may cover pages. I try to imagine what a character's life story—early environment, childhood experiences, etc.—has been before we encounter him in the play. Joe Bonaparte, Odets tells us, is cross-eyed, a trait to which I paid no attention because besides being precariously "comic," it was something the audience would be unable to see unless made grotesque. But Joe may have suffered being called a "sissy" because as a boy he carried a violin in a neighborhood where other boys sported baseball bats. Fuselli, another "wop," also found the going tough till he learned the trick of terrorizing people.

The more detailed the background the director imagines for the play's characters, the richer the performances become —with good actors! The antecedent life histories are only helpful to the actor if they lead him to kindred material wrought from his own imagination. The director's intentions, howsoever interesting, may leave the actor untouched. In either case, what is imagined should stem from certain elements in the playwright's script. "My" characterizations derive from three sources—the script, the actor's imagination, my own nature.

The characters' spines had best be stated as *active verbs*. The spine is an active response to a wish: the characters *want* something and *do* something to satisfy that wish. They are often impeded in that satisfaction; sometimes they succeed in satisfying it or are deflected from it by either more pressing desires or a realization of the vanity of what they had previously wanted. The simultaneous wishes, aims and actions of all the characters cause the conflicts which create the play's argument.

For a production at one of the Moscow Art Theatre's studios, Michael Chekhov who, if I remember correctly, directed it, chose "to play with life" as the spine for *Twelfth Night*. This also suggests the *style* of that production. The director's next step, in that instance, was to specify in what way each of the play's characters plays with life. It certainly cannot be the same for Malvolio as for Sir Toby.

To repeat an already cited example*: My spine for *Desire Under the Elms* was "to possess the Farm." The "Farm" in that play is the actual object over which the characters struggle, but it is also the symbol of the land, the country. The play's theme might be translated metaphorically as "Who or what force shall possess America?" How and by whom is the struggle waged? Each of the play's characters wants to gain possession of the farm in his or her own way. Those who despair of ever owning it—the two elder brothers—go west to gain a similar benefit: gold.

Not all directors, again I repeat, commit their thoughts to a notebook, or not to the extent that I do or to the much greater extent that Max Reinhardt did. But nearly all directors think and plan in a similar fashion though they may not use the specific terms I employ. Many work largely by "instinct." The *formal structure* which my interpretation of a play takes *is a personal guideline and not something to be spelled out, read to the actors or literally insisted upon at rehearsal.*

The notation of the play's spine and characterizations pre-

---

* Repetitions are unavoidable and necessary in this essay because its various elements overlap, each being integral with the other.

cedes the drawing up of the director's "score." When rehearsals begin, the director has already digested all that he has thought or written about in his preliminary work with the script. He may not even refer to it again, till perhaps after the production has opened. In a state of puzzlement as to the drift of a production, I have at times looked back to my notes to remind myself of my original intention. On reading my published notes for Miller's *Incident at Vichy** after the play had closed, Joseph Wiseman remarked, "You know, Harold, about eighty percent of what you had in mind was actually accomplished." Regardless of whether this estimate was true or not, I was immensely pleased. I am relatively content when only half of my production idea is realized.

From the director's notes to the stage there is a long, long road. The production may prove inferior or superior to that which has been adumbrated beforehand. The plan and the execution are of an altogether different nature. They are in different "languages." The production is composed of real bodies and concrete materials, not of verbal and intellectual imponderables. I cannot too often repeat that the director's work is not a solo performance: it is a graph for and, at best, an inspiration to his collaborators—the acting company and all the other members of the production staff.

Theatre is not an accumulation of ingredients: it is a composite organism greater or lesser than its several components. That is what makes the discernment of how it has been wrought a most difficult if not a wholly impossible undertaking. But in this we approach the area of theatre criticism, about which comment must wait for a later chapter.

The search for and the conclusions as to the nomenclature and composition of the play's various spines, style, theme, "philosophy," relevance, its atmosphere and mood, the social and historical background from which it springs, the imagined biographies of the characters antecedent to the play's

* The *Incident at Vichy* notes will be found on p. 242.

events—all these are still only the first steps toward the director's "score." The foregoing procedures are indispensable;
they are not the thing itself.

The director's working script is his score. It follows the play
scene by scene, line by line. I arrange it in the following way:
I insert a blank sheet of paper facing each of the pages in the
play's text. I divide the clean sheet into three more or less
equal columns.*

The first and most important column notes the particular
action of the moment. It states what each character—in silence
or through speech—is doing, or, more precisely, what he wants
or intends to do. These actions, too, are always designated by
active verbs: to warn, to plead, to threaten, to reprove, to
punish, to heal, to flatter and so on as the case may be.

The prescription to use an active verb for each specific
action may appear arbitrary and didactic. But it is, if not
mandatory, extremely helpful. It avoids such generalizations
as "getting angry," "being modest," "feeling hurt": these
tend to encourage histrionic clichés. Stanislavsky described
the first step in embodying love on the stage as "to pay attention," and at a later point of its emotional development as
"to take care of" or "to care for"—actions. He decried the use
of phrases which describe behavior in terms of abstract sentiment: to love, to hate, to be kind, etc.

When Ophelia, for example, is coarsely teased by Hamlet
at the play which is to catch the conscience of the King, she
is not simply to act "wounded"; rather she protects her dignity, that is, she does something definite, acts in some positive
fashion.

This leads to the second column of the director's notations
in which he sets down the manner in which the basic action
is to be carried out. The first column states what is to be done,
the second how it is to be done. Actors speak of the instructions given in the second column as adjustments. To use the
previous example, we may then say Ophelia "protects her

* Examples of this arrangement of the script are to be found on pp. 269-289.

dignity" with such adjustments as "in a pained voice" or "in sad reproof" or in whatever given manner befits the character and the scene. If Ophelia, as some directors have audaciously conceived her, is not the pure creature we ordinarily take her to be but a girl corrupted by the hypocrisy of the court, her action might be "to counter the thrust" (in the first column) and (in the second column) "provocatively" or "flirtatiously."

Continuing with the same scene, let us suppose the director sees Ophelia slapping Hamlet's possibly searching hand, the slap would be noted in the third column. This is the column in which the director indicates the *overt physical activity* which manifests both Ophelia's action and adjustment. Hamlet's use of his hand in speaking of "country matters" would also be inscribed in the column devoted to activities.

To reiterate in strict order: the three columns are (1) the basic *action*, (2) the attitude or *adjustment* which colors the aforesaid action in the circumstances of the scene and (3) the *overt physical activity* which accompanies the action.

I speak of an activity accompanying an action rather than extending or completing it because there are activities which are not organically related to the action. Thus Bessie (the mother) in *Awake and Sing* while chiding her husband and correcting her children's behavior (actions) is setting the table, which may be said to relate to her spine ("to take care of everything") but not directly to the action of chiding her husband or correcting her children.

In the same play Ralphie, Bessie's son, *sings the praises* of his girl friend's charms ("She's like French words"), which is his action, while at the same time putting on a new pair of trousers. This last is an activity but hardly a direct consequence of his action, though he is preparing to visit the girl. The juxtaposition of the boy's lines and the activity given him are not simultaneous in the script.

When, however, Moe Axelrod in *Awake and Sing*, the petty racketeer who boards with the Bergers, learns that Hennie Berger, with whom he has had an affair, is to marry another man, his·casual reply has the action "to hide his feelings," while he bites into a thick slice of cake he has bought for the family. The biting of the cake at that moment is the activity he resorts to to appear casual and to hide his feelings.

There is a scene in Odets' *Paradise Lost* in which a young violinist comes to end his relationship with the girl he had hoped to marry. He must explain that he is too poor for matrimony. As he enters, she waits for him anxiously at the far end of the room. He approaches her hesitantly. The action might simply come under the heading "to greet" with an adjustment of tension. They both wear glasses, a minor touch in their characterizations. When the young man comes face to face with the girl he removes his glasses, she removes hers— and they kiss. These activities (or bits of business) were not part of the original script; they were the director's invention.

Actions are not always obvious in the author's writing. They occasionally seem to contradict the dialogue's surface connotations. In the park scene of *Golden Boy*—often used for film tests and by students for class exercise—many of the lines suggest a tender love scene. But the girl, who has been sent by her lover, the boy's would-be manager, to persuade Joe to take up professional fighting, studies Joe *to discover* how best to carry out her objective. Joe, self-absorbed and dimly aware of her purpose (these are his adjustments), pays little attention at first, then begins *to probe* into her character and attitude toward her lover (this is his action) in an aggressive manner—a further adjustment. The scene as a whole, with short lapses in which Joe muses aloud about what music means to him as well as about the high-powered motor cars (further actions), has something in the nature of a conflict about it. The scene ends with Joe brashly proclaiming (action—to decide or resolve) that he'll enter the fighting game.

It was, I believe, the Russian director Vakhtangov who suggested that every scene be given a name or a descriptive tag to provide keynotes as an aid to director and actors in finding the right actions and adjustments. I have occasionally taken advantage of this "pointer," calling one scene "The Trap," another "The Showdown," still another "Release." This is especially valuable when the descriptive titles do not superficially appear to correspond to the actions indicated by the lines alone but reveal the scene's true character.

A production I directed in 1949 with the Habimah company of Israel, Emmanuel Roblès' *Montserrat* (a translation of the original text, not the Lillian Hellman adaptation), ends with a duologue between two officers of the Spanish army, which has been sent to South America to suppress Bolívar's struggle for independence. One of the officers is an embittered authoritarian, contemptuous of "the people," the other an idealistic humanist. The scene read like a debate. To preserve the intellectual mode of the writing would not only have crippled the play's climax but would have struck the audience as wearisomely wordy. This was the only scene written by Lillian Hellman which I filched from her version (a scene, incidentally, that she cut in her production of the play). In my script I called the scene "The Last Battle" and directed it as if each of its speeches was a fierce blow. It proved a great audience success.

The quizzing of a murder suspect in a film I directed, a whodunit called *Deadline at Dawn* (RKO, 1945), contained little more than a series of questions. I called it "The Seduction," an attempt *to woo* the suspect into an admission of guilt.

A scene running to several pages of text may be comprised of only one or two basic actions. An action doesn't change with every spoken line, although the adjustments may do so, diminishing or gathering intensity as the scene progresses. An action changes when it is fully carried out, in which case another action ensues, or when it is interrupted by the unexpected entrance of another character, the ringing of a telephone or the intrusion of an unexpected event, or simply when a character changes his mind.

In *Death of a Salesman* Willy Loman comes to see his boss

to request a less tiring job. He is hesitant and circuitous in his effort to explain his situation but his action is interrupted by the boss's tactics aimed to deflect Willy from what he guesses is Willy's intention. These tactics are an action. The action continues till Willy's outburst, which then turns into the action "to protest" or "to denounce." The scene would be impossible to play if Willy and his boss were obliged to change their actions with every line they speak. Each of these characters has only two or three actions in this relatively long scene. It should also be noted that every scene or *unit* (sometimes called a "beat") of a scene has its own climax.

The great Russian director Meyerhold had something else in view when he declared "Words in the theatre are only a design on the canvas of motion," but his dictum may be applied here. Writing is not the theatre's last word! Stage business is born of free association on the part of the director and/ or actors from the premises of the script's basic actions.

It is certainly no recent discovery that theatre may be expressive without the use of any verbal text, though today some folks talk as if it were. The point impressed me in a special way when Ray Bolger remarked that he didn't dance with his legs and feet alone. The dance he was referring to was the moment in the musical *Where's Charley?* which, he explained, sprang from Charley's dilemma: how to get away from the girls' embraces so that they wouldn't discover his real identity while he was posing as their aunt. The answer led not to words but to twists, leaps and a delightfully complex choreographic routine, in itself a whole scene.

The fanciful antics of Peter Brook's *Midsummer Night's Dream* are suggested by Shakespeare's text, "A man is but an ass, if he go about to expound this dream . . . And those things do best please me that befall preposterously," lines which offer a clue to the extravagance of the whole production. When Brook placed ladders on both sides of the stage on which characters ascend to a rostrum above the stage or descend from it, he was doing what the goblin Puck says of himself, that he is constantly going "Up and down, up and down. I will lead them up and down—."

The third column of my working script, the activities column, is usually left blank before rehearsal. There are, however, certain "high moments" which I do prepare and note in the script in advance of rehearsal. After the production has opened, the stage manager, as my assistant, writes down all the business which the actors and I have devised together. There are directors who invent all or most of the business beforehand. I do the greatest part of this during rehearsals. There is no particular value judgment attached to either practice. It is a question of the director's disposition, the kinds of gifts he has, how he "operates."

The removal of the eyeglasses preceding the kiss in *Paradise Lost* occurred to me in the preparation of my script. When directing the end of the second act of *Uncle Vanya* in which Yelena eagerly anticipates playing the piano, I staged the scene as follows: She sits down at the keyboard, opens the piano; Sonya enters and tells Yelena that her father (Yelena's husband) in the next room objects to her playing. Yelena quietly closes the lid and looks up helplessly at Sonya. This, too, was planned before rehearsal.

Some such notations of business—such details as setting the actors' positions, moments where actors are to cross from one point of the stage to another, where they are to sit or rise, in other words, the whole job of blocking—may be found in my working script, but not many. I find that observing the actors in rehearsal suggests more elaborations or expansions of action than I am able to foresee with nothing but the script and the model of the setting before me.

Notations on lighting, tempo, offstage sound and music are also set down in the third (activities) column. These all concern the production's physical life.

In the last phase of his career Stanislavsky—of whose teachings and their influence I shall say more further on—

spoke of actions chiefly in terms of *physical problems.* This has been called the technique of physical action. Such actions as "to protect," "to flirt," and the like provoke physical impulses. Even a man sitting in a chair preoccupied by an unexpressed thought manifests minute "unconscious" physical activities: we detect them in his eyes, his breathing, his half-realized or suppressed desire to rise and changes of position of the head or body as he sits apparently "doing nothing" but thinking. The action, set down in the first column of the working script, may be translated into such problematic questions for the actor as "How will you prevent this or that person from approaching you?", "How can you get rid of that fool?", "What can you do to convince this man?" and so forth.

The disputes over such refined distinctions as to the best procedure in this matter so passionately engaged in by teachers and theoreticians may be of interest and importance but they are not vital to my present exposition. There are more ways of dealing with actors at rehearsal than have been dreamed of by readers of Stanislavsky's or anyone else's discourses. Stanislavsky himself said so.

At least four to six weeks have passed in the preliminary work I have described. The director has made himself ready for the first rehearsal. Let's get to it.

CHAPTER 8

Early Rehearsals

WHEN THE ACTORS are called for the first rehearsal, the director has, as we have learned, already done a considerable part of his work; the actors are only now beginning theirs. The director and playwright must bear this in mind. To overlook it will obstruct progress.

After greeting the actors and introducing them to one another, I ask the designer to explain the model of the setting. It becomes more meaningful and the actors' interest in it increases after the play has been read several times.

The actors have all read the script privately. Now for the first time they are to read it together. With permanent companies the actors become acquainted with the script through a reading by the playwright or the director, depending on which of the two is the better reader.

If the director and playwright have agreed on textual cuts

made at their early conferences, it is advisable that the actors take note of them before they begin their first reading. On this occasion it is preferable that they read from complete scripts rather than from individual part books or "sides." It troubles actors to cut lines which they have already committed to memory. There will be more cutting required at later stages of the work; in fact, there is almost always more cutting to be done than one suspects. The earlier the cuts are made, the better for all concerned.

Faced for the first time by the director, the playwright and the producer, the actors tend to suppress too overt an expression—of anything! They are "hiding." English actors at first readings are bolder and more fluent than Americans. This is due in some measure to the English actors' "professionalism"—which simply should be taken to mean more practice in the profession. Their facility is also due to the greater emphasis on speech and voice in their training.

Early in my career I used to instruct the actors on these occasions to *talk* the lines of the play to one another and to make themselves heard by the company around them. Speaking the lines as conversation, I explained, is the first step toward truth in acting. Whatever validity there may be in this explanation, what I really intended was to allay nervousness, to let the actors know that they were not required to impress anyone. (According to Equity regulations an actor not signed to a run-of-the-play contract may be dismissed on the fifth day of rehearsal.) But I soon learned that there was little point in giving the actors at the first readings any instructions whatsoever. They should be allowed to read in any way they will and should not be interrupted unless they become inaudible or strain to produce an effect. It is a routine joke with me to say, "If any of you are great right away, I shall have to fire you: it will leave me with nothing to do!" A well-chosen company—and I always assume complete confidence in the players I have cast—requires no special admonition.

Ten-minute breaks are taken after the reading of each act. The play of average length is read for the first time in little more than two and a half hours. We then retire for lunch which, according to the Equity contract, is to be not less than an hour and a half in duration. Since the tension of the first reading is tiring, I allow for a longer lunch (or rest) period. The company, I trust, will be comparatively relaxed when called back for the afternoon reading.

The time allowed for the entire rehearsal process differs with various companies. In certain European theatres a play may be rehearsed for twelve weeks or much longer. The actors in these theatres usually appear in other plays of their repertoire during this time. Rehearsals at such theatres rarely run more than five hours a day. I consider this the ideal length of time for daily rehearsals. Peter Brook rehearsed his *Midsummer Night's Dream* for eight weeks.

In our professional productions we allow four weeks of rehearsal for a "straight" play, five weeks for a musical. Equity demands that rehearsal time be limited to seven out of eight and a half hours daily. This may be extended to ten out of twelve hours during the week before the first public performance. The day prior to the opening night the rehearsal time is unlimited—always provided that twelve hours elapse between rehearsal calls.

If the producer chooses to prolong rehearsals beyond four weeks he may do so if he pays the actors full salaries or not less than the Equity minimum. But this can only be done if the actors have agreed to such an arrangement. Due to the present high cost of production, extension of the rehearsal period, without the support of paid performances, may prove exorbitant.

Even the four-week rehearsal period is not as much time as it appears to be. The first three weeks are computed on the basis of a six-day week. These first three weeks of seven rehearsal hours daily, conducted on a bare stage or whatever space has been procured for the purpose, must allow for cos-

tume fittings and the like. The next three or four days are
devoted to dress rehearsals on the sets, in costume and
makeup, with lights, etc. These are held in preparation for
either an out-of-town ("road") tryout or previews in town.
The previews or road tryouts are paid public performances.
During this time only four hours a day (except for the usual
two matinee days) are allowed for rehearsal.

It is necessary to keep this information in mind to understand some of the problems in craft and personal "psychology" which arise due to the pressures of time. The Group
Theatre's first production, Paul Green's *House of Connelly,*
was rehearsed for approximately twelve weeks, its second
play, *1931,* was rehearsed for eight weeks, and Sidney Kingsley's *Men in White* for ten weeks. All three plays were directed by Lee Strasberg. Because of altered circumstances I
was only permitted the regulation four weeks for all my
productions except for Odets' *Paradise Lost* (six weeks), the
same author's *Golden Boy* (five weeks) and, more recently,
O'Neill's *A Touch of the Poet* (five weeks).

The scheduling of my productions in regard to time is, as I
have said, typical of the commercial theatre. I have never been
obliged to postpone an announced opening. I should, nevertheless, quote a remark an actor who appeared in one of my
productions once made: "Harold rehearses a play as if there
were never going to be an opening night!" This says something about my "method": I refuse to create a sense of haste.
But for any but the most rudimentary script, four weeks of
rehearsals are insufficient. Apropos of this, I cannot refrain
from citing a Stanislavsky quip: "No matter how long one
rehearses one always needs two more weeks."

At the second reading of the play the actors may read
even less securely than at the first. It does not matter. They
are getting acquainted with the play and a little more accustomed to each other's voices and faces. They may even listen
better.

During both of the first day's readings, as already noted, I offer no advice. I make no comment; I listen and observe. I study the material: the script as read and the nature of the readers. My routine joke at the end of the day—by which time, to the actors' astonishment, I have hardly uttered a word—is to say, "You must admit that the direction today has been perfect." It is true! The director should shut up and allow actors and script to "merge" without interference.

This "treatment" is repeated on the morning of the second day. The actors even then may not read any more convincingly than on the first day, but they are more capable of listening to one another. They are now eager for word from the director. This, in my case, usually follows after lunch on the second day, that is, after the third reading. The actors are now sufficiently familiar with the script to gain something from a discussion of it.

Many directors and actors consider general discussion of a script superogatory. They want "to get to work" right away. This is particularly true of English actors; they wish to "get on their feet," that is, proceed to the staging immediately after the first or second reading. But I am speaking here of my customary practice. I have on occasion yielded to the habitual inclination of such an actor as, for instance, Ralph Richardson, who is somewhat discomfited by any talk which doesn't directly lead to blocking—the assignment of stage positions, crosses from one place to another, etc. Dogmatism in the theatre is debilitating.

My first talk deals with the character of the play we are producing, its general import, its relevance to the world we live in. In speaking of the "world" I include the actors themselves as part of that world. With a foreign play or an old play (out of a past epoch or such a play as Shaw's *Saint Joan*) I discuss its national and/or historical background. Apropos of Williams' *Orpheus Descending* I spoke about the South, which I had visited, read about and learned about from what

Williams had told me. For Miller's *Incident at Vichy* I read accounts of the Nazi occupation of France and made inquiries in Vichy itself, and I spoke about my findings.

My remarks may be sociological, psychological, "poetic." I avoid the dry sound of scholarship. The purpose of the talk is to arouse a feeling of the worthiness of our project, to create enthusiasm. The first rehearsals are the honeymoon period in our love affair with the play. The world of the theatre is the whole world, and nothing human is alien to it. No one need blush to approach production in this manner. Experience has taught me that the stimulation of these early exchanges bears fruit in the performance. They contribute to its "aura," without which it often remains arid, lacking in glamor.

I speak, too, of the play's style, the dramatist's individual touch, his habit of mind, his rhythm, the kind of acting his play demands. I illustrate this by references to the character of the writing, the play's structure. In the early years of my career I also spent considerable time analyzing each of the play's characters. This was not done with diagrammatic rigor. There was little specific mention of spines or main actions. I do not employ terms which may be meaningful only to me. The intention is to stir the actor according to his individual nature.

In speaking to actors about their parts some directors think it best to talk to each of them privately. This may be advisable at a later stage of rehearsal. But when describing the play's general lineaments and how the various parts constitute the play's general design, I prefer to address the company with everyone present. It enhances a sense of the collective character of the undertaking, for each part affects the other.

These first talks are a banquet of ideas: each actor can pick what he chooses from the fare. Authors and actors usually enjoy them and participate in them at my invitation. But they used to go on too long; there was too much to digest.

Some of the actors would note the gist of what I said, especially as it impinged on their own parts. I encouraged but did not insist on this. In productions subsequent to 1949 I have reserved many of my insights for those moments during the reading or the playing of scenes or whole acts when they might imprint themselves more firmly in the actors' consciousness. Nowadays my first "address" to the actors lasts little more than an hour.

We then proceed to readings with "interruptions." After a passage or a scene has been read I explain in what way my previous generalizations apply to what has just been read. These interruptions, which admittedly have often been too protracted, continue through the reading of the whole play. The actors begin to see the play and their parts in sharper perspective.

Something else I attempt to accomplish during this formative stage of work is to trace the progress of the play's inner action: how each segment and scene reveals the development of the characters' and the play's continuing action so that the pattern of the play as a whole becomes evident.

When one or more of these "interrupted" readings have been completed, the company reads the play once again without interruption. A certain experience of the play is achieved in this way. The actors are now prepared to "get on their feet" and "walk" the play. Through the readings the actors have acquired a solid *theoretical* knowledge of the play, though actually it is now something more than that.

Formerly I used to conduct the early rehearsals in the manner just described for a whole week. Later, due to an ever tighter rehearsal schedule, I reduced the period to three or four days. With *Golden Boy*, when a five-week rehearsal time was made available to me, the readings continued for two weeks! But they were, as we shall see, something more than simple readings.

Some directors, particularly in England, expect the actors to commit their parts to memory before rehearsals have begun. This may be necessitated by the fact that in the English theatre blocking commences on the first or second day of rehearsals. One director I know calls for a complete run-through of the play (with ad-libbed blocking) on the third or fourth day of rehearsal.

Though there may be nothing inescapably disastrous in such practices, I have never engaged in them, nor have any of the other directors whose first important productions were presented under the Group Theatre's auspices (Lee Strasberg, Elia Kazan, Robert Lewis) done so. We virtually forbade our actors to learn their lines prior to rehearsals. On the other hand, it is probably desirable for actors to do this in the case of plays by Shakespeare and other verse plays. But none of the directors just mentioned have directed these kinds of plays. We believed, and I am still inclined to believe, that actors learning the text by heart apart from actual work at rehearsal fixes preconceptions and hardens readings into set molds so that receptivity to their fellow players' impulses is impaired. The actors, under these circumstances, hardly listen to one another, and something mechanical in the acting results.

The actor must always remain resilient, be free and open to change and new adjustments. This becomes much more difficult to do if he has learned his lines before contact with other members of the company. He will abstract himself from the all-important human context, the "team." Still, I know that some actors who have memorized their parts before rehearsal manage to remain responsive to all the contingencies of production. In this as in other theatrical matters there is no "absolute."

The first rehearsals permit the director to learn something about the kind of direction which best befits each of the actors. He studies the actors' strong points and weaknesses. Some virtually demand direction; others are disturbed by too much talk even when it is good talk. Many like to discover everything—except for technical matters—by themselves. Talk, they feel, interferes with their creative process, their pleasure in discovery. They are often right, and their inclinations should be respected. I have known actors who were reluctant to do certain admittedly interesting bits of business because the director was the first to suggest them!

Not everything the cleverest director suggests is useful to the actor; the wise director recognizes this. Direction is not to be equated with giving orders. The teacher-student relationship is to be eschewed. I have occasionally been reproached for and indeed found myself guilty of doing too much for the actors or *saying* too much to them. I have had to learn to repress my natural volubility. Some actors—particularly Americans—may be equally disturbed by the mute director, one who too strictly keeps his council. Actors want help; they want to be worked with. This has recently become so marked a tendency that my hope is that the actor will take the initiative and strike out on his own. It is a matter of pride with the director to be able to inspire the actor; it would be a greater joy if the actor was able to inspire him.

On the other hand, the type of director actors call "traffic cops," those who confine their direction to the externals of the craft with here and there an "editorial" comment, must be deplored. A veteran English actor in the cast of *Tiger at the Gates* said to me, "You are the first director who has actually *directed* me since Granville-Barker." Many English directors, the actor went on to explain, believe their function to consist of little more than the arrangement of the physical elements of the production—blocking, grouping and the like. The actor is supposed to provide the rest by virtue of his talent. Such a division of duties is unsound.

I remember an occasion when a seasoned actor stopped me on my offering a suggestion about some seemingly small point at one of the early rehearsals. "You needn't tell me that," he admonished, "I know my business." I insisted no further. I decided to say nothing more to him for several days. Following a short passage of time the actor came up to me during a lunch break and complained, "You are directing everybody else; have you nothing to tell *me?*" He was ready to be directed.

Direction and acting compose themselves into a reciprocal exchange, a two-way relationship, a kind of marriage. The most important thing that should result from the initial work period is an understanding between actor and director; each learns how to put up with and deal with the other. This becomes increasingly vital in the subsequent stages of rehearsal.

CHAPTER 9

More Rehearsals

THE READING REHEARSALS of *Golden Boy* went on for two weeks. They did not, however, consist of daily repetition of the same thing. Every step in production entails another. As actors were wooed, prodded or inspired by the director, they became ever more imbued with the sense of themselves as characters in the play and with the play itself. They were possessed by it. During the second week, although they were still "only reading," they sprang to their feet and with "book" still in hand, accosted one another, pleading or threatening, warning or soothing, teasing or provoking—in other words, *acting*. Drama was already present. Very little time—approximately five days—was required to block the entire play.

The moral of this incident suggests a rule for rehearsal: **Do** not move on to a second stage of work until the first has **been**

satisfactorily completed. The first thing well done will naturally develop into the next. To work for everything at once—
immediately to achieve "tempo," for instance—while the actors are still seeking to make their actions true will induce
falsity.

One should not demand "pace" in the early readings. Perhaps, as I shall later explain, one should not insist on it at all:
it is a consequence, not a cause. Some of the best actors are
inordinately "slow" at the outset of rehearsals. It is a foolish
director who from the first whips his company with the command "faster, faster."

Before further pursuing this exposition I must pause to
remind the reader that there is an entirely different rehearsal
procedure which may be followed. There are in fact several.
But I shall confine myself to the mention of one which to
some slight extent I undertook, as, to a greater degree, Lee
Strasberg did, in the early Group Theatre years. It is the
method of improvisation, a method which calls for more time
than is ordinarily available to us at present.

There are at least two different types of improvisation. Before describing either of them it should be immediately stated
that improvisation does not signify "doing anything you want
to do." Improvisations should always be based on a plan or a
"scenario" the director has outlined, a goal or an objective he
seeks. What is left to improvisation is the path by which the
projected end is reached.

After the play has been read and its general dramatic line
has been established, the director, instead of going on to the
blocking of the scenes, asks the actors to improvise in either of
two ways and, at times, in a combination of both.

The first type of improvisation consists of positing imaginary situations which parallel the mood or action content of
a scene which occurs in the play. For example, one asks the
actors in *Awake and Sing* to improvise a typical dinner at the
Berger apartment. The improvisation will undoubtedly last
longer than the analogous scene in the play. It is important to

give such an improvisation a special dramatic "twist" by telling one of the actors—without notifying the others—of some disturbing occurrence during the day which affects the other members of the family and of which they had been unaware.

Through such an improvisation the actors learn something of the characters' customary behavior, their interrelation, their essential traits, their possible reactions in moments of surprise or consternation. The director then comments on the degree to which the actors have understood the nature of the character which they are to play.

An improvisation may involve a single character alone. In *Awake and Sing* I asked Morris Carnovsky, who played the grandfather, to sew the torn visor of his cap—a real, not an imaginary cap—and recount to his grandson some hitherto unrevealed episode of his life, something which might serve as a cautionary tale for the boy. Carnovsky profited more from this little improvisation than from anything I might have said by way of description or explanation of the old man's nature. The sewing of the cap was later used as a minor stroke of characterization in the performance.

A more elaborate improvisation emerged as one of the most impressive scenes of Sidney Kingsley's *Men in White*. A young woman is due to undergo surgery. Lee Strasberg thought the actors playing the surgeons and their assistants ought to witness an operation at a hospital. He then asked them to repeat what they had observed. The play script itself called for no more than a short scene preceding the operation, after which the curtain fell. The actors' improvisation or recreation of the operation procedure, the washing-up routine, the pulling on of surgical gloves, the handling of the instruments, was so awe-inspiring that it was incorporated in the production and lent it something close to grandeur.

Certain improvisations have only a peripheral relationship to the play. One of my first attempts at directing a play (it was never produced) dealt with the Russian Revolution. I felt the need to arouse in the actors some of the tensions of such a crisis. The improvisation took place on a quiet country road. I asked the actors to move in march formation carrying banners with insurrectionary slogans. Without warning the marchers, I instructed another group of actors to come out of hiding and assail them as the repressive military might do.

For the same play, and for similar reasons, I had the players enact a "scene" following an explosion in a coal mine with the miners' relatives gathered around the pit to learn the men's fate.

Such improvisations are of doubtful value, because to be at all truthful they might require as much rehearsal as would the doing of an original play. I mention them not only to indicate their limits but to move on to the second and more practical type of improvisation which Stanislavsky has described and which Lee Strasberg made use of with signal success on several occasions.

The play is done scene by scene following the basic situation and circumstances in each of them. To avoid the possibility of staleness through repetition the director adds ever new adjustments and circumstances designed to arouse new perceptions and responses within each situation. But the line of action remains identical with that of the play's text.

At a run-through of *Men in White,* after five weeks of rehearsal, the whole play was acted with hardly a word of the author's dialogue spoken. The words were almost all the actors'. But the play was essentially there. Sidney Kingsley was appalled at first, and then impressed.

Such improvisations necessitate true connection among the actors. It obliges them to listen: they cannot set their reactions mechanically. They cannot take the other characters' movements and manner of address for granted. The give and take among them is spontaneous, fresh, alive.*

The physical line of action under certain given circum-

---

* I am not at all sure that this type of improvisation can be employed to advantage in producing Shakespeare.

stances to which the director adds nuances and variations is the major substance of a staged play. Playwrights themselves recognize this principle. An anecdote I once heard is worth telling in this connection. The story has it that one day Racine entered his salon where guests were awaiting him. When asked what prompted his apparent elation, he replied, "I have just finished my new play: all I have to do now is to write the dialogue."

I shall have more to say later on about the approach to acting and directing just outlined. What must be immediately stressed, however, is this: there is and should always be a degree of improvisation in the making of a production no matter how traditional the rehearsal methods. If such a margin of freedom were not allowed, the theatre would be reduced to the mere recitation of lines in conjunction with the most primitive sort of illustration. And that, no matter how elegant, precise and intelligent the reading or the illustration, would hardly constitute theatre.

After whatever number of readings the director deems sufficient or has the time for, the actors "get on their feet": blocking begins. The stage manager and his assistants trace the ground plan of the settings, in accordance with the scene designer's working drawings, with tape, chalk or paint on the floor indicating where the entrances are to be made, where steps and platforms are to be placed, etc. In addition they "rustle up" benches, chairs, tables, couches, wherever they are able to find them. The same is true of such properties as dishes, cutlery, playing cards, firearms, swords and what not.

I refer to professional American productions where no permanent technical staff—carpenters, electricians, property men —is employed. In these respects, much of our professional theatre is miserably amateurish. In the run-of-the-mill setup under which most of my colleagues and I work, the use of adequate props, furniture, even such utensils as glasses, plates, forks and knives, entails payment of regular wages to stagehands at the union scale—a costly and more often than not a prohibitive item. Paper cups, knives, forks and all sorts of paltry substitutes take the place of what is actually needed. Couches and wooden benches which only approximate the dimensions specified by the designer as required for accurate staging are all the actors may work with. This is also true of armchairs, beds and the rest.

Such arrangements are extremely discouraging as well as inefficient. Imagine a love scene in which the actors are so constricted that every emphatic gesture they make puts them in peril of falling off their seats! The inadequacy of the furniture and most of the hand props leads to a waste of time in a specifically technical sense. One does not handle a paper goblet as one does silver, a stick is not wielded as a sword, slices of beef tongue are not cut, chewed and swallowed in the same way as fine meats. In all such instances timing of lines which accompany the various activities becomes mere guesswork. At the dress rehearsals when the proper paraphernalia is brought in, the matter of coordinating dialogue and business has to be rehearsed anew.

There is a comic side to all this: the actors who after a few days manage to achieve some ease in the use of the crude props provided at first become embarrassed at dress rehearsals when these objects have been replaced by the "real things."

Where the rehearsals occur on the stage of a theatre the lighting consists of a thousand-watt electric fixture which barely gives sufficient illumination to read by. The actors are immersed in a dismal atmosphere. If more light is demanded, it is made available—at a price, the price of an electrician's wage.

The director usually knows where he wants each of the actors to be discovered for the opening scene. The placement is often indicated in the script, though this, too, is subject to drastic change. Blocking in its barest outlines is not as complex a task as the inexperienced director may suppose; it is dictated in large measure by the designer's floor plan: doors, furniture, essential props have been set accordingly. Much of the placement may be altered when necessitated by previously unforeseen business and movement. But such alterations, as mentioned earlier, are not always feasible. That is why, whenever possible, director and designer are well advised to wait on the progress of rehearsal before making the contours and detail of the settings definitive. But occasions for such a procedure are extremely rare.

Manuals exist which lay down ground rules for blocking a play. They instruct the director not to have several actors stand in a straight line parallel to the "footlights," not to have an actor walk on a "laugh line," even what foot it is best for him to put forward on making an entrance! Certain areas of the stage, according to these textbooks, are most desirable for the playing of love scenes, others for scenes of violence; crucial speeches should be read from stage center, etc., etc. A director, highly regarded in his day and under whose direction I acted in my nonage, always avoided having scenes played at the center of the stage because he thought it was "old-fashioned." It was the only technical rule he seemed aware of and about which he was dogmatic! It should go without saying that most such rule-of-thumb prescriptions are absurd.

The audience's attention must be directed to the focal point of interest in every scene. There are a number of means by which this may be accomplished: gradations in the intensity of lighting is the most obvious. But there can be no strict rules for blocking. Even "stage center" is not a fixed position: all depends on the design of the floor plan—and the theatre's architecture. In side seats of certain arena theatres, stage center is at a considerable distance from the spectators. What is most decisive in blocking is maintaining flow and variety of movement. A fixed position within a limited area produces visual monotony and decreases the audience's power of attention. All visible stage space should be used in the course of an evening. Incessant movement, however, distracts.

It is my practice to remove virtually every property or piece of furniture which has no function in the play's action. During the early blocking session I sit on or very close to the stage. I move further back from it with the progress of rehearsals. The director ought to check his blocking from all parts of the house, although it is vain to hope for wholly propitious sight lines and grace of composition from every point.

Famous paintings and the manner of their creators often serve to inspire various directors in their stage pictures. Meyerhold spoke of finding the colors for his production of *La Dame aux Camélias* in Manet and Renoir. There was something of Brueghel in Peter Brook's staging of *The Visit*. Rembrandt's lighting is a frequent model. For study of dramatic movement, Gordon Craig recommended Giotto, Masiliano and Michelangelo; for facial expression and costume, Fra Angelico, Franz Hals, Teniers, Hogarth and Rembrandt; for Shakespeare, Carpaccio. But conscious "borrowings" of this kind, though legitimate, are alien to my habit.

As previously stated, some directors plan their blocking in advance of rehearsals. They map out every cross, change of position, move upstage (away from the audience in a proscenium theatre), downstage (toward curtain line). This may save time. Stanislavsky said he worked this way as a beginner. He gave it up later.

I concern myself with the climactic points of action: those movements or pieces of business crucial to my vision of the play. For the rest, to begin with, I allow the actors to ad lib their crosses and the moments they find most suitable for sitting, standing and pacing. Still, I regulate this "freedom" to assure myself that the blocking makes sense: that besides being conducive to the actors' effectiveness, it corresponds to the dramatic needs of the play and helps in the control of audience interest.

I remember an occasion when I was called in to redirect a play which had already opened out of town. During one of the rehearsals I asked an actress to make a cross at a different point than she had become accustomed to under the former staging. "But," the actress protested, "I feel so comfortable doing it the old way." "*You* may feel comfortable," I countered, "but the audience doesn't."

Looking back and recalling the actual conduct of my rehearsals I find that what I have just said is not strictly accurate. After the first "go" signal in blocking, I am careful to designate where I prefer the actor to cross, sit, stand, etc. I find that my suggestions in these matters are soon firmly established and rarely require change through the actors' request or because of my own dissatisfaction. Christopher Fry, who translated two Giraudoux plays I directed, expressed surprise that I made so few alterations after the initial blocking. John Gielgud, who directed Fry's *The Lady's Not for Burning*, kept revising his blocking almost daily, Fry said, and had on occasion to be stopped from doing so just before the curtain rose on the opening night.

Still, I warn my company and stage manager that my early blocking is by no means to be considered final: that I am prepared to alter it as I observe visual awkwardness or physical inconvenience to the actors. They themselves sometimes make suggestions for changes in blocking which are indisputable improvements.

A whole act may be blocked in rough outline in a few hours. This is particularly true of the ordinary realistic play. I have known directors who were able to block an entire play within two or three days.

After I have worked out my first blocking in patches, with repetition of each bit reasonably complete, I have the actors run through the whole act uninterrupted, except where they fail to remember what they had just rehearsed. The stage manager, having noted the blocking in his prompt script, reminds the actors of what had been previously set for them to do.

This run-through is followed by still another and then a

third. With each repetition the movement becomes more fluent. Then, often to the company's astonishment, I ask the actors to sit down and read the act through once more. My comments on the motivations of actions, scenes, lines, are now more minute. I try to stir the actors to a greater awareness of character traits or to the implications of certain actions which may previously have escaped them. They are now better able to understand the drift of my interpretive suggestions through having actually performed the basic externals of the act.

The company is then asked to run through the act again "on their feet." They apply whatever they are readily able to from the reading and discussion just held. I make still further suggestions. Still another repetition follows, but this time I stop from moment to moment to alter, refine, enlarge the earlier work.

This may go on for two or three days with just the first act. I have not yet insisted on any histrionic profundities or creative "heights." The actors have probably been rehearsing with book or "sides" in hand, although they have gradually absorbed their lines through the numerous readings. On the fourth day I expect them, through home study, to know their lines and to be able henceforth to rehearse without the "book." The act is run through once more, though recourse to the prompting stage manager is still inevitable.

What I have described is by no means an ideal procedure. It would be far more advantageous for the actor never to have a script in hand when he is actually trying to play a scene. This is possible only if he is allowed to improvise. In this case the blocking, to begin with, would perforce be loose, with little attention paid to precision in timing, etc. But we are not speaking of an ideal situation but one dictated by the limitations of time in the context of the ordinary American theatre organization.

Many directors, having blocked one act, go on immediately to the blocking of the next and then the next. They wish to view a rough sketch of the entire play without delay. This mode of work has its merits but I half suspect that it is actuated by fear. The director is being spurred by the producer and the playwright, who are anxious to see "what we've got." They are forever straining toward the semblance of a performance; they want to be sure they have a *show*. But hastening the process of gestation frequently produces a stillbirth.

I do not proceed to the second act till I've achieved a fair "draft" of the first. There have been occasions when I've withheld blocking of the last act till the fourteenth day of rehearsal. This so alarmed one producer (not to mention the playwright) that he reminded me that the tryout opening was imminent. "Oh," I said, "I never rehearse the last act of any of my productions." The jest was not appreciated till I drew out my notebook in which the rehearsal schedule as I had planned it showed that I was due to begin work on the final act two days later.

The blocking of the last third of the play is usually the least arduous for director and actors. Work on the earlier parts of the play has already habituated them to the stage layout and familiarized them with the interpretation and interrelationship of the characters.

Suppose, then, that the first act has been run through three days after the blocking rehearsals have begun. The evening before we are to block the second act (on the fourth day) I ask the company to reread it at home because as we have "neglected" the second act for three days it may no longer be as fresh in their minds as it should be before blocking is undertaken.

The same plan which obtained for Act One is adopted for Act Two. We skip Act One for a day as we devote a whole day to blocking the second act. Following this we resume work on Act One while concentrating on Act Two. Soon we begin devoting half a day to Act One and the second half to Act Two. Finally we go on to the third act. When all three run smoothly as far as the physical life of the whole is concerned, the rehearsals rise to a new level of study and effort.

But much more has been going on in the preliminary stages of rehearsal than just the perfecting of mechanics. The completion of one task, I repeat, achieves more than its specific aims. The measures taken to polish the externals are virtually inseparable from inner "psychological" considerations. It is merely a convenience for the sake of exposition to speak of both aspects of production as if they were distinct entities.

CHAPTER 10

Rehearsals Continue

IF THERE WERE little more to stage direction than blocking it would be a comparatively simple matter. Blocking by itself gives a production bone structure. The heart of direction, the brain, blood, nerve and spirit, give it life. People who have observed me at rehearsal have found me impatient with details, hesitant in blocking. Audiences and critics, however, have rarely complained about the mechanics of my staging. The finished product usually looks good—at least as far as blocking goes.

What chiefly concerns me is dramatic meaning, character, mood and feeling. This is essentially a matter of work with the actors, individually and collectively. Without the actor there is no theatre.

Apropos of the relation of the actor to the matter of blocking I am reminded of a story told me by Charles Laughton.

Ellen Terry was being directed by a "traffic cop" who instructed her as follows: "At the rise of the curtain you are seen at the table knitting. After a count of fifteen you rise, go to the window and look out. You then light a lamp on the mantelpiece. After that you return to your seat at the table and resume your knitting." "Yes," the actress responded, "and in the meantime I'll do all those things for which I am paid so much money."

There is, to be sure, the story of another actress, typical of certain English stars, which has quite another significance. The director asked her to pause after a certain phrase, then to stress a particular word in one of her speeches. "Young man," the actress said, "don't tell me when to pause and what word to stress. I shall pause when I please and stress what I choose." This kind of exchange recurred several times. The abashed director, his authority jeopardized, protested, "But Dame E., what am I expected to do?" "Don't worry, young man," the actress replied, "we'll find something."

"Oh," Molière exclaims in his play which shows him conducting a rehearsal, "how hard it is to lead those unruly creatures—actors!" Yes, indeed; but not really as unruly as the layman imagines. Unless an actor is perverse by nature or, as is more frequently the case, spoiled by show biz, he wants to be helped. Actors know that they cannot see their own performance (not on the stage, at any rate) and they hope for a trained eye, sympathetic as well as knowing, to judge and correct them. As a director I never find fault with, never "criticize," actors. I work with them, try to aid, if possible, inspire them.

I must recapitulate some of the items alluded to in the previous chapter. One advances from the general to the particular. During blocking sessions, while the actors still carry their scripts, they should not be asked to "give out," to act in any complete sense. They need only apply themselves intelligently to their tasks with just enough sense of the basic action to justify the moves they make, to understand why these are required. It is a mistake to exert pressure on the actor in the beginning.

One does well to assure the actor that if an indicated move is either inconvenient or uninteresting it is subject to change. The first steps are preliminary to the subtler aspects of the work. Some directors will not go on till each piece of business is perfected. I do not insist on this. I am chiefly intent on establishing flow and continuity.

I seldom encounter resistance. There are, of course, actors who find themselves at a loss unless told from the beginning precisely where they are to stand, sit, move, at each moment. This is not necessarily a sign of insecurity but the result of previous experience with directors who regard every rehearsal in the light of a complete performance. It is a way of work which is reassuring to many producers and playwrights. I am inclined to believe that it produces a certain stiffness, an absence of natural "breathing" in the actor.

One should not ask actors to speak to the last row of the house or to achieve pace from the start. The full voice, the right pace, come with the actor's familiarity with his part. With the progress of the rehearsals he becomes ever more imbued with the spirit of the play, gains confidence in it and in himself. One must simply make sure that sloppiness in technical matters does not become a constant. There are actors who whisper or mutter their lines at first. This may help them but is frustrating to their partners. I discourage the practice as it is antithetical to the give and take which is at the core of truthful acting—ensemble playing—but with certain very talented actors I am tolerant of it for a time.

"The actor is not a machine," Jean Vilar has written. "This is a truism that has to be shouted in people's ears. The actor is neither parrot nor robot. The director must assume from the start that his players have all the necessary talent." The actor gains confidence from such an attitude: it leads to freedom. Without freedom the actor remains a stick, no matter how polished.

Freedom, we all know, does not mean license. The actor cannot just do anything. " 'Anything,' someone heard Stanislavsky say, 'is the enemy of art.' " The actors' guide lines are the actions of each scene truthfully and completely carried out according to the given circumstances of the scene, the spine and characterization of his part and, above all, the spine of the play.

In directing Kazan in *Golden Boy* I explained that Fuselli, whom he was to play, was motivated by a drive to possession and power. The understudy, who played the part well during most of the play's London engagement, suggested an amendment to this interpretation. Wasn't it true, he asked, that Fuselli was fiercely possessive with everyone but the "golden boy" to whom he was strongly attracted? This was perceptive but, I pointed out, if emphasized it would prove false to the play's context. Even Fuselli's love for the boy was affected by his will to "ownership." How was this to be embodied?

The answer to the question illustrates a number of points about business and characterization which I have hitherto left vague. Joe Bonaparte expresses anxiety and dissatisfaction about the boxing racket. This occurs just before a match on which Fuselli, who owns "a piece of the boy," has bet heavily. Fuselli wants to soothe the boy while at the same time warning him against any "tricks." When Joe has calmed down, Fuselli manifests his pleasure by touching the boy's hand, a touch which is both a caress and an admonitory slap.

A single scene or passage may be repeated two, three or four times consecutively till it plays correctly. The same is true of each act. These reruns are of two kinds: one is stop-go, the other a straight run-through. The stop-go rehearsal is one in which the director interrupts the scene to explain what is amiss, how it is to be improved, what new adjustments ought to be considered. This constitutes the work on detail for director and actor. Even after a scene—twenty lines or several pages—has been repeated as many as three or four times the actor may himself request that he be permitted to run it through once again because he wants the satisfaction of feeling that he has mastered it. Some scenes are so difficult that the director will go over them innumerable times.

It is sometimes advisable to work on such scenes with only those present who are directly involved in them. The time taken for such rehearsals affords other members of the cast an opportunity to attend to their own needs—to study lines, be fitted for costumes, experiment with makeup or just rest. I am told that Kazan rarely permits members of the cast to sit out front in the house as observers. He doesn't want to make "critics" of them—critics, that is, of their fellow actors. Rehearsal may be called for an individual actor alone. This is done for intimate consultation, for "special treatment" of individual problems.

Should the director suggest his ideas or personally demonstrate them by "acting" them out? I believe such demonstrations dangerous. Yet they are inevitably resorted to. The peril in demonstrating to an actor how something is to be done is that it leads to imitation on the actor's part. If the director is a poor actor the result may be grotesque. If he is an excellent actor—Stanislavsky, Meyerhold, Reinhardt, for example—the actor becomes "crippled," hopeless of matching the director's brilliance.

An actor in *Tiger at the Gates* confessed he didn't know how to justify a crucial transition in his part with no more support than a single line to mark a total change of attitude. Throughout a long scene Ulysses has been telling Hector that he (Ulysses) can do nothing to avert the war; yet at the very climax of his argument he agrees to attempt doing so. The reason for the sudden change, I explained, is that as Ulysses speaks to Hector he is moved by Hector's passionately idealistic rebuttal. "Yes," the actor asked, "but how can I do this so the audience will understand that motivation?"

A pause was needed in which Ulysses' change from diplomatic regard to compassionate respect for Hector had to be *acted* before Ulysses could go on with the line expressing his conversion. I demonstrated the transitional moment. Silence ensued. "But I shan't be able to do that," the actor responded. I could not tell whether he meant I had acted skillfully or very badly. I only know that he finally managed to play the scene clearly and convincingly. I flatter myself that, in one way or another, I contributed some measure of assistance.

I demonstrate more than I believe fitting or desirable. (I was myself an actor for a brief period.) I usually preface my demonstration with an apology. "I'm going to do this badly," I begin, "don't imitate me. All I mean to do is to indicate an intention. It may prove clearer than anything I might be able to say. But *you must find your own way of carrying out the intention.*"

I rarely ask an actor to prove immediately that he has grasped the idea. "Work on it," I tell him, "it may take you a week to arrive at what we want." When the actor insists, as he frequently does, on effecting what I have asked for right away and fails, I reassure him, "Tomorrow will be time enough." Tomorrow is often a long time off.

In Miller's *Incident at Vichy* Hal Holbrook, an actor of gentle nature and benign appearance, was cast as a regular German army officer under orders from the Gestapo, a part for which no one considered him the "type." The character's troubled conscience sparked vindictiveness in him. I explained this over and over again. I demonstrated and demonstrated through readings and other means. When a director demonstrates by reading the actors' speeches he had best improvise the lines; instruction through exact readings of the text may be logically clarifying but rarely succeeds in evoking true responses in the actor.

For a while Holbrook made little progress. However, I saw him alone working hard in the corridor adjoining the rehearsal hall. Then one day he came to me and said, "I understand what you want. If you don't lose patience, I'll get it." A few days later he did "get it"—magnificently.

Generally speaking, the director should not read lines for

"...the playwright is the director's closest collaborator."
The author with Arthur Miller during rehearsals for
Incident at Vichy.

"For my production of Robles' Montserrat at the Habimah
Theatre in Israel, the designer ... was an artist whose work
I did not know. I therefore instructed him minutely on
every aspect of the set and costumes." The author's sketch
for the setting.

"For Anouilh's The Waltz of the Toreadors (*top*) *I
suggested that Edwards seek inspiration in Cezanne's and
Vuillard's colors. When in a similar vein I suggested
that Aronson make the set for Inge's* Bus Stop (*bottom*)
*look like an Edward Hopper painting, his rejoinder was,
'Why not like an Aronson?' " (Photo courtesy of
Ben Edwards; photo courtesy of Boris Aronson, by
Robert Galbraith)*

Top: *"It must seem constructed of metal and stone.
Its locale not too specific. . . . Something hard,
mysterious, 'Kafka-like desired.'" The model of Boris
Aronson's set for* Incident at Vichy. (*Photo courtesy of
Boris Aronson, by Robert Galbraith*)

Bottom: *"Ben Edwards' setting for my production of
Eugene O'Neill's* A Touch of the Poet *owed nothing to
any instruction from me. O'Neill's stage directions and
text were his sole guide."* (*Photo courtesy of Ben Edwards*)

Top left: *"In Odets'* Golden Boy *there was a difficult choice to be made in casting the role of Joe Bonaparte. He is a musically inclined youth who also happens to be endowed with a physique and the skill for boxing."* Luther Adler in the title role, with Lee J. Cobb, Phoebe Brand, John Garfield, Morris Carnovsky, and Frances Farmer. (Photo courtesy of Alfredo Valente)

Top right: *"The mood of this 'romance' is* loneliness. *Every element in the play, the physical environment (the setting), the heat, the 'love affair,' the 'sexiness,' must express the basic loneliness."* Morris Carnovsky, Eleanor Lynn, and Luther Adler in Rocket to the Moon. *(Photo courtesy of Alfredo Valente)*

Middle: *"Bessie (the mother) in* Awake and Sing *while chiding her husband and correcting her children's behavior (actions) is setting the table, which may be said to relate to her spine ('to take care of everything'). . . ."* Stella Adler as Bessie, with John Garfield, Morris Carnovsky, J. Edward Bromberg, Luther Adler, Sanford Meisner, and Art Smith. (Photo courtesy of Vandam Studio)

Bottom left: *"There is a peculiar turbulence in the air, a constant nervousness, everyone is impatient with the other, impatient with himself."* Richard Basehart and Joseph Wiseman in Uncle Vanya.

Bottom right: *"This play cannot be acted through the lines. A skein of emotional impulses must be woven. A web of odd sentiments which have only the 'logic' of feeling."* The Los Angeles Center Theatre Group's production of Uncle Vanya.

Left: *"Faced for the first time by the director, the playwright and the producer, the actors tend to suppress too overt an expression—of anything! They are 'hiding.' English actors at first readings are bolder and more fluent than Americans." The author with Ralph Richardson and Mildred Natwick during the rehearsals of* The Waltz of the Toreadors.

Below: *"Couches and wooden benches which only approximate the dimensions specified by the designer as required for accurate staging are all the actor may work with. . . . The inadequacy of the furniture and most of the hand props lead to a waste of time in a specifically technical sense." Early rehearsals of* Truckline Cafe.

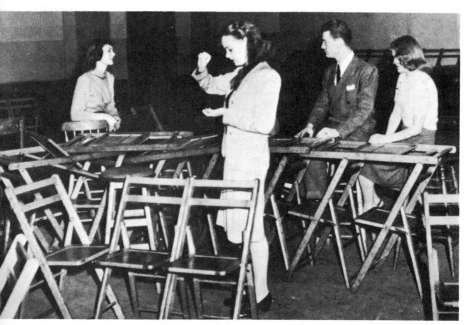

Left: *"The first rehearsals permit the director to learn something about the kind of direction which best befits each of the actors." The author with producer observe Kim Stanley and Helen Hayes during rehearsals of* A Touch of the Poet.

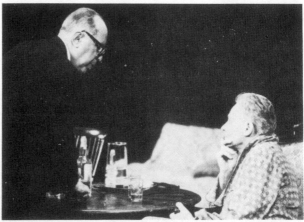

"Dress rehearsals are among the most hazardous and troublesome periods in the production of a play. The rule 'one thing at a time' . . . is particularly applicable at this juncture." The author giving final notes during the dress rehearsal of the Japanese production of Long Day's Journey into Night.

actors. As just noted, a paraphrase may serve to suggest the action or feeling of certain speeches. Though for certain people—theologians of the Method—directing an actor by reading lines for him is a cardinal sin, it becomes mandatory at times and practically inevitable. I once apologized to Fredric March for presuming to read a line for him. "No! No!" he encouraged me, "your readings help me."

When I asked Stanislavsky, "Do you ever read lines for an actor?" he replied at once, "Of course, whole speeches sometimes. One does everything, *anything* to arrive at the desired result." And it is chiefly from Stanislavsky that the notion has arisen that a director's reading lines to an actor is harmful! Still, for the neophyte director I advise "proceed with caution." It is better to evoke than to command.

I have just quoted Stanislavsky to the effect that one does anything to arrive at a desired result. Directors have been known to take the most outlandish measures to achieve their ends. One might fill many pages with instances of directors' "tricks" designed to stimulate the actor when ordinary methods—explanations, improvisations, demonstrations—have not availed.

One such instance, unorthodox to say the least, occurred during rehearsals of my short-lived production of Maxwell Anderson's *Truckline Cafe* in 1946. I had cast a young actor of twenty-two. He had been recommended to me by Stella Adler who praised him highly as the most gifted of her students: Marlon Brando. I had never seen him on the stage but I trusted Miss Adler's judgment and went to "look him over" in John van Druten's *I Remember Mama* in which he played an adolescent. He was certainly interesting but the nature of his role in this play was so different from that of the returned G.I. in the Anderson play, who on learning of his wife's infidelity kills her, that I wasn't at all sure he would suit the part.

I had him read for the author, the producers (Elia Kazan and Walter Fried) and myself. He read poorly, his head sunk low on his chest as if he feared to divulge anything. Yet there could be no question: he was peculiarly arresting. We decided to use him.

He mumbled for days. I applied myself so strenuously to his problem (I really couldn't determine what it was) that after a particularly arduous session—he listened attentively—I cried out, "All the actors here are witnesses: you will be a star someday and I shall demand that you support me when I'm a broken down old director." We all laughed. But he didn't improve.

The author's agent and wife suggested I recast the part. Anderson was a gentle and fair man and told me about this. "What do you wish me to do?" I asked. "Do what you think best," was his reply. I said I had faith in the boy and I would continue to work with him. But I was worried: the boy couldn't be heard beyond the fifth row.

His difficulty, it seemed, was that he could not give vent to the deep well of feeling which I sensed in him. He could not overcome some inner resistance: he would not "open up." The use of affective memory—a term I shall explain in a later chapter—did not help.

One day I asked everyone in the company to leave the stage and retire to the dressing rooms. I turned to Brando and said, "I want you to *shout* your lines." (For this I chose the crucial scene in which the young man tells how he drowned his unfaithful wife, whom he still loved.) Brando raised his voice. "Louder," I ordered. He complied. "Still louder," I insisted. This was repeated several times and my command for ever greater vocal volume began to exhaust the actor and to rouse him to visible anger. Then I yelled, "Climb the rope!" as I pointed to a rope which was hanging from the gridiron above the stage. Without hesitation he began climbing the rope while I urged him to keep shouting his lines. The other members of the cast came rushing onto the stage, alarmed at the terrifying sounds they had heard while still in their dressing rooms.

When Brando let himself down, he looked as if he were ready to hit me. "Now," I said quietly, "run the scene—normally." He recovered his poise and did as I bid him. He "spoke up"—effortlessly. In a few days he played the "moment" beautifully. On opening night—and every night thereafter—his performance was greeted by one of the most thunderous ovations I have heard for an actor in the theatre.

I am not at all sure he wouldn't have come through without the "beating" I administered. I never again tried another such device—and I certainly don't recommend this method. But at the time it seemed a noble and triumphant experiment!

In the building of characterizations I draw, as I have already noted, from three sources: the dramatist's script, the actor's being, my own imagination. In speaking to an actor about his part in Odets' *Paradise Lost,* I remember inventing a long story about the character's past: the oppressive poverty, shame at his lack of education, embarrassment about his accent and foreign looks. As I spoke I observed tears shimmering in the actor's eyes. I later learned that without my realizing it I had described much of the actor's early youth.

Knowing the springs of an actor's temperament is an asset in developing inner characterization for him. The actor should be encouraged to recreate in his own mind an imaginary past for the character he is to play (and possibly a future). For whatever one imagines, no matter how fanciful, always has its origins in one's own experience. The imagined past the actor creates for himself may parallel the secrets of his own subjective being without the actor necessarily being aware of it.

The clues to outer characterizations are objectively numerous. It often happens that an observed external trait (even a particular costume or makeup) leads to a feeling for the inner man, though it is probably preferable to work from the inner characterization (dictated by the part's spine, etc.) to the outer. (I have heard that Alec Guinness appears to get the feel of a part by imagining how the character would dress his hair!) Then, too, the actor may begin with a model: a person he knows or has seen somewhere, a painted portrait, a newspaper photo. I remember a self-portrait by Paul Gauguin which suggested both an outer and inner characterization for a character who was not an artist or a Frenchman, but only an unhappy businessman.

The games people play, which consist of answering such questions about a person as "What kind of music is he like? What food? What town? What painter's style?" etc., may stimulate the actor in his search for a characterization. What prompted Odets to suggest that the professional arsonist in *Paradise Lost* be played with a Swedish accent? It may have sprung from some dimly remembered chance encounter in the past which made a sinister impression on him. I saw the same character with bright red hair, wearing a black leather finger protector! Was it the "devil" I had in mind? I'm not at all sure—and it doesn't matter, if the image works.

Racial origins may lend character traits (too often conventional) to the building of an outer characterization. Certain historical periods known through representative paintings may also contribute ideas for characterization. Illnesses, habits and occupations casually mentioned in the play's dialogue or in the dramatist's stage directions may be further hints to characterization. Chekhov tells us that Uncle Vanya on his first entrance wears a "fancy tie." The actor or director must ask himself why this one item of clothing should have been important enough for the writer to mention: what does it signify for the total characterization? There is something more to it than a manner of dress. Tolstoy tells us that Karenin in *Anna Karenina* is in the habit of cracking his knuckles. It is a sign of something more than just a tic which displeases Anna.

The director must not overlook variety and development in characterization. A characterization should *grow*. It is not something the audience is immediately to perceive which remains constant throughout the play as a static condition. A characterization must be seen to develop in stages and should only become perceptible in its entirety with the resolution of the play.

In the first act of *Uncle Vanya*, Voinitski has come to realize that he has wasted his life on behalf of his selfish and pedantic brother-in-law. In the second act he despairs. In the third act he rebels—ineffectually. In the last act he painfully resigns himself to his state.

Laurence Olivier has a penchant for disguising himself. He specializes in variety of nose shapes even when they appear un-called for: the shape of the nose means something to him and will, he trusts, do something for us. Russian actors almost always employ some external feature to make their characterizations more vivid. (See the illustrations of Stanislavsky in a variety of roles to be found in his *My Life in Art,* each with a distinct and altogether different "face.") American actors, on the other hand, usually avoid sharp external characterizations. They consider them hammy. It rarely occurs to many producers that actors may invent special physical features. Such producers seek *the* type: the fat actor must play the fat man, the cadaverous-visaged character will be played by someone of that breed. Besides being a by-product of the commercial theatre's need for quick results, this shying away from overt physical characterization is part of a theatre thinking which is largely geared to realism, the "natural" rather than the expressively theatrical.

External characterization need not be strikingly graphic. Donald Cook played a jet set Frenchman of possibly aristocratic lineage in the Marcel Achard-Harry Kurnitz whodunit *A Shot in the Dark.* A practiced comedian with a talent for crisp delivery and timing as well as a dry humor, he was superb in the part when it tried out in New Haven. Unfor-

tunately he died there of a heart attack. Walter Matthau replaced him. There was much head shaking; he was certainly
not the "type."

The directorial task was to find some not too obvious facet
of characterization which would convince the audience at
once that here was a character who would behave and speak as
the authors had him do. Since Matthau once mentioned that
he was responsive to music, I asked him to choose the record-
ing of a piece which struck him as "super-elegant." He was requested to play it for himself at home and then to walk
rather than to dance to it. (I never inquired into what piece
he selected.) His gait was ever so slightly altered at the next
rehearsal. At the preview before the opening the producer
asked that the "walk" be eliminated. I insisted that it be retained and Kurnitz agreed. Silently, Matthau glided onto the
stage as if his feet were caressing the floor. The opening-night
audience roared with laughter: the characterization had
acquired a base.

There was no caricature in this. It became second nature to
the actor. Such idiosyncrasies may be even more minute than
Matthau's gliding walk. In Reinhardt's production of *Danton's Death* Vladimir Sokolov's Robespierre became memorable to me through his dry, staccato delivery of lines, but
most of all through the two fingers he kept tapping ominously
on the lectern in front of him as he drove home his arguments.

There is such a thing as an external characterization (or
makeup) which overwhelms every other element of the por-
traiture and is therefore false. Funny accents sometimes have
this effect. After the worldwide success of the Vakhtangov-
Habimah Theatre production of *The Dybbuk* (part mystic
romance, part social commentary), in which the actors' faces
were rendered awesomely weird, the Habimah company was
afflicted for years with mask mania: all roles were stylized to
the point of distortion. This was so much a trademark of the
Habimah company and others who modeled themselves on it

that when I was asked my opinion of Israeli acting at a lecture in Tel Aviv I replied, "You have talented actors but many suffer from a certain peculiarity: if you tell such an actor 'You are to play a lawyer,' he will inquire eagerly, 'With a limp?' " It was therefore a really original stroke when an Israeli played Richard III without crookleg or hump.

The special walk which Matthau assumed in *A Shot in the Dark* might be set down in Michael Chekhov's terminology as a "psychological gesture." Chekhov explains that every person has some special manner of speaking or moving or watching which reveals something of his inner nature. When this remarkable actor played Chlestakov in Gogol's *The Inspector General* he seemed—especially after he had been mistaken for a V.I.P. by the local gentry—to be walking on springs. When he began to lie about his exalted position in St. Petersburg society he positively danced. I have found the discovery of psychological gestures for various characters of considerable value in developing character delineation not only because they are visually or aurally specific, but because if assimilated they lead to deeper insights.

The temptation to adopt the psychological gesture as a gimmick may be grotesquely illustrated by an incident in the direction of an actor who played a businessman in my Habimah production of *Montserrat*. For some time he floundered about without "finding" the part. The man, I told the actor, takes everything into himself, to his stomach as it were, and holds it in safe keeping there. The actor thereafter held his hands over his belly as if he were guarding his possessions in that spot. Now, he said, he knew how to play the part. But lo, one day I came to rehearsal and saw several other actors committed to the same gesture!

A play's action is fleshed in stage business. The elaboration of business, the byplay or outgrowth of action, is the chief attribute of drama in performance. It clarifies, intensifies, gives body to what is sometimes referred to as the play's *subtext,* the action believed implicit in the dialogue. It gives texture and vivacity to the play as spectacle. It is often hyperbolic and fanciful. The fame of certain directors and actors is founded on the imaginative quality or resourcefulness in their invention of business. Comedians often evince genius in this respect. As with everything else, business may be overdone, become too profuse.

Business may also be defined as the physical extension in minor activities of the major action in each passage or "beat" of a scene. In a production of a Danish play when Michael Chekhov cried out, "I shall defend myself," he used his fists, his feet, chairs, cutlery and every other available object to do just that. When Hume Cronyn in Molière's *The Miser* reached for the smoke from someone's pipe in order to "save" it, the audience appreciated the gesture as a crazy metaphor of Harpagon's avarice.

When Hermia in frustrated rage in Peter Brook's *Midsummer Night's Dream* jumped high onto a bar suspended from the flies and kicked her feet furiously she was very much like the "puppet" Helena called her.

Yelena's closing of the piano lid at the end of Act Two in *Uncle Vanya* (previously cited) tells us more clearly than words that her failure in life is the outcome of her constant obedience. When Julie Harris as Frankie in *The Member of the Wedding* spoke of her dream of going all around the world, she whirled herself around the stage imitating the sound as well as the slightly swaying motion of an airplane. She lent vivid substance to the thought I had expressed one day at rehearsal that children imitate what fascinates them. The written line could have been spoken as a point of information or as a yearning but Miss Harris made it *theatrical,* that is, dramatically visible. Eric Portman as Melody in O'Neill's *A Touch of the Poet* flinging his pistol into the mirror after momentarily posing in front of it while reciting Byron was a dynamic image of his self-contempt and defeat.

All such pieces of business, I repeat, may be planned in advance by the director, they may appear spontaneously during rehearsal or they may issue from the actor's response to a director's challenge when he says, "I need something unusual to be done at this point. Can you think of something?"

Every theatregoer speaking of a play or a performance he has enjoyed will remind you of what this or that actor *did* at a particular moment. The *doing* is more indelibly memorable than what the actor said. Though it was as long ago as 1926 I can still remember the German actor Albert Basserman as a famous painter in a play by Gerhart Hauptmann because while asking each of his several pupils such questions as "Have you read Goethe?," "Do you know Shakespeare?" and the like, he pinched the cheek of one, prodded the ribs of another. He was chiding and teaching them with respect, concern and paternal affection.

As rehearsals advance and take on genuine quality greater attention will be directed toward matters involving speech, timing and pace. A former reviewer on a New York daily newspaper could describe direction in no other terms than "fast" or "slow," the one signifying good direction, the other bad. It is silly to discuss the subjects of speech, pace and voice as if they were unrelated to all the rest. It is as much sheer ignorance to concentrate on these facets of acting and theatre art as to overlook them.

I pay close attention to them in the final weeks of rehearsal when the groundwork of the production has been laid and is nearly complete. If an actor has some special defect in speech, a disturbing vocal shortcoming or a disquieting mannerism (in which case one hesitates to cast him), one should do something about it as early as possible only if one is convinced that the fault may be corrected within the four weeks of rehearsal! Ordinarily, it should be taken for granted that an actor is adequately equipped or well trained in voice and diction. There are lamentable exceptions.

I find the question "How should one speak Shakespeare?"

somewhat absurd, as if it is of little importance how one speaks in a contemporary play. Laurence Olivier's speech and voice are as fine in Ionesco's *Rhinoceros* as in *Henry V*. Shakespeare doesn't call for a special type of speech; he demands besides an ear for language a particular emotional adjustment or style, in the way Pablo Casals asks his musicians to play Bach "with honor."

When the great Italian tragedian Salvini said that the three most potent factors in acting are "Voice! Voice! Voice!" he was enunciating a salutary apothegm—and an egregious simplification. It is like saying that to be a good pianist one must possess a good piano. There have been extraordinary actors with faulty or ruined voices (the Sicilian Giovanni Grasso of whom Stark Young wrote so beautifully comes to mind) and others with peculiarities of diction (Henry Irving), though, it is true, they are very few in number. Excellent speech and voice should be the stock-in-trade of every would-be actor before he embarks on acting as a profession.

Proper stage speech is largely a consequence of right thinking, of understanding the operative words in sentences, and partly of a feeling for language and literature and of being aware of sound and rhythm in relation to meaning. These in turn depend on the thorough execution of each of the play's actions or, to put it less technically, clarity of intention. Given a normal vocal instrument, actors need not shout to be heard: they need to know what they're talking about, what, *dramatically speaking,* they mean. Opera singers capable of producing magnificent sound and actors with "piped-in" voices are often unintelligible on the stage. They make no sense; they do not *act.* To fashion readings of elegance, euphony, grace and shapeliness are among the final tasks to which the director need devote himself.

Pace and tempo are usually taken to be synonymous with speed. They are not achieved by "going fast" but by change and variety of attack. But apart from this bald axiom, it should go without saying that pace is established through the nature of each particular action and the adjustment to it. I once saw an actor who made an exit prompted by the need to call a doctor for someone who had suddenly fallen ill. He moved at a pace which convinced me he wished the stricken person dead!

The director may well shout "Faster!" or—more rarely in the United States—"Slower!" and this may at times prove useful. But such commands are only short-cut remedies to correct a failure in understanding the nature of specific actions and adjustments. An actress in class once did a long speech from Shaw's *Misalliance* for me. Everything seemed right in regard to her understanding of content; her articulation and voice were unexceptionable. I asked her to increase the pace of her delivery. She frowned at this deviation from what she took to be my "credo," but she did as I bid her. When she was through, she agreed along with those present that her "fast" reading not only made the speech more entertaining but more "real." The reason for this, I explained, was that the rhythm of Shaw's thinking, his mental agility and the sparkle and fluent energy of his writing were attributes of his style, *part of his meaning.* Every play has its own basic rhythm, its ground tone. Reference to these aspects of the play should be made at the inception of rehearsal discussions but are to be insisted upon only during the final phases of production.

Then there is the question of *pauses.* In the early stages of his efforts an actor should be permitted to take his own sweet time and pause as often as he deems fit; if this threatens to become habitual he should be warned against it as an obstructive mannerism. The justification for such forbearance on the director's part is the recognition that the actor is still unsure of himself; he gropes for the "something" which still eludes him. He needs time to find himself in the part.

Some actors will protest that what makes them pause and pause again is that they are "thinking." Occasionally I retort with a long spiel of intellectual verbiage and then conclude with "You can't say I haven't been thinking as I spoke." The actor's forethought should be done privately—at home. Though rehearsals, as Vakhtangov once said, are the period reserved for mistakes, it is also true that rehearsals are intended to reveal the effects of one's thinking. When the actor retires for the day he should think over what has been said and done during the day's rehearsal.

There is really no such thing as a pause on the stage. What we call a pause, apart from breathing space and the "leap" toward a stress, is the time when nothing is *audible* but during which we see or feel what is going on. It is a form of suspense; something *is happening* and we await the outcome: what is going to be done or said next. If the audience's expectation isn't aroused, the pause is "dead air." A play's action must never stop. When the actor is really thinking—itself a specific action—we watch him with interest. This explains the legitimate use of the close-up in film: the actor's eye is telltale. The general imperative in staging, apart from variety of movement, tempo and sound, is, as already noted, to keep the audience's attention on the crucial points of action. The placement of the actors, the groupings, the stage "pictures," should all be calculated with this end in view.

The first major run-through of the entire play usually takes place approximately three weeks after the first rehearsal. Producers have urged me to hasten to the occasion. I have sometimes countered, "I'll show you two acts within twelve days and will also go through the last act with the actors reading from their scripts."

At this first run-through—a nervous time for everyone—we find the director, the playwright, the producer and their various secretaries taking notes. For this latter occupation I call on the services of one of the stage managers, an understudy or a student volunteer. I mention this because I rarely take notes in the early rehearsal period.

Following the first run-through the director, playwright and producer (along with a stage manager seated discreetly by their side) gather in conference, each with his own packet of comments, criticisms, questions, suggestions and advice. On these occasions I say little; I listen. Many of the producer's and playwright's notes are already to be found in mine. I assuage their expressed and unexpressed fears, I promise to remedy the faults and rough spots they have complained about. By reasoned argument I am sometimes able to convert dissent into acceptance of directional details to which objections have been raised. I occasionally contradict certain criticisms so emphatically that my colleagues abandon their argument. Absolute conviction is rare.

I sometimes nod agreement to a criticism without the least intention of doing anything about it. There is no disdain in this. I know that certain "troubles" automatically right themselves through further rehearsal. Very often an objection which has been made is based on a momentary subjective reaction and will be forgotten by the very person who raises it.

I generally find my colleagues' suggestions helpful and I am grateful for them. Producers are not always dumb; some of them are quite smart, knowledgeable, even wise. The great majority of my production conferences have been carried on with the utmost cordiality and respect on everyone's part. The only time I am upset by criticisms or suggestions is when they are offered while I am still in the thick of work and I have not yet had time to observe the results. There is a proverb, "Never show a fool work half done." Playwrights and producers are rarely fools but their nervous impatience frequently provokes them to premature critical counsel. I am not a "temperamental" director, though in driving home a point I have been known to become vociferously oratorical. It's all fun—or should be.

Directors are sometimes dismissed after the first unfortunate run-through or after a disastrous preview or out-of-town opening. This has never happened to me. Other directors, disheartened or disgusted by their own or their collaborators' dissatisfaction, have resigned from a production *in medias res.* I never have.

The morning after the "big" conference the company is

given the notes agreed on by the "governing trio." When cuts have been recommended and approved by the playwright, the first order of business is to dictate them to the actors. Then all criticisms and suggested changes in staging (which may have to be specially rehearsed) are presented by the director alone. The director may ask the playwright to add something of his own personal views. If possible, the playwright should be encouraging. But he should never say anything specifically in the way of direction.

Work continues and after another three days there is another run-through and another conference, following the pattern just described. The intervals between these run-throughs are usually devoted to rehearsal of the more difficult scenes, the "rough spots" and to private work with particular actors. My usual practice is to do this polishing every morning of the last week and to run through the entire play every afternoon—for myself alone. Actors gain confidence, strength and fullness through repeated run-throughs. No amount of discussion or criticism is as productive at this point as playing the play.

The last run-through before the beginning of dress rehearsals is generally bad, unless an audience of friends is invited to witness it (this audience should not consist of theatre professionals). The guest audience at this point helps keep the company on its toes.

CHAPTER 11

Dress Rehearsals, Previews, Tryouts

DRESS REHEARSALS are among the most hazardous and trouble-some periods in the production of a play. The rule, "one thing at a time"—the admonition not to correct everything at once—is particularly applicable at this juncture.

Though three or four days (a week for musicals) are sup-posed to be devoted to all the necessary adjustments prior to the first paid previews, the fact is that during these days the stage is largely given over to the carpenters, electricians, prop men, the designer and, if the designer does not light the show himself, to the lighting expert. There are also present dress-makers, milliners, hairdressers and wardrobe ladies as aides to the costume designer. They help the actors look presentable at the first dress run-through. The cast spends hours in trying on the costumes, wigs, shoes, etc.

While these technical matters are being attended to the cast is called to the theatre lounge, or to a large room in a nearby hotel, where the director goes over the notes made at the last run-through. Though the actors know their lines they may be asked and even wish to run them all once again. There may be some difficulty in remembering them when for the first time the cast finds itself in the play's setting.

English directors take pride in lighting their productions. In America lighting specialists have become prevalent. Certain scene designers—notably Joe Mielziner—do their own lighting. Very few directors do. A brief lighting conference attended by the director and the lighting staff usually precedes the dress rehearsal period. The designer and others responsible for the lighting have at an earlier time watched several run-throughs to familiarize themselves with the placement of the actors in the play's climactic moments. As soon as the "scenery" is safely in position, the light men begin their jobs.

I know what I want in lighting a play but I am unfamiliar with the precise designation, the number and the exact disposition of the lighting paraphernalia. For this reason I do not join in the preliminaries of lighting. I am confident of those in charge of the task; I am also sure that after several dress rehearsals the actors and I will find the stage too dark and the actors' faces in shadow.

It is a truism that designers are chiefly concerned, at first, with lighting the set so that it makes an impressive "picture." But one can hardly blame them for this. A play cannot be adequately lit till the actors are in place, and their figures, features and costumes closely studied in movement. Work on lighting therefore continues through most of the dress rehearsals—often disturbing the actors—and frequently goes on up to the last moment before the curtain rises on the official opening night.

I ask the actors, before the first dress rehearsal begins, to come on stage and occupy all the chairs and couches they are to sit on, to open and close doors through which they are to pass, to mount and descend whatever steps and platforms they are to use—in short, to acquire the habit of the play's physical environment. The request is hardly necessary; if they are at all experienced they will do this on their own. But it should be done even before they don their stage clothes. Each step—the testing of the set, the putting on of costumes, the application of makeup—should be separately effected before they all become part of a single routine. It is doing "one thing at a time."

The altered circumstances of dress rehearsal seem at first to be more of an impediment than a help. Time must be allowed the actors to achieve ease and comfort. Though the actors are acquainted with the set in its model, have moved within its dimensions, and have been informed where they are to find the needed props, they are usually "thrown" when they first encounter the set. They may even find the "real" settee designed for their playing somehow less convenient than the substitute bench which tormented them during the first days of rehearsal. The desk isn't quite high enough or it is too low, the chair not deep enough, the doorway not wide enough and so on. The complaints are sometimes well founded and alterations are made within hours or in a day or two. But the plain fact is that even when the actors declare themselves satisfied with the setting, the furniture, etc., the new conditions of the dress rehearsal discomfit them and time is required for complete adjustment.

Every marked change in the actors' working conditions affects them adversely. Not only laymen find this hard to understand, but even some producers and directors. For example: A producer who was entirely delighted with a run-through he had attended asked me to arrange for another on the following day to pick up the last bit of backing for the show from a lady who wanted to see the play before investing in it. I agreed to arrange for the special run-through. The only hitch was that this time the run-through would have to be held in a different theatre than the one in which the company had been rehearsing for more than two weeks.

The special run-through was a failure. The actors appeared ill rehearsed. The producer was bewildered. "What's happened? They were great yesterday. It was awful today." I explained that the change of theatre and stage was responsible for the difference. Though the man had produced many plays he still could not understand. Only a few theatre professionals learn from experience.

Whenever one makes a pronounced change in the conditions of performance—such as a change in spatial distance on stage and in relation to the auditorium—the acting will be disturbed though the actors themselves may not be aware of the cause. On this account I ask stage managers of companies on tour to have the actors speak some of their lines and run some scenes the night before the opening in every new town they play, no matter how long the tour.

Actors should be given the opportunity to wear their costumes before the regular dress rehearsals begin. The first rehearsal on the set should take place unencumbered by anything but the indispensable props. It should go without saying that the actors have tried on their costumes at a special "dress parade" onstage or in the costumer's shop at least a week before dress rehearsal time. (The actors of the Moscow Art Theatre wore their Roman dress for its production of *Julius Caesar* for many weeks prior to the play's opening.)

I prefer the actors to rehearse without makeup when they try their costumes on for the first time at the dress rehearsal. Makeup, even of the simplest kind, is another factor which contributes to their self-consciousness at dress rehearsals. "How do I look?" the actor asks himself, his fellow actors, the director, the designer. Even when satisfied that he appears no different than his natural self, he seems a little different to the other actors, a little strange. If the actor has put on a character makeup (a beard, a wig, a scar) or changed his hair style, he not only loses some sense of his own identity but even that of the character he has been working so carefully to create. After all, *that* person (the character) didn't look that way before! And if the actor seems strange to himself, he must seem even stranger to his partner. "Who is this man or woman I'm acting with: it's a new person, an unknown!"

Speaking of costume and makeup, I cannot refrain from telling one of my favorite theatre stories, not alone for its humor but for a point connected with the question of characterization. European actors, as already noted, are happiest in the disguise of pronounced characterization which often entails a change in facial and bodily look. Not so Americans. They prefer to appear "natural"—to be themselves. That is one reason why most American actors, particularly those who have embarked on their careers in the past twenty-five years, aren't adept at makeup and require assistance.

But to my story. In 1924 when Joseph Schildkraut played Edwin Justus Mayer's *The Firebrand,* a sex comedy presumably about Benvenuto Cellini, he was uncertain as to how that famous sculptor and rake should be made up. (Schildkraut's early theatre experience had been Viennese.) The author and director, never having thought of Cellini as anything but a darling playboy, as conceived by New Yorkers in the twenties, suggested that Schildkraut consult a portrait of the man in a book about Renaissance art. He did so. He was not surprised to find that Cellini was blessed with a formidable beard. On the evening of the first dress rehearsal he carefully applied that appendage to his face.

Rudolf Schildkraut, Joseph's father, himself a veteran of Max Reinhardt's productions and one of the finest actors of my theatregoing experience, had been present at several of the earlier rehearsals to keep a watchful eye on his son, who worshipped him. When the old man saw his Joseph at the dress rehearsal enter the stage for the first time as a bearded Benvenuto he rose from his seat and cried out in astonished German, "Beard! Beard! Where are you running with my son!"

There are makeups, costumes and characterizations which proclaim the actor's performance and run away with it. Period authenticity in costumes or makeup is of minor importance; what matters is dramatic relevance, not historical congruity. The criterion for judgment in these areas is the individual role and the actor cast for it. The habiliments worn in most productions which call for period dress seem to be fit for costume balls only. Costumes in the theatre must be, first of all, *clothing*.

When the actors run through the play for the first time in a complete dress rehearsal they should be warned to do very little in the way of acting. If they attempt to act in the full sense, they will frustrate themselves as well as disappoint the director. Despite all the good will possible, they will concentrate chiefly on overcoming the hurdles of setting, lights, costumes and makeup which have been supplied to aid them. No matter how well the actors speak, the director barely hears them. He, too, is chiefly conscious of the new faces, the lights, the costumes, which do not quite meet his expectations, or he is admiring a costume or makeup so much that he cannot see the actor. Usually nothing works as it should. The director may decide to stop the action because an actor has forgotten to shut a door (they were only imaginary doors before), and when he does close it, it opens again of itself. But there is no time to stop to attend to such momentarily trivial matters; the rehearsal continues, yet the director can't keep his eyes from the gaping hole that the open door cuts in the set.

A light cue is late or the light isn't of the right color or intensity, it doesn't hit the right spot, there is bad shadow on the leading lady's face and everything is either glaringly bright or, more often, dismally dark. The designer is busy whispering instructions to the electricians backstage; the costumer is exasperated because this or that actress didn't put on the right dress or has put on the right dress the wrong way. An actor complains that his jacket is too tight for him to make the telling gestures he did when he wore his own suit. Some scenes must be restaged for mechanical reasons and the curtain never falls at quite the right speed or on the right cue.

The occasions on which I have not found the first dress rehearsal exhausting and dispiriting have been rare. Technical notes are given the stage manager, as well as to various designers and the heads of the stage crew (carpenter, property man, electrician). Each of these makes his own notes.

The second dress rehearsal always begins later than the scheduled hour but it is usually a great improvement on the first. The technicians always require more time than anticipated to make the necessary adjustments. There are generally two dress rehearsals on the second day. The one called for two-thirty begins at four. If the stage crew is called between twelve and one the management is obliged to pay overtime; if the rehearsal lasts beyond midnight there is more overtime payment due. In any case, the crew must be paid for a minimum of eight hours a day.

And so on through the afternoon of the third day to the opening performance that night or, if one is lucky, on the night of the fourth day. The days before the first New York preview or the first out-of-town opening being hectic, the director's main job is to continue working as calmly as possible. If he is unduly nervous he must make every effort not to betray his condition. Nor must he try to "pep things up" with an impassioned speech about the seriousness of the occasion. I laugh the moment away by saying, "Tonight we rehearse the audience." The actors need not be reminded, as some silly producing fellows will, that they must do their best and a little better. Actors for the most part are responsible people.

If they are not a total bust these first performances out of town or at previews are always instructive. (Most "straight" plays nowadays are previewed in New York; the road or out-of-town tryout has become too costly.) If the play is a comedy, the actors may have learned through the presence of guests at the pre-opening run-through where laughs are to be expected. But there are always surprises: what tickles one audience may fail to amuse another. The duration of the audience's laughter is not calculable in advance. Then again the audience may laugh in the wrong places, and it is not always easy to understand what provoked the inopportune reaction. An ill-advised phrase or an incongruous gesture at a tense moment may give rise to guffaws. At the first preview of *Men in White* the audience found a passing reference to the moon funny. They understood only too well that an affair between a lonely intern and a pretty nurse was to follow. It took a while to discover that it was the word, not the scene, that had caused the "bad" laugh.

One soon learns which scenes drag, either because they need partial or total cutting or because they are not being properly played. Most such difficulties are readily overcome overnight or within a few days, provided director, playwright and producer maintain poise. Theatre folk are prone to alarm. They overreact to everything which in any way smacks of a setback or someone's displeasure. If a production at an out-of-town tryout receives an adverse review, even from a person everyone pretends to dismiss as a fool, a dangerous chain reaction is set up. What's to be done about this, that or the other? My own first decision, unless I agree with the reviewer's or the audience's reservations, is to do nothing.

As we approach that "moment of truth," the New York opening night, the number of people ready to proffer advice on the production increases. Everyone has an "idea." The playwright thinks you have cut too much, or too little. That actor is not playing as directed. One of the actors is miscast: fire him!

That astute agent, and the author's representative, Audrey Wood, confesses that after the first days of the Philadelphia tryout of *The Member of the Wedding* she advised Robert Whitehead, the producer, to postpone the New York opening: the show, she opined, was "not ready." The show opened on schedule in New York almost immediately after this advice was given—and was a decided success.

Judgments and criticisms on these occasions are not always misguided but the atmosphere in which they occur is overwrought. There is fierce, nerve-racking pressure—financial, egotistical and, worst of all, "corporative." Everybody gets into the act: show biz mentors, husbands, wives, boy and girl friends, other actors, other directors, other writers—experts all! It is my invariable practice to warn everyone concerned with the production against giving credence to these well-wishers and, if possible, not to listen to them at all.

It is panic time, and the director must keep his own counsel. There is no arrogance in this: he must realize that he knows the play and its problems better than anyone else. He should and will heed advice thoughtfully offered by people whose theatre knowledge or instincts he respects. But he must resist even the playwright and the producer if he believes them in error. He may "experiment," try new approaches. He usually has at least two weeks of previews or out-of-town performances (much longer with a musical) to do this. This gives him the opportunity to test a suggested change. The director should keep himself pliant, but he must not run scared. Presumption of infallibility is out of order because there is something unpredictable about the life of a play on stage before an audience. It is this "mystery" which is what makes play production so fascinating and frightening. The fright and the fascination (each is part of the other) are the cause of theatre superstition.

A director must cultivate the virtue of patience: patience with others, patience with himself. He must believe in himself and in what he is doing, but he must also know himself subject to error and gross miscalculation. What follows are some examples of what I am alluding to. It is pleasant to speak of those instances which refer to the production of *The Member of the Wedding,* for whatever difficulties we underwent in its making, we were rewarded by a happy ending.

There was Ethel Waters' trouble in remembering lines. It was not the ordinary trouble with a poor memory, but with coordination. When Miss Waters remembered the lines, she forgot the business; when she remembered the business, she forgot the lines. Julie Harris, who played opposite her, was very patient. (She is always generous with her fellow players.) Robert Whitehead, the producer, and I were worried. At the last run-through before the Philadelphia tryout Miss Waters was still far from having mastered the text.

I said nothing to indicate dissatisfaction or nervousness. I appointed one of the stage managers to go over the lines with her privately, repeating the exercise again and again and again. On opening night in Philadelphia (the coaching went on in her dressing room during intermission) she was still uncertain and occasionally "up" (stage slang for failure of memory), even though her acting was magnificent.

Though she gained confidence through enthusiastic notices, it took many days before she achieved verbal security. After returning to New York from Philadelphia, further rehearsals were called before the opening. Miss Waters suffered a relapse into uncertainty. I sought an explanation. She had pains in her stomach, she said. I reassured her: "You are simply nervous because of the approaching opening night." She then referred to the responsibility some actresses feel which is not entirely personal: she was referring to her race.

Still, this was by no means the knottiest problem which confronted us at the time. The Philadelphia opening ran till midnight. This was partly due to two scenes in a cheap barroom to which twelve-year-old Frankie, the play's central character, repairs, scenes which necessitated a mechanically difficult shifting of sets. One of the scenes was cut on the second night. I was strongly urged to cut the other as well. I objected. Increasing pressure was put on me, but I was obdurate. I argued that the barroom scene conveyed something of the town beyond the kitchen kingdom in which Frankie and her seven-year-old boy friend John Henry played together. The author, Miss McCullers, said nothing: she had no theatre experience. But everyone else, Robert Whitehead, his partner Stanley Martineau and their associates, pressed their point unremittingly. I was not to be moved.

Then one afternoon two local high school boys came to interview me. They told me how much the play had moved them. Their reaction was touchingly genuine. One of the boys timidly asked if the scene in the bar was needed. I did not answer; I was convinced. That evening I cut the scene.

The audience plays a vital role in the theatre, but one must be careful. There are those in the audience like the gentleman at the first New York preview of *The Member of the Wedding* whom Robert Whitehead overheard saying to his companion, "I don't see anything at all to recommend in this show." An actor friend of Julie Harris' assured her in Philadelphia that she needn't be ashamed to appear in the show: "It should run at least six weeks." But of audiences later!

During the out-of-town run of O'Neill's *Desire Under the Elms,* Bob Whitehead one night declared himself a little unhappy about the performance. The actors were doing the right things and the direction, too, was well conceived; still, he felt a certain emotional hollowness in the production. There was not enough "inner life." Would I do something about this; would I not work harder? I nodded assent. Five days later Whitehead returned from New York, saw the performance, and was elated. He congratulated me. I never told him I had done nothing. The fault which had disturbed him had corrected itself, as I knew it would, through further playing. Repeated performance is the actor's most valuable instructor, if the play's interpretive foundations have been carefully planned in the first place.

I have often been pleaded with, virtually commanded, "to work harder." In most cases there exists a certain misconception—I hesitate to say ignorance—about the solution of acting problems by "hard work," a persistent hammering away on the same nail. The director must work well, not "hard." After prolonged effort, periods of rest and apparent nonchalance are more salutary for the actor than hitting him again and again with direction.

During the Philadelphia tryout of Arthur Laurents' *The Time of the Cuckoo,* on a day when four hours of rehearsal were available to me, I announced to the cast that they could take the afternoon off. I was going to hear the Philadelphia Orchestra, I said, and the actors were invited to do the same or anything else they pleased. Laurents may have been perplexed; he told me that Whitehead, hearing of this in New York, was furious. Well . . .

I call Bernard Shaw to witness. In a still unpublished letter dated July 11, 1905, to Arnold Daly, his first American producer, Shaw wrote: "Under the pressure of that awful responsibility, and the conviction carefully instilled by me that each member is the particular one on whom the whole performance depends, they all get into such a state that I sometimes have to beg them [the actors] to take it easy, and to remind them that, after all, a failure will not be the end of the world. The one thing they never feel is that they are working for an employer, or that they are simply to do what someone else conceives. When things go badly and a general terror that the play will not be ready on the night seizes us, I suggest golf and a holiday. As to saying 'we must work at this till we get it' such an outrage never suggests itself to me. The moment there is any difficulty I drop it. It [the solution] always turns up spontaneously two rehearsals later if it turns up at all; and if it doesn't, no grinding at it will make it possible."

Spoken like an artist of the theatre, not a shop foreman.

Part II

CHAPTER 12

The "System"

ANYONE WHO HAS HAD any contact with theatre folk in the past thirty years will know what the title of this chapter refers to: in America it has come to be known as the "Method." It is the overall tag for the teachings of Konstantin Stanislavsky, co-founder and co-director of the Moscow Art Theatre.

The moderately informed have surely recognized that what I have outlined in the foregoing chapters is a directorial procedure largely influenced by what I have learned from Stanislavsky's writings and from personal contact with him as well as with the most knowledgeable exponents and witnesses of his activities.

I do not propose to paraphrase even in the sketchiest fashion the material of Stanislavsky's three seminal books, *An Actor Prepares, Building a Character,* and *Creating a Role.* My purpose here is to dispel some of the misconceptions about the System, or the Method, which have resulted not only in twaddle but in malpractice.

We ought to remind ourselves that Stanislavsky did not establish his theatre with the System in mind. He had been acting and directing for a long time before the founding of the M.A.T. His aim was to set up a permanent company (a "collective") which would bring artistic probity to a theatre community infected by dead conventions and shabby and false methods or lack of method. Stanislavsky and his collaborator, Nemirovitch-Danchenko, a playwright and teacher of acting, proposed to bring art to the people, and by "the people" they meant chiefly the educated middle class of Russia and perhaps, too, the advanced working class of their day. By art, Stanislavsky, in particular, meant honest, heartfelt, moral expression.

Stanislavsky was acutely aware of inadequacies in his acting, though he was from the first an accomplished actor. Truth in acting was something he could recognize when he saw it or when he momentarily experienced it in his own playing, but he found it difficult to define and to capture. Was there no way, he asked himself, that the elusive mystery of acting could be made more than a matter of chance and happy accident? By close observation of great actors and by scrupulous examination of his own acting, he arrived at certain conclusions which he was able to formulate sufficiently to be of use as a system of training and of practical work in the theatre.

It wasn't till 1909, with the production of Turgenev's *A Month in the Country* that the System was consciously applied for the first time in the direction of a play. For those who still persist in thinking of the system as a "foreign" or "un-American" phenomenon, it is worth remembering that the actors of the Moscow Art Theatre were, to begin with, not only somewhat skeptical of it but resistant.

Still more astonishing was Stanislavsky's statement to Stella Adler in 1934 that the System had never been thoroughly practiced at the Moscow Art Theatre. It was only in the theatre's Studios, particularly in the Third Studio directed by his "prize pupil" Vakhtangov, that the System was consistently employed. And, be it noted, Vakhtangov's style was not realism. Some members of the Moscow Art Theatre company, Stanislavsky said, understood and appreciated the System but did not practice it.

I myself am convinced that the Stanislavsky System, or, if you will, the Method, has never really been practiced in the United States. It is understood by some, it is taught by many, but it has never been completely employed. It has influenced the American theatre more than any other outside of Russia and those countries in its artistic orbit. I am certain that its general effect has been far more beneficial than harmful. But I would also emphasize that its practical implementation has always and everywhere been sporadic and piecemeal.

The reason for this is simple. One cannot wholly follow Stanislavsky's precepts and procedures under the conditions which obtain on our stage: there is just not enough time. One has only to read Stanislavsky's suggestions on building a character to realize how complex are his demands and what protracted and arduous effort they require. Even in the Soviet Theatre rehearsals rarely exceed three months now, which does not compare with the time spent on rehearsals in Stanislavsky's day.

But we study the System and are right to do so. It is the only thoroughgoing formulation of the actor's craft. Its tenets are neglected at the theatre's peril. This does not mean that all good actors have been trained in the Stanislavsky "canon." It is, I repeat, from the study of great actors that Stanislavsky derived the basis of his lessons.

The System is not a style. As an artist, Stanislavsky was a realist, though it should also be recalled that in 1911 he set up a studio at his own expense to broaden the theatre's range, to progress beyond realism. He said:

Briefly, the credo of the new studio was that realism and local color had outlived their use. It was the time for the unreal on the stage. It was necessary to depict not life itself as it takes place in reality, but as we vaguely feel it in our dreams and visions, in moments of spiritual uplift. It was this spiritual state that it was necessary to portray, just as it was shown by modernistic painters on their canvases, by musicians of the new school in their compositions and by new poets in their poetry. The works of these painters, musicians and poets have no clear outlines, no definite and finished melodies, no clear thoughts. The strength of these works lies in the combination and blending of colors, lines, musical notes, and the euphony of words. They create a mood that subconsciously infects the audience. They give hints which compel the spectator to create a picture in his own imagination.

Meyerhold [whom Stanislavsky appointed to head the first attempt at a studio] knew how to talk of his dreams and thoughts and found good words for their definition. From the reports and letters I saw that we agreed in our fundamentals, and that we sought for things which had already been established in other arts, but not yet in ours. . . .

I saw no means of creating the things I felt in my own imagination, saw in paintings, heard in music and read in new poetry. I did not know how to incarnate on the stage those delicate shades of feeling which were hardly expressed in the much more developed medium of words. I was powerless to bring to life the things that interested me then and I thought it would take actors tens, hundreds of years, perhaps a whole new culture, to traverse the road that had already been traversed by the other arts. . . .

I believed that every generation had something of its *own* that could not be seen by the generation that preceded it. Perhaps that which we cannot find, which we can only desire, will be normal to them . . . the new art needs new actors with a new technique. . . .

The experiment failed. "A good idea, badly shown, dies" was his comment on this initial try at overcoming the limitations of his own realism. "But," he added, "we, Nemirovitch-Danchenko and I, already saw that we were at a crossroads, that we had to bring new blood into the company. . . ."

Though he adapted his system to the performance of opera, Stanislavsky never wholly achieved a new style. Still, the starting point or basic approach of the outstanding non-realists and even those who apparently opposed him stems from a core which he was first to enunciate and systematize. Vakhtangov and Grotowski have repeatedly affirmed this though their productions have aimed at different aesthetic objectives for which they discovered new or additional means.

Such a question as "Is X a technical actor or a Method actor?" makes me gag. The system *is* a technique, it is not an end in itself. Nor is it a *theory*. It exists and has value only in practice, in the work of the actor, the director, the company. What is called the "technical actor" is one who has mastered the peripheral attributes of acting: the problems of voice, speech and body and the various devices for effective projection. Stanislavsky does not neglect or reject any of these capacities but they are not central to his technique.

I have never spoken about acting without being asked: Can the System be used in comedy, in musicals, in farce, in fantasy, in the theatre of the absurd, in Brecht, in the non-verbal or ultra-contemporary theatre, whatever that may be. The question betrays a fundamental misunderstanding: the System wasn't conceived to produce a particular stylistic result, such as realistic truth; it is a means whereby a particular artist or group of artists may most authentically and completely manifest whatever they wish in the theatre.

One of the most unmistakably non-realistic theatre forms is the Japanese Noh. It is still appreciated by many Japanese today, most of whom barely understand a word of the archaic language it employs. It is preeminently a theatre of movement, song and speech which is closer to chant than to dialogue. It is one of the most abstract of theatre modes. When one reads the tracts of the actor Zeami (1363–1444), the Noh theatre "Shakespeare," one imagines one is reading Stanislavsky in poetic apothegms. "If, because the actor has noticed that old men walk with bent knees and back and have shrunken frames, he simply imitates these characteristics," Zeami writes, "he may achieve an appearance of decrepitude, but it will be at the expense of the 'flower.' And if the 'flower' be lacking there will be no beauty in the impersonation. . . . The 'flower' consists in forcing upon an audience *an emotion which they do not expect*."

The truth or the "emotion" of a Shaw play is not that of one by Maeterlinck, Chekhov, Pirandello or Beckett. The so-called Method director, unless he is an ass, will not aim at the same objective for Shaw as for any of the others. Brecht, influenced, he said, by the Noh theatre, did not seek to create the kind of truth or the moods which Stanislavsky did, but the System does not propose only one kind of mood or truth, not even "emotion," in all plays. It only leads to ways and means to induce assent of spirit, credibility and conviction on any level desired.

The Method teaches the actor how he may discover in himself the causes which lead to proper effects. Such effects exist in artificial comedy as in everything else. Realism, in its day a new style, is the style fashioned to create a semblance of actuality. It might even be argued that it is the most extravagantly artificial of all styles. For who but a yokel or a madman confuses a realistic play with real life?

When an actor exhibits sorrow or rage, nobility or exaltation, without our feeling something of their reality within him, we who employ the vocabulary of the System say he is playing the *result*: he is demonstrating what he wants to believe he is expressing. But unless we are guileless we fail to believe him though his demonstration may be executed with remarkable expertise. What he is doing may be superb imitation or illustration; it is not creation. Lightness, fancy, wit, eloquence, vivacity, daring, may be as fraudulently exhibited on the stage as the so-called deeper sentiments which the innocent or ignorant among actors and spectators associate with the System.

The System comprises two main divisions. The first is "the work on the self," the *training* of the actor; the other, for which the System is specifically designed, is "the work on the part," that is, within a production. Young people who study the System in theatre schools, colleges or studios are enlisted in the first of these divisions; in other words, they are hopefully equipping themselves to practice in the second.

We have no theatres, as there are in the Soviet Union and elsewhere in Eastern Europe, where the System is regularly part of production. Those of our actors and directors who have received some training in the System, and they are now legion, help themselves as much as possible with it—and, if wise, shut up about it.

When an actor mumbles, behaves in all sorts of unseemly and distasteful ways, grovels shamelessly, forces his soul grotesquely, cries out and roars to the point of unintelligibility, it is not because he is a "Method actor" but because he is a bad actor. No English or French theatre schooling has ever been as exacting in its insistence on vocal flexibility, control, euphony, clarity, force and beauty of speech as Stanislavsky. Reading the sections devoted to these subjects, in addition to the one on tempo-rhythm, in *Building a Character* and *Creating a Role,* one gathers the impression that the man must be exaggerating. The severity of the prescribed discipline is exhausting—even to read about.

I was convinced that Stanislavsky meant all he said on this score when he spoke with respect but unmistakable dissatisfaction about the actors' voices at the Comédie Française, a theatre which has always been regarded as preeminent in this respect. He himself, Stanislavsky added, could speak Pushkin's poetry as it should be spoken, but not Shakespeare's. His ideal for Shakespeare was the projection of something like an entire vocal score in itself, a thing of beauty but organic with the dramatic content and function of each speech and scene.

When Stanislavsky asked me which of the players at the Moscow Art Theatre I had most admired in the spring of 1935 and I named an actress who had played the leading role in Tolstoy's *Resurrection,* he dismissed the praise with a grimace and said, "But she speaks so badly."

My essay assumes that the director is dealing with capable actors who are not in production for pedagogic purposes. Still, I feel impelled to go on with these remarks on the System. I curse the day the subject was introduced to public discussion because certain of its aspects are the source of endless confusion among directors as well as actors.

The System is not nor was it ever intended to be a static body of knowledge. It kept changing not only through the practice of the epigones, but with Stanislavsky himself. He was always enriching it with new insights based on his experience as an actor and director. When Stella Adler complained that the System disturbed her, he said, "If it really disturbs you, forget about it. But perhaps you do not understand it." He then proceeded to rehearse a ten-minute scene with her for five weeks.

It may be useful to enumerate the three stages in the System's development. In the first, Stanislavsky's emphasis was on affective memory or the *memory of emotions*. I shall not discuss this in detail. For my present purpose it is enough to say, as I did in a brief discussion entitled "The Famous Method" in my book, *Lies Like Truth,* that in the exercise of affective memory the actor recalls some personal event in his past in order to generate true feeling in relation to a particular scene in a play.

I need only remark in this connection that in the cultivation and use of affective memory (interrelated with memory of the senses) Stanislavsky found the authentic stuff of life with which acting must be informed. Robert Edmond Jones defined acting as "a gradual half-conscious unfolding and flowering of the self into a new personality." In the memory of emotions Stanislavsky discovered the usable "roots" within the actor's person which might be guided toward the making of that new personality which is a particular role of a play.

The purpose and goal of this technique was to fulfill the *play*—not just the actor. Those who suppose that Stanislavsky was not concerned with the dramatist's work simply don't know what they are talking about or they have mistaken

Stanislavsky's apes for the man himself. Indeed, what Meyer-hold, Vakhtangov and others criticized in Stanislavsky was that he was too dependent on the mere interpretation of scripts. Over and over again Stanislavsky reiterates that the System exists for the "super-problem"—that on behalf of which the play was written, the dramatist's purpose.

In the United States the stress on emotional memory was embraced as a saving grace, as a universal answer. It became a fetish. It was what we all sought, were in need of: *feeling*. That is why the Method for many American actors is no longer a technique but a therapy. At a party I once heard an actress under the illusion that the System had great curative powers ask Grotowski if the Method mightn't be of inesti-mable value to a mentally disturbed person. Grotowski's im-mediate rejoinder was, "Such a person doesn't need a director, he needs a doctor."

After the initial insistence on the primacy of affective memory in lending substance to the actor's "living a role," Stanislavsky progressed to another means for arousing the actor's imagination and for stirring truthful responses in him. He spoke of the "magic 'if.' " When an actor found himself unmoved by a situation as presented in the script, he was asked to do whatever was called for by the scene *as if*—and here to interpose a substitute condition in the scene or "moment" which would make it come alive for him. The actor's imagi-native faculty—his unconscious, if you like—would awaken in him an emotion corresponding to what was required by the scene. For example: "You enter this hovel *as if* it were a cathe-dral," or "You listen to the proposal *as if* you were tasting peach brandy," "You address the man *as if* you feared he might attack you with a concealed weapon you suspect he car-ries."*

This new implement in the System led to its third stage,

* To quote Stanislavsky: "An actor must never say about the given action of his role, 'It could never happen to me,' or 'It could never happen in life,' but he must naively believe in that magic 'if' and freely and easily imagine he would do so 'if' he ever found himself in that circumstance."

one to which I have previously referred—the concentration on *physical problems.* This third stage finally became predominant in Stanislavsky's work with the actor but we should not overlook the fact that the three stages compose a continuum. Each is vital to the other.

"One must never speak of feeling to the actor," Stanislavsky says countless times. The prime element, the motive power of acting, the entire System, is based on *action.* By action Stanislavsky meant not only psychological action—the desire which prompts us to act—but the physical steps through which the desire may be aroused and fulfilled. "One must be a virtuoso in these physical actions," Stanislavsky told Stella Adler, "believe in what we do. But everything must be completely true—*to the very end.*" Stanislavsky chose the physical actions implicit in the play. "For emotion," he went on, "I search in the *given circumstances* [the particularities of each of the play's situations] never in the feelings.

"If I try and do the psychological, I force the action. We must attack the psychological from the point of view of the physical life so as not to disturb the feeling. [I translate literally from the French he spoke.] *In each psychological action there is some physical element.* Search for the line, *in terms of action,* not in feeling.

"For example: I want to drink water but I am told there is poison in it. Before I drink, I question myself: 'Who has put it in, do I want to die, why should I drink, why should I die?' Your imagination must understand each of these things. . . . Do you see the character's life with your eyes (not your feelings)? How does the character get up in the morning? What was she like yesterday, what is the layout of her house?"

In his plan for the production of that highly emotional play *Othello,* and in his instructions to the actor who was to play the role, he wrote, "For God's sake don't think of the psychology, of the feeling, of emotion—work on the physical problem, the action."

Stanislavsky had always maintained that feeling, though

" 'tis a consummation devoutly to be wished," was most elusive and beyond conscious control. It could only be summoned by indirect means. He defined the System as a conscious technique to lure or awaken the super-conscious. To act means to will: one can prepare oneself to will solutions for specific technical problems.

All this has a special relevance to the *esthétique* of the new avant-garde theatre. In this theatre, we are assured by its exponents, life isn't "imitated." The actor doesn't interpret a character, he enacts "functions." Actors change from one "role" or "function" to another many times during a performance. Meaning is communicated through the various actions the actor is called upon to do. This leads to a particular style intended to embody something of our present mode of behavior. So be it! But this does not contravene the System, though it puts very special limits on it. I repeat: There is nothing in the System which dictates or necessitates a particular sort of play or performance—except an empty one. Most of the plays of the "new theatre" are certainly not the kind Stanislavsky would have cared about, but that is a personal, not an objective, consideration.

When we reduce acting to physical behavior alone (though that is just as impossible as totally abstract art) we are certainly in tune with the times: it is a social symptom. But action without motivation or without objectives other than itself, performed by beings without background or whose background is taken for granted as that of "anybody" in situations assumed to be common experience, rarely carries much impact—no matter how startling it may be. Such performances stir us to the degree that we might be stirred if a pistol were shot without our knowing who did the shooting, why it was shot and at whom it was aimed.

The removal of broad human scope from acting does not eliminate it, but it takes away much of its power to touch us. That is one reason the so-called new theatre has not yet produced any outstanding actors. Still, we may go so far as to admit that if the physical actions performed in such plays were dazzlingly, breathtakingly executed, they might produce the kind of exhilaration we sometimes experience at a bullfight or at an especially fine circus feat. We find perfection of this sort in certain dancers. But everyone familiar with the dance knows that the classical ballet as much as the modern dance calls for something more than physical aplomb.

The purport of my argument is neither to extol the virtues of the Stanislavsky System nor to uphold a traditional view of the theatre—neither is threatened by the new theatre—but to make clear that in the creation as well as in the judgment of theatre we must first of all understand what goal is being sought, what the artists are endeavoring to communicate. No holds are barred in the theatre, but we must believe in what we see and ascertain what value we attach to what we see and are asked to believe.

I believe in the Noh theatre, I believe in the great clowns. I believe Edward Villella's leaps, I believe Violette Verdy and Allegra Kent, Martha Graham, Merce Cunningham. I believe the superb acrobat. All have their reality—as well as deadly imitators. Whether we think of their different realities as an "imitation of life" or not matters little except to pedants: they are manifestations of life. What do we expect from the theatre? It is not merely a question of novel techniques for these must be ultimately judged by their contribution to our human needs, our aspirations, moral concerns and philosophies. These questions lead to the role played by the audience in the theatre.

CHAPTER 13

The Audience

WE HEAR MUCH TALK nowadays about the theatre of partic-
ipation, in which audience and players fuse and become part
of one another. The impulse which prompts propaganda
for that sort of theatre is a healthy one. It harks back to the
theatre's origins. Its recurrence now as a battle cry of the
younger generation has social meaning. But it should escape
no one that the theatre is and always has been the product of
such fusion. The theatre is inconceivable in any other terms.

Theatre is a particular mode of expression through which
a community realizes itself. The audience is the theatre's well-
spring, its leading actor. This is not a metaphor, it is a historical fact.

The theatre is an outgrowth of the rites of primitive communities engaged in prayer or invocation to the gods. These
communities beseeched the gods to supply them with those
things without which they could not live: rain, plentiful har-

vests, a successful hunt, *et al.* Every member of the community or tribe was involved. The gods were feared as well as
loved; along with pleas for sustenance there were magic cere-
monies of appeasement enacted in gestures of worshipful
praise. When the tribal pleas were granted, there were fes-
tivities. The communal rites developed ever greater variety
of form. Some of the rites were "reports" or symbolic reenact-
ments of the adventures, perils and triumphs attendant to the
tribal pursuits. Relief, fervor, ecstasy, as well as sheer pleasure, imbued these manifestations. Men cannot live without
venting the energy aroused by their deepest needs, desires
and drives.

Each tribe had its own identity; everyone shared in a common ground of anxiety, hope, appetite and faith. A leader always emerged from within the tribe. He may himself have
contributed to the ritualizing of ceremonial activities or
chosen a favored "qualified" person to help him do so. Rites
took place where it was natural or convenient for everyone to
participate in them. Whatever sites were selected for these
occasions were the first settings or stages, just as the leaders
of the tribal "performances" were the first directors.

Since language had not yet sufficiently evolved, primitive
men expressed themselves chiefly through gesture, mimicry,
movement and sound which became dance and music. With
the development of speech, magic words came into being:
poetry, "literature." Whoever extracted them from the welter
of tribal experience and ceremonial action was an embryonic
"playwright." Or perhaps the leader alone with the aid of his
subordinates chose the scheme of the "play" and determined
which of the spontaneous improvisations were most impressive as movement, sound and speech.

There may have been a time when there was no leader at
all—only the group unit. But not all its members could engage in the main pursuit: not all could hunt, plant seed,
gather crops, fight. They served complementary functions "at
home." The folk mass as a whole was therefore divided into

those at home and those who depicted their way of life through ordered celebration. Those who sat and watched—if they were capable of such passivity—must at least have swayed in sympathy with the "actors." The least directly engaged, let us say the old, were close kinsmen to those who were central to the ceremony.

It would have been unthinkable for a community which lived by the hunt to develop a rite centered on the need for grain or for one which depended on abundant rainfall to inspire themselves with the "play" of sun worship. The material and content of the various rites were always in accord with tribal needs. Art as such was not a consideration.

The foregoing is a wholly unscientific, crudely fanciful summary of what every history and book of anthropological conjecture tells us. What is almost never told us is the bearing such studies may have on our present understanding of the theatre. They proclaim the theatre's monistic essence, its oneness. The actor, the dramatist, the director, the designer, are interrelated in a single organism. They all originate in the community which they serve, they are all parts of the so-called *audience*. Actors are not born in Equity.

With the theatre's development from the unifying rite to the later mysteries and morality plays along with the street fairs, troubadours, clowns of the marketplace, and minstrels of all descriptions, to the theatres of sovereigns and nobility and then to the commercial theatre, the functions begin to separate, to assume independence and to arrogate to themselves special and divisive airs and privileges. The various craft unions of our contemporary theatre are signs of this baleful evolution. When each grouplet represents a separate interest, it becomes more inimical to the theatre as a whole. Monetary considerations, if nothing else, may force our new theatre groups to restore some of the lost unity by having actors, directors and even some playwrights serve as technical and administrative staff as well.

In our pluralistic society the audience is no longer homogeneous. The establishment in some countries of workers' theatres, political theatres, religious theatres, theatres for poets, guerrilla and hippie theatres, are attempts to recover harmony, to wed audience and players.

There is a practical significance in all this. It explains why a pleasant little comedy like John van Druten's *The Voice of the Turtle,* played by an excellent company headed by the enchanting Margaret Sullavan, succeeds in New York and fails in London with the same cast and production. The play, which had its New York premiere in 1943, dealt with the philanderings of an army officer on leave. The war with its daily devastation was no laughing matter to the English. They were not merely unamused by the play, they resented it. The audience was badly cast for the play. It rejected its part.

How explain the enormous success of Brecht-Weill's *The Threepenny Opera* in Greenwich Village beginning in 1954 after its failure on Broadway in 1933? Why, following its long New York run, did it fail once again when it was taken on tour in large theatres outside New York? The audience for a Macdougal Street theatre, though it is made up of people who come from different parts of town, is not of the same disposition as the Broadway audience: its financial estate is different, its social and intellectual physiognomy and its taste are dissimilar.

The Trial of the Catonsville Nine, about the destruction of draft board files by the Berrigan brothers and their followers, is acclaimed by public and press when produced at a small church only to collapse as a Broadway show. The audiences which pack the house for *Promises, Promises* or *Follies* are not likely to be attracted to a debate on the moral issues raised by the Berrigan action.

Strindberg, I venture to say, will never be a popular dramatist in the United States except in university theatres or with other special groups. Neither will Pirandello. Brecht has never been a success on Broadway, but he has been played in America more often than anywhere else in the world—played, that is, to audiences receptive to his art, which are found mainly in universities and in certain regional theatres. O'Casey's plays, by no means abstruse, have never enjoyed a long run in New York.

One reason, I believe, for the emergence of musical comedy as an eminently American theatre form is that productions of musical comedy unite talent of kindred nature and similar training in a form embodying American ebullience, commitment to fun, energy, industry and an optimism fostered by prosperity. Our musicals, if nothing else, are marvelous machines of entertainment. And that is what the big undifferentiated American audience wants above all in the theatre.

To everyone's astonishment, the Theatre Guild became a thriving organization in the twenties. There had been sophisticated, cosmopolitan people in New York prior to that period with a wider range of interests and tastes than the earlier American theatre had led us to suppose, but a theatre audience composed of such people became conscious of itself for almost the first time in 1915. When America was transformed into a world power in ever closer contact with Europe as a consequence of the First World War, its theatre entered a new stage in its history. A new audience formed itself through this development, an audience which brought about a "renaissance" in all our arts. The Theatre Guild was able to organize an audience on a subscription basis and attract large numbers of theatregoers for plays by St. John Ervine, Andreyev, Molnar, Shaw and O'Neill. Before 1914 such dramatists would have been caviar to the main body of our theatregoers.

"When the audience is not there," I once heard Jacques Copeau say, "the actors aren't there either." He was not referring to box-office receipts. A play achieves resonance when all its actors are bound together in a common faith and consciousness. The play receives its echo from the audience. To put it even more simply: if the audience won't play, there's no game.

What does this mean in the practical conduct of the thea-

tre? What has·it meant to me as a director? It has been basic
to all my practice. The playwright I choose to direct must be
"mine," and I, in a sense, must be part of him. We must be of
the same audience, of the same community, not in a parochial
way but in the widest sense of sharing a common vocabulary
of thought, feeling and ideals. In the broadest understanding
of this proposition, it applies to the plays of the past and to
foreign plays as well.

I do not cast actors on the basis of talent alone; I endeavor
to choose talents compatible with the playwright and myself. We know the sort of people we wish to address and to act
as our collaborators. Our audience is one which looks forward
to what we may have to say, with whom when we find ourselves in present conflict we hope to be able to persuade on
the grounds of common assumptions and proclivities. It is
this audience we believe it possible and desirable to move
and to please.

The theatre which scorns its audience is doomed, is, in fact,
no theatre at all. Does this connote conformism? Does it mean
that we follow the crowd or that Ibsen's "compact majority"
dictates the rules of our game and that we trip to its measure?
The man who believes that the audience (the *customer*) is always right, and he who believes the exact opposite by proclaiming the mass an ass, are both mistaken. The confusion
arises from ignorance with regard to the audience of which
they are part. They do not know to what segment of society
they belong. They are cut off from their fellow men, except
by the ties of animal need or, more appositely to our time,
money. Unless we are masochists, we always hope that our
audience is as large as we anticipate—or larger! I understand
what Goethe, as theatre director, meant when he admitted
that he hesitated to produce a play he felt had no chance of
success.

A director or a producer who believes he can count on an
audience of no more than a hundred people for ten nights
and finds such an audience is a success. Ionesco's *The Bald*

Soprano is a huge success in Paris: it has run for over ten years at a theatre which can only be described as minuscule. I scheduled Saroyan's *My Heart's in the Highlands* for a run of five performances under the Group Theatre's auspices; when we were able to extend its run to six weeks I found its success remarkable. I was disheartened when people who liked it bemoaned it as a flop. I could not help feeling sorry to find that such nice people's thinking was so tightly bound by Broadway calculations. "If a man does not act as he thinks," I have read somewhere, "he will end up thinking as he acts."

To the question often put to me in one form or another, "How conscious are you of the audience when you direct a play; if a situation arose in which you felt your own taste demanded one kind of direction and the assumed taste of the audience another, would you try to please yourself or the audience?" My answer always has been, "But I am one of the audience or, at any rate, a particularly conscious part of it." I choose a play for a certain audience, and the actors for that play. I do not consider myself alien to the audience. We are a family more or less in accord. I assume that the audience wants to see and hear what I do, that it will laugh when I do and be moved where I am moved. When I am disappointed by the audience's reactions, I try to understand the reason; I investigate the cause of the discrepancy.

If I am convinced that the audience is justified in its discomfiture or objection, I try to remedy the fault. When I believe I may override their objections, I persist on my path till proved wrong, though absolute proof is rarely possible. There are, after all, the previews or the weeks of tryout to test various solutions to unresolved problems. But I never proceed from contempt. At times I will allow myself to fail if failure is the cost of my convictions. I do not believe in gaining favor by self-betrayal. My normal attitude is exemplified by the incident of the two high school boys whose innocent and modest query about the barroom scene in *The Member of the Wedding* persuaded me to cut it.

No discussion of the audience should neglect the influence of the critic. It is not easy in our society for the critic to exercise his true function which is to serve as an enlightened go-between for artists and audiences. The reviewer on a large-circulation daily is chiefly responsible to the journal which employs him and its impact on the theatre profession *as a business.* His relation to theatre as an art and to theatre workers is, in the main, fortuitous. Ideally (and why not speak occasionally in that vein?) the critic should be something of an artist himself (*as critic*) with a particular aptitude for the "optics" of the theatre enhanced by experience and study. With innate sympathy for and understanding of the theatre's craftsmen such a person may serve as the audience's knowing eye and conscience.

When we speak of the theatre audience today we are referring to a conglomerate. Actually there is a great variety of audiences. The critic must know to which of these audiences he is most truly related or what sort of audience he would like to create. In his day Shaw helped create an audience for Ibsen and the then new theatre of England. In the fifties Kenneth Tynan waged a battle for John Osborne, Arnold Wesker, Bertolt Brecht and other writers, as well as directors and actors who were upsetting the West End theatre establishment.

We must judge a critic not so much by his particular opinions as by his standards. The chief issue is not the critic's separate likes or dislikes but what he believes and is as a man, what he strives for, in what sort of world he desires to live. I am distrustful of the critic who only wants "good theatre." Good for what, I ask, for whom? In what way is it good and what part of me is it good for?

The sound critic is not wholly "free." He is limited, as Shaw put it, by his prejudices. He must reveal them and "fight" for them. I have admired conservative, socialist, religious, Marxist, impressionist, analytic, anarchist and mystic critics. They have all been more useful in the formation of my own tastes and judgments than the affable creature who is equally and blandly, or even enthusiastically, receptive to everything. He signifies nothing because he stands for nothing: he merely fills space in a column which usually resembles pleasant or unpleasant chitchat. Such a person, at best, acts as a privileged consumer's guide.

The critic must know what a *play* (not simply its plot) signifies: he must be equipped to judge the script, the acting and the direction. Each of these has its own content, yet must be understood in relation to one another. He must be able to assess the "weight" and import of the theatre event as a whole. And he should be judged by his ability to see the play in the perspective of what lies "outside" the theatre, i.e., the world in which we live, the world which has brought the occasion into being. The critic most illuminates what he sees through the fullness of his own perception of life. That is how he may help make the audience a more creative participant in the theatre's festivity.

This has little to do with "raves" or "pans": they only concern show business. But who in hell thought of the theatre as a business in the first place? That is a sure way to eliminate it —even as a business!

CHAPTER 14

Questions and Answers

IN LECTURING on direction and related subjects I am asked many questions. Though most of my answers are implied in the foregoing chapters, I shall set down here a few summary replies to the questions most commonly asked.

1. *If the sources of the theatre are rooted in the community in which it is situated, does this not restrict the choice of plays to the narrow interests of the local scene?*

Though I deplore a theatre which neglects the patrimony of the past, I confess a predilection for the newly created. Not because the latter is superior to the old—obviously this is not so—but because the art of theatre, an art of *presence*, is also the art of the present. Shakespeare and other masters of the past are, as Jan Kott and others have pointed out, our contemporaries. Their greatness transcends the limits of time and many cultural differences. In the *theatre* they reveal their contemporaneity only when they are felt and projected in response to our innermost needs. This is not to be construed to mean that they must be made "topical," e.g., Julius Caesar as Mussolini, Shylock as an East Side peddler or King Lear as an example of latter-day nihilism.

The theatre is not a museum, a treasure house to commemorate ancient wonders; it is a vehicle for the manifestation of the joys and travail of our existence. The greater the scope and profundity of its revelations, the more universal it becomes. But it always begins with the *now*.

2. *What do you do about the resistant actor, the one who disagrees with your interpretation of a part?*

Before answering the question point blank it is important to realize that refractoriness in an actor has diverse, not always immediately recognizable, psychological causes. Vanity may enter into it, or a too-great susceptibility to criticism, a fear of disapproval, a "star" complex, unfamiliarity with the director's mode of procedure and other peculiarities.

Every director invents or improvises "tricks" to deal with the individual actor's hang-ups. An actor in whose talent Stanislavsky believed lacked self-confidence. He was always breaking down with a sense of inadequacy after his finest flights. Stanislavsky instructed his company to prepare placards on which were inscribed something like "Y is a superb artist." Whenever Stanislavsky noticed that an attack of inferiority tremens was about to overpower the actor, he would call on the others to parade around the despondent man. This always produced the desired effect: the actor felt refreshed.

In directing Thomas Mitchell in the touring company of *Death of a Salesman* I found that no matter how brief a remark I made about some small point, he would elaborate with extended comments of his own to show me not only that he had understood what I had said, but that he understood more and better. After all, he was a veteran actor and director many years before I had begun my career. I realized that if I betrayed impatience or attempted to silence him he would resent it. On the other hand, if I let him continue to interpolate his disquisitions at every bit of direction I proposed, the rehearsals would deteriorate into hours of futile discourse.

I ceased offering him any direct guidance. I would turn instead to whomever he was playing a scene with and say something like this: "You are annoyed because your father [Mitchell] has just reprimanded you," or "Willy [Mitchell] has begun to plead with you so touchingly that you answer in kind," or "You see in Willy's face the clouds of anger gather and you try to calm his impending fury." In other words, I directed Mitchell through his partners in the scene. The stratagem worked.

But my principal maxim in cases of personal difficulty with an actor is: Never, never, never win an argument with him, never persuade him that he is "wrong," just get him to do what you want! The director who beats an actor down by the force of his own authority does so at his own cost. The director-martinet is an obsolete phenomenon today—and should be. A director who insists that he is always absolutely right is indulging his own ego. Much rehearsal time is wasted through such indulgence.

Still! When an actor tells me that he differs with me, I usually say, "Don't talk, *show me*." If his demonstration fails to convince me, I explain why what he has shown me doesn't fulfill the play's or the scene's demands. Or I choose two or three other possible directives, not previously proposed, which he may follow. The actor more often than not will then turn back to the directorial suggestions which he had initially rejected.

Though I am given to close analysis of all the interpretive problems which may arise at rehearsal, I am aware that too much cerebration of this sort tends to be redundant and obstructive.

In casting *The Time of the Cuckoo,* I had Katina Paxinou in mind for a certain part. Arthur Laurents, the author, had reservations on this score. We chose another actress: Lydia St. Clair. But the Paxinou image persisted in my thinking. I directed Miss St. Clair as if the Greek actress were playing the role. After the first major run-through Miss St. Clair said, "I'm bad in this role. If you want it acted as you have directed it, you should have cast Katina Paxinou." "I never thought of such a thing," I lied. "Please show me how you would prefer to play the part." She did, and was excellent. Thank heavens she "won"!

The actor is seen on the stage, not the director. It is also important to realize that there is a moment—very late in the rehearsal or preview period—when the actor knows more about the part he is playing than the director. The director must be ever vigilant in seeing that the actor doesn't become sidetracked in his performance; he must be kept "in line." But the role is finally the actor's possession.

An actor, after due compensation of course, may be dismissed. I have very rarely had recourse to this method of improving the quality of a production.

3. *Does the director call additional rehearsals after the play has opened?*

He should. It is difficult to keep a production in shape after three months of playing. We rejoice in a long run, but it is artistically debilitating. A director should check on his production *at least* twice a month.

I say this glibly, but the truth is that during my first years as a director I positively loathed seeing one of my productions after it had opened; I was nearly always disappointed at my failure to accomplish all I had hoped to. But since then self-discipline has prevailed.

Apropos of this, I recall speaking to the brilliant Czech director Ottomar Krejča about his beautiful production of *The Three Sisters*. Though I admired it, I found much in it subject to cavil. A year later, on seeing it again, I told him that I now liked it much more. "Ah, but we've been working on it ever since we opened," he said. The play, to begin with, had been rehearsed for many months. It was in repertory.

Kazan once told me that after six months of a continuous run actors are unable to retain either the glow or the just proportions of their original performance: they lose their resilience. I agree.

There are exceptions. I saw Walter Huston in *Desire Under the Elms* four times over a period of twelve months. Each performance was better than the previous one. One day after many months of playing in *Awake and Sing* I noticed Stella Adler examining the "book" of her part. I asked her why. "I'm looking over the notes I took at rehearsal," she answered. "I'm trying to see if I've lost something of the original intentions and if there are new ways of recharging the 'battery.'"

4. *Are there any ground rules you bring to bear for comedy versus tragedy versus "straight" drama versus fantasy, etc.?*

The basic tenets of direction remain the same for all productions. Only emphases change, that is, styles. Before I undertook the direction of my first independent production, *Awake and Sing*, Elmer Rice advised me to direct it "for comedy." Several other established theatre people told me I must stress the pathos. I found both counsels meaningless. I directed the play for the qualities I perceived in it—without "labels." The results depend on the choice of actions, adjustments and characterizations. What counts is the director's vision and temperament.

In the direction of musicals, certain technical considerations are extremely important: they have to do with concision, overall rhythm and proportions in the relationship of music and dance to dialogue. There are directors who are peculiarly suited to the task. I have directed only one musical: Rodgers' and Hammerstein's *Pipe Dream*. It was not a success: serious mistakes in casting were made, and the piece itself was far from the team's best. Would the outcome have been happier if George Abbott, let us say, had directed it? He is adept in the field, but *Me and Juliet,* the Rodgers and Hammerstein musical which preceded *Pipe Dream,* had also been a failure.

5. *Can a good director handle anything from* King Lear *to* Burlesque?

Theoretically, yes. Actually, I doubt it. An artist's limitations are integral with his talent. I can't truly say which of my productions I regard as the "best." Was it *Awake and Sing, Golden Boy, The Member of the Wedding, The Waltz of the Toreadors, Bus Stop, A Touch of the Poet, Tiger at the Gates, Incident at Vichy,* or—? Perhaps one of my failures was as good as any of these. What is the "best" anyhow? I work as scrupulously on plays I do not particularly admire as on those which I do.

6. *How have you managed to direct plays in such languages as Japanese and Hebrew, of which you are totally ignorant?*

Apart from the use of an interpreter, my methods do not change in these cases. Technique sustains me. After several readings and the repetition of scenes for a week or two, I begin to associate the foreign sounds with the script in English (or with *Monserrat,* in French). I am able to detect errors in readings and even, incredible though it may seem, faults in diction. This was no doubt also Tyrone Guthrie's experience in Israel with *Oedipus Rex.*

7. *Do you assume that for any play an ideal production is at least in theory possible?*

No; a production is ideal only in relation to its director's vision of it and to a particular spectator's taste. "A play," Vakhtangov said, "must be directed with a view to the company and the audience to whom it is to be presented." I have seen productions which have troubled me in regard to interpretation but which I respected for the excellence of their craftsmanship and their imaginative originality. A play is new with every fresh view of it. We would all be horrified, I am sure, if we were able to see *Hamlet* as it was done at the Globe Theatre in the Shakespeare-Burbage production!

8. *Do you ever lose your temper?*

Very rarely. Usually it does little good—unless the temper is feigned and is suitable to a particular situation and actor. (Directors are often expert "hams.") But an atmosphere of genial cordiality coupled with earnest effort serves best. Blame, recrimination, anger, a display of anguish, are hardly ever in order.

9. *Can an actor direct as effectively as a good nonacting director?*

An actor had better not direct a play in which he appears himself—unless his role is a subsidiary one. But what of Stanislavsky or Orson Welles? There are many notable exceptions. Should a playwright direct his own play? Those who are qualified should. Bernard Shaw, Noel Coward, George S. Kaufman and Bertolt Brecht directed their own plays with signal success. Each in his own way was a consummate theatre craftsman. Very few contemporary playwrights are, though some believe themselves to be: ask their actors.

10. *Should a director have acting experience?*

It is most advantageous, even if the director should not have proved to have been a good actor. The more general theatre experience the would-be director acquires during his apprenticeship, the better. I frown on those who, having just graduated from a theatre school, attempt direction on an ambitious scale.

11. *How much of an "academician" must a good director be?*

An intelligent person need never fear learning. The more extensive the director's general study, the more equipped he will be for his profession. "Direction," Meyerhold said, "is the broadest specialty there is." But one must learn how to translate one's knowledge into theatre. Direction is not achieved solely through verbal concepts. For stage embodiment words alone do not suffice.

12. *Can directing be taught?*

To a certain extent, yes. It certainly can be learned. But a college course alone is inadequate for the purpose. One should attend many, many rehearsals of many different sorts and eventually take some active part in them. It is best to study direction under a variety of theatrical auspices. Assistant stage management and, later, stage management in several productions under different directors provide good schooling. Working for or directing a stock company, a community theatre or a modest but professional experimental group is also a valuable preparatory step. A theoretical approach alone will not do.

The simplest answer to the question is: you can learn directing if you have a talent for it.

13. *Should theatre people be aware of sociological or political problems?*

The answer is the same as to question eleven. The director today, particularly with a permanent company, tends to become an educator as well as a director. The theatre is not a school, but work in it should constitute a schooling. I applaud Tyrone Guthrie's dictum: "Unless you're a rounded citizen, you're a square theatre person."

14. *What other "lines of work" are comparable to directing?*

Directing is often compared to conducting an orchestra. The parallel is only partially apposite and there is one very important difference. While a conductor knows the exact properties, possibilities and limitations of each instrument, the director is never certain with the actor whether he is to be stroked, scratched, plucked or thumped!

15. *Are "stars" easier to work with than "unknowns"?*

An experienced and talented actor is easier to work with than an unpracticed one. He knows more and has more to offer. The amateur or novice is often extremely touchy and cocksure when he is not self-conscious. (But children are sometimes "born" actors.)

After years of work with the Group Theatre's acting com-company I found Fredric March, Melvyn Douglas, Julie Harris, Maureen Stapleton, Michael Redgrave and several other stars most amenable and appreciative of direction. The test of the actor is innate creative resourcefulness which is intimately associated with receptivity to suggestion. Perhaps I've been lucky, perhaps I've known how to choose the right people.

16. *What are the chief qualities a director must have?*

The first of these surely is the ability to deal with people. "Direction," a French critic has said, "is criticism transferred to action." Yes, but the director, I repeat, does not influence by verbal explanation only. There are eloquent directors and some who are very nearly mute. In one way or another the director must impress his company, make it feel that he merits his leadership and their confidence.

The director does not achieve his effects only by means of physical staging, the visible and audible signs of his invention, knowledge and skill. I have observed many directors in rehearsal. Even in the case of those who said little and seemed to be "doing" less, I could detect their imprint in the completed production. There is something of a mystery in this of which the director himself may not be conscious. It is an emanation which we inadequately designate as "personality." It goes beyond the demonstrable specifics of the craft.

Did not Reinhardt's productions breathe a Viennese gaiety, a baroque sensuality and glamor, a peculiarly mid-European warmth, a cordially humorous Jewish skepticism? Was there not something of the cunning necromancer, the diabolic magician, in all of Meyerhold's productions? Guthrie's wide-ranging playfulness, his vaulting freedom, his amiable mischievousness, shines through all his work. We cannot fail to recognize the muscular energy added to common sense in Kazan's best efforts on the stage, or the adventuresomeness, the love of prestidigitation and the bravado in Orson Welles' stage exploits.

The director's essential qualities as a human being, which he perhaps unconsciously communicates, cannot be pinned down. There are no lessons for acquiring this inalienable personal touch. This is only another way of saying that a director must be a creative person, he must be *somebody*. Otherwise he is only a journeyman.

But we must never lose sight of my first proposition: It is not the director alone who shapes the production, he employs everyone's talent. He chooses those whom he may be able to inspire and those he believes will aid and inspire him. As a leader, he must be a knowing follower. Like all good artists, the director must also be a canny plagiarist.

17. *What should a director avoid or prevent?*

Though the director must at all times leave himself open to suggestion and be prepared to accept correction, he must never release his command. Though a collaborator in a collective effort, he must always remain at the forefront of his troupe. He must not permit the playwright or the producer to speak to the actors about their roles—unless he requests them to do so. It is confusing to actors to receive direction from several sources. Moreover, playwrights and producers rarely employ the actor's vocabulary, that is, they seldom know what is exactly the right thing to say to the actor and the right moment to speak. The director and his company develop a common language through their long and intimate exchange during rehearsals.

Previews and out-of-town tryouts are the periods at which the actors are most vulnerable and susceptible to infection even by the most kindly or innocuous comment. Actors will

listen to almost anything at such times. They should be quar-
antined from friends and relatives.

I directed Morris Carnovsky in Odets' *Night Music* in the
role of a New York detective, the fount of wisdom in the play.
He was to speak his lines, I told him, in a gravelly voice and
to apply a makeup that would give him an almost bestial look.
He chose the bust of a grim Roman emperor as his model.
The combination of compassionate sentiment in the dialogue
with the forbidding mask contributed to an unusually interesting characterization. Odets was most favorably impressed.

A friend or a relative—perhaps an out-of-town critic—found
the voice and the makeup "unsympathetic." Slowly and un-
knowingly Carnovsky began to modify both. It took me a
while to realize that by the time the play opened Carnovsky
had gone back to his own natural, clearly benevolent and
dignified physiognomy.

Still another example of interference from an outside
source came to my aggrieved notice after the opening of *Golden Boy*. Luther Adler, it struck me, had lost something of
the boyish innocence with which, as directed, he had endowed
his part. When I questioned him about this he told me that
an actress whom he greatly and justifiably admired had reminded him that he was playing an *artist*. I winced in pain.
All through rehearsal I had insisted that Joe Bonaparte was a
kid who might conceivably become an artist. If he were already an artist (how does an artist behave?), the play's story
might be considered incredible. Actors and directors must
protect themselves from the hot air of chance guidance.

18. *Do you place more emphasis on the eye or the ear in
your productions, that is, are you more visually or orally
oriented?*

As this question is put, I cannot answer it. Certain directors
compose beautiful or striking tableaux or visual patterns. I
never consciously attempt to do so. I direct for the idea or intention of each scene and for the play as a whole, and seek
whatever combination of means will best convey them. I di-

rect for the actor and through the actor: he is body and voice, movement and feeling, and something more than all these. The actor, like the production itself, is an indivisible totality. I do not conceive a production in "departments." I seek the integration of all the theatre's elements to form a unified effect and meaning.

Speaking of his production of Beaumarchais' *Marriage of Figaro*, Stanislavsky said, "The style was hardly French: it is impossible for Russians to achieve a true French manner. There were crudities in the acting and in some of the staging. Not all the actors were well cast. The sets weren't all they should have been. But somehow the production worked, it was alive." The same must have been true of the first Moscow Art Theatre production of *The Seagull*—which made history.

Perhaps the overall answer to the question should be stated hyperbolically: The director should listen with his eyes and see with his ears.

19. *What are the director's special satisfactions?*

For all his preparation and particular competence the director works "blindly." He cannot really be sure as he concentrates and polishes each bit what effect the play will ultimately produce. There are occasions when it never comes to life till the audience has acted with, on, or in it!

The director experiences his greatest satisfaction the moment he realizes that he has contributed to the magic of a birth, and that what has been born possesses something of the nature he hoped it might have.

20. A sixteen-year-old student once asked me, *"What is the worst thing that happens to a director?"*

My answer was: "You see from all I've told you how thoughtfully, how painstakingly, how sincerely and how knowledgeably I labor on a production. Yet for all that my efforts to bring about the hoped for result may be in vain. The magic doesn't happen. I fail."

"What do you do then?" the candid youth asked.

"I forgive myself."

Part III

DIRECTOR'S NOTES FOR

Rocket to the Moon

by CLIFFORD ODETS

(First presented by the Group Theatre at the Belasco Theatre, November 24, 1938.)

The mood of this "romance" is *loneliness*. Every element in the play, the physical environment (the setting), the heat, the love affair, the "sexiness," must express the basic loneliness.

The loneliness is also a social phenomenon. Stark's office, his practice, his daily pursuits and habits, his income and his marital life create his need for Cleo or someone like her. These are all part of the play's poignancy.

The setting must suggest a kind of mystery. Always the feeling of night, of secrecy, a hidden place, an enclosure, "mysterious" sounds: the gurgle of water from the cooler, the hum of the electric fan, rain.

The spine of the play: to seek love (search for love).

Spine: to make things (his life) approximate the condition of love.

He has always been poor; his childhood was spent in an orphanage. He has had to accommodate himself to the "reality" of lower-middle-class inevitability. "Aren't you always right?" he says to his wife.

But even after he has accommodated or accepted this sort of reality, he somehow resists it. He suggests that with his father-in-law's aid he might open a new office with new equipment. "All night I didn't sleep thinking about it," he says, but when his wife demurs, he weakens. "Let's forget it, Belle." Nevertheless, he keeps pressing his point. When Belle rejects his arguments he surrenders, "You win, you win!"

His lower-class timidity overcomes him, both here and at the end of the play. "It's settled."

His life is a long forgetting: "I came over to the water cooler," but he has forgotten his objective. "I wanted *to do* something." "I have a bunch of answers for that, but I won't give them . . ." because they won't avail. He even kids his ineffectuality. To his wife's remonstrances he replies, 'Yes, m'am."

He has forgotten the struggle that has made him forget. He has almost forgotten his child's death.

He is embarrassed by his own and other people's emotion. It is too sharp a reminder of the feelings welling within him —feelings and impetuses which he has suppressed or have been suppressed in him.

His *smile* is the sign of his embarrassment.

He is boyish, sometimes almost childishly jubilant. He is naive, and on a mature emotional level, inexperienced. He is guileless, lacking aggressiveness. His perpetual state of economic disadvantage makes him habitually neglectful of himself: he doesn't eat on time, for instance.

There is withal a certain stubbornness in him. Though he

renounces many things, he depends on his desires. What he has desired was something to help him toward love.

He is irritable, but his irritability, being without positive consequences, gives way to depression. After Mr. Prince, his father-in-law, leaves him, he admits to himself all the secret desires he has denied in Mr. Prince's presence.

Mr. Prince depresses Stark because he sees in him a completely despairing man, and Stark isn't that as yet.

Stark's naiveté is the result of his continued surprise by the evidence of life. He is amazed that his old, financially successful father-in-law should have wished to be an actor. He thinks of a secretary as a simple employee but Cleo, his secretary, opens his eyes to himself.

Stark doesn't believe that Mr. Prince has ever been a faithful husband. He envies Prince, jealous and attracted to him because of his sexual freedom.

He defends his own status quo because he has accommodated himself to his own defeat.

Stark's relation to Cleo: in the first act Stark doesn't really see Cleo. He notices Cleo as a woman because Prince has done so.

In the first scene of the second act his (Stark's) questioning of the girl begins to arouse his sexual interest in her. "Life must be very pleasant for you," he says. That is because he sees in Cleo the possibility of fulfillment. She is in conscious quest for love, therefore closer to it, and through it, to life in general.

His inactivity has become a habit. His unhappiness is a habit.

Finally, he dares to love her. Life has forced this upon him. Cleo teaches him the insufficiency of his way of life. She urges him to change this. She makes him realize how wrong his wife's pushing him about is. He protests; he is jealous. He's afraid to lose her. He takes her.

He is unable to change his condition. His life's "reality"

is too strong and he ends defeated. But somehow because of his desire (implied in his spine) and his experience with Cleo he has been brought closer to life and love. Forever after, even if he "forgets," he will be a deeper, perhaps an ennobled man.

CLEO SINGER

Spine: to seek love—the essential action of the play.

Her quest is not simply the desire for a mate, a sexual partner. All the men offer her that. She wants a release from the drabness of her surroundings—physical and spiritual. She wants a free world of true contact with everything which is humanly worthy. Though "lost," she is richest in aspiration and in the experience of her aspiration.

Her lying is a lyric flight to an imagined world of beauty and a free life. She admits she lies, doesn't know anything; she likes "big" words, high-sounding ideas, because they move her beyond herself toward the world she yearns for. Still, they leave her empty as the people who use them are empty. She wants them concretely embodied in real people and actions. Someday, somewhere, she hopes to find them.

When she lies in a sort of daydream, she "dances."

To begin with Cleo thinks of Willy Wax as an "artist." But soon she realizes he loves only himself—not even his art, only himself in art.

BELLE STARK

Spine: to keep her man "right," in order, safe and secure in their small world.

Background of emotional insecurity, quarrels. She too is an "orphan." Her father and mother did not speak to each other. She turned against her stern father. But she wants a father.

She wants safety, steadiness. She has become "practical," conservative, she wants everything to proceed on an even keel.

Her relation to Stark is based on admiration for his fundamental kindness and fineness . . . but he must be made "steady" (her father was a gambler, a bankrupt).

She can't stand adversity. She wants to save money, to keep things neat. She wants the world's "respect." Her thoughts are turned toward keeping Stark a good provider and making him a less perfunctory, distraught lover. When she is able to arouse him in this respect she sends him back to his job again.

The loss of her child makes her feel inferior, a feeling she hides even from herself. She imagines her husband blames her for the loss, but she never talks to him about this.

She, too, is hungry for love. Through frustration, everything centers on *her* man. Cleo's yearning for love extends beyond a man. Only her husband exists for Belle.

She is secretive about her feeling, she is *lonely*.

She is proud of her ability to make Stark work and keep in line.

"No man deserves me!" Because I am competent, intelligent, practical, faithful, warm, protective, "romantic."

She is insensitive, through her exclusive concern with her own problem or her husband's. Only their world is real to her.

She is jealous of other women. Disapproves of them. (Jealousy isn't nice: lacks pride.)

"Your terrible wife": she realizes that she nags . . . feels superior and inferior. Coquettish: "You like me anyway, don't you?"

She wins her battle. But she will forever be locked in her dilemma.

She is suspicious of everyone who deals with her husband, including her father.

MR. PRINCE

Spine: he wants to find something to *do*.

"I like to do some good to a man who needs it, a lovable being"—a real connection.

He has no "philosophy." He learns only by a certain type of practical experience (success, etc.). But he has learned that the "right" answer is wrong.

He began as an "idealist," married a good-looking girl . . . then he encountered frustration of the sex impulse in marriage. No warmth. Only work was a release. Frustration of his vaulting imagination. There is a bit of the aesthete in him. He likes beautiful fabrics, colors, opera, music . . .

He broods a good deal. Lives in his past. "How did I miss my boat, a man of my fire. What did I do with my life! Where was my mistake?"

He has a sense of failure, the paradox of his failure.

Love is the only thing which really interests him. But being worldly-wise, he got "stuck." The result is cynicism. He doesn't altogether believe in anything. Yet he doesn't quite believe in his own cynicism, his own "fake" or that all there is is a fake! Yet what is there? What is the truth? He, too, is embarrassed (like Stark) but he knows one must *do* something, one must take the leap into life, unafraid. And somehow, if you're lucky, you'll have lived. But he didn't live.

He is still a sort of idealist. (Why didn't he have extra-marital affairs? Because he was honest, because he was baffled. Because just sleeping with a woman doesn't interest him even now. He was faithful, he was "stuck" even in that regard. Yet he doesn't really know what kept him faithful.)

His energy seeks an outlet. He's generous with money. He is given to large gestures, a certain panache. He is shrewd because as a businessman he has learned that there is nothing sure but money and the power it gives.

He appears to be a misogynist—because of his bad marital experience. But he loves women: tenderness, warmth, beauty. He needs companionship.

Frustration: he wanted to be an actor. He laughs at this, it is only a symbol for the kind of life he desires. Occasionally a cry is torn from him, the cry of a deeply suppressed longing.

He "resents" his age. He doesn't like being old when he's still young! It hurts him when Cleo says he's old. But being both proud and "sensible," he takes no notice of this. He toys with the idea of declaring his desire for her. He wants, wants, wants to live. And laughs at this. But thinks about death.

He dislikes himself. But he is too strong to allow any sense of inferiority in himself. He sees the fraudulence in himself and in others. This is *his* honesty.

He's still potent. And he hasn't been with a woman for a year. He is almost morbidly curious about sex. His humor and gaiety are edged with sexual repression. His cynicism is hearty. He's mischievous.

He's clownish. His alert and disturbed mind has no coherent and definite object. He has thoughts and sentiments unworthy of himself, thoughts he would be ashamed to acknowledge. When these thoughts show, he pretends he is only joking.

In the end, he bursts forth—*fights*. He has found something to do: he's even willing to buy Cleo. He's realistic about it: "I'll leave you money, give you what you dreamed about." But he's missed the boat.

Perhaps he'll commit suicide.

COOPER

Spine: to solve a problem. (If he can solve this problem he will be able to find love.)

But he is a man unused to and ill equipped for problems.

He is boyish, good-natured, almost jovial. He is never sore. A well-liked American middle-class boy. All the fellows at high school and college liked him. Never gives trouble. Always optimistic.

He doesn't do anything besides work.

He is bewildered, helpless, without protest. The heat enhances his inner discomfort.

He can hardly believe his bad luck: it has stolen in on him
imperceptibly.

He worries about his creditors. But hardly believes they
will *insist* on collecting—is surprised and hurt when they
do. Expects everyone to be as considerate as he is.

Background: two great shocks in his life. (a) *His wife's
death.* He's utterly helpless without her. He doesn't know
what to do with a kid. He's a man who should be married
and have someone to take care of him. (b) *Unemployment*—
loss of his practice. Puzzled and intimidated, frightened by
the unexpected breakdown. Hysteria.

He's also sentimental. If he weren't fundamentally healthy,
he would be maudlin.

He jokes a lot, kids.

His drinking is a minor offense. He doesn't think he drinks
much; he slips into the drinking habit.

The last thing he does in the play is to kiss Cleo.

FRENCHY

Spine: to keep going.

Poor. Intelligent, independent. Lives on his energy.

Without direction because he lacks love, hasn't found any
"real" love. He's turned away from any true contact with
women, except as sexual playmates. He doesn't like "janes"
or conniving girls. He's looking (but not very hopefully) for
a *real girl,* a girl for this tough world.

He loves Stark because he is without malice, helpless, lonely
and tender.

He (Frenchy) also is lonely. He's attracted to Cleo, looks for
her whenever he enters. "You're like a magnet." He's jealous of the Cleo-Stark relationship, partly out of his desire for

her, and partly because of his concern for Stark's well-being.

If it were not for his desire to avoid becoming entangled in the mess of life he would become a bum. But now he works at his job. Lives "animal-fashion"—eats, sleeps, observes people, reads a bit. He is alone a good deal of the time.

He's something of an "anarchist" because most of his reactions to life are negative. He's waiting for a world in which he can safely connect himself with people. But now responsibility is too much for him. He's a lone wolf.

He hates phoniness, pretense and softness (as exemplified in Wax).

He is a little shy . . . arising from a fear of any connection which is not effected on his own terms. Yet he longs for connection.

I see him wandering, hovering, lolling about, breezing in, retiring with regret, yet hurriedly.

WAX

Spine: to please.

The inferior man's sense of *superiority.* This is constant even when he disparages himself.

Terribly nervous. Never contacts others except to make himself liked. He actually *sees* no one.

Eager to succeed, to get ahead, to make himself known in the rat race. This has made him overwork himself. He suffers constant strain, tension.

He cannot really enjoy his work, only his dream of it (a bit forgotten). He is sustained by his illusion that he is better than anyone else. He has no time for *devotion* to a woman. His only concern is with getting ahead and reassuring himself. He tries to impress everyone (himself included) and to please young girls.

He envies genius—chiefly among the deceased or the foreign. He's observant, even keen, malicious or sweet by turn —according to his egotistic need.

A very hard worker. Eats in. Stays alone a good deal of the time. Doesn't frequent places like Sardi's or the Algonquin. Quasi-contemptuous of ordinary theatre folk. "Kind" to radicals, but not one of them. Has heart-to-heart talks with promising young writers, musicians. Laughs a little at "arty" groups, minority communities, etc.

He rather likes Stark. He's no threat to his ego: Stark is poor, honest, and reads Shakespeare!

DIRECTOR'S NOTES FOR

The Member
of the Wedding*

by CARSON McCULLERS

(First presented in New York, January 5, 1950, at the Empire
Theatre by Robert Whitehead, Oliver Rea and Stanley Martineau.)

What is the audience to enjoy?

The poetry of first impulses expressed naively, sweetly, directly. The first "shoots" of life and emotion (adolescent longing) appreciated by grown-ups thinking back on the purity of
their first contact with life.

The production style: poetic—which means concentrated:
every moment visually significant of the inner state.

The spine of the play: to get "connected."

It all happens in a hot summer atmosphere. The world is
"dead"—the people suspended. Everything is slightly strange,
not altogether real.

"Lets us have a good time," says John Henry. He seeks

* First published in *Directors on Directing*, edited by Toby Cole and Helen
Krich Chinoy, Bobbs-Merrill Publishing Co., 1953, rev. ed. 1963.

"connection" but there's so little to connect with in this environment.

People who seek connection and aren't able to—ache. Frankie aches all the time. Her sobbing in the first act is the climax of an ache delicately indicated all through . . . part of the loneliness inherent in the main action.

(Frankie has no one to talk to about her resolve—so she talks to strangers: the Monkey Man or to a cat. . . . She wants connection with the whole wide world of experience.)

A stage direction reads: "Frankie scrapes her head against door." These strange gestures of children make one think that they are reenacting man's past living through the ages—animal-like, weird, primitive. More of such "gestures" must be invented for Frankie. "Flying around the world together"— Frankie will "fly" through the kitchen.

A mighty loneliness emanates from this play. It is as if all the characters were separated from the world—as if the world were only a mirage in a vaporous space making wraiths of the people.

THE SPINES FOR THE LEADING CHARACTERS

FRANKIE

Spine:—to get out of herself.

Getting out of herself means *growth.* . . . She has "growing pains": she is both tortured and happy through them. . . . The juices of life are pouring through her. She is a fragile container of this strange elixir.

Growth twists and turns her—as it does us—gives us new shapes. Frankie twists and turns. The play is the lyric drama of Frankie's growth. At the end of the play, she runs or twirls out—"to go around the world." She has achieved her aim— imaginatively. She is ready "to get out of herself."

THE MAIN CHARACTERISTICS

(1) Frankie is tomboyish. (She puts on no shows with kiss-

ing. Her father is a "widowman" with his nose to the grind-stone. She has no mother, no "social" environment.)

(2) Frankie is crazy with first love: literally head over heels: the love of the *wedding*.

(3) She is intense. She's trying to see underneath every-thing, seize its essence, "cozen it in her mind"; she even tries to seize the atmosphere of heat as a unique experience. "The kitchen's the hottest place in the U.S." she says.

Thus she is a "poetic" character. She is terribly aware of every little thing: Berenice's fur, Frankie says, has "a sad, fox-wise face."

(4) All the above produces an awkwardness that is weird an occasionally graceful.

(5) Frankie is hostile. You hate what you can't connect with and want to hurt it. Or you want to hurt yourself for failing to make the connection.

(6) She is given to self-examination. She is self-absorbed in relation to her desire for connection and wanting to "get out."

(7) Her torture comes from a sense of a past vaguely re-membered, troubled and painful—and the future—wondrous, void, unrealized and therefore frustrating. "I have this feel-ing," she moans.

(8) She is imaginative. Her mind and spirit leap: they stretch, lift, dart, fly . . . to whatever place she wants to go. When the destination is too vague, she explodes or drifts in all directions.

(Remind Julie Harris: The main action makes her a very active character. She is straining to get out. When she fails, she has one sort of emotion; when she almost succeeds, an-other.)

Frankie is fascinated by Honey. He is romantic, exciting, lightfoot. He's been "out."

BERENICE SADIE BROWN

Spine: To do her deed (work) . . . "normally." For her to live is to be connected.

A woman who is naturally and easily connected. Once she was connected with Ludie Maxwell Freeman. He died. "It leaves you lonesome afterward." After that, she sought connection with scraps and bits of what she loved—even to a madman. Now she's alone, relatively unconnected. But she manages somehow to connect with her community, with T. T., with Honey, with John Henry—but some people she doesn't desire connection with (Mrs. West, "them Germans and Japs," Mary Littlejohn). Of John Henry she says, "We enjoys him." It's as simple as that. Everything is approached without fuss, without sentimentality, without "eloquence."

She is plain—direct, earthy, quiet. Hers is the poetry of the "prosaic!" She's basic: "Two is company," she says.

Her life: "We just talks and passes the time of the day"—that's enough.

"Stop commenting about it," she tells Frankie. She does not need to "comment" to make things real to herself.

"Sunday will come." Sufficient unto the day—

When people want to go away from her—John Henry or Frankie or Honey—she just lets them go.

Unnaturalness ("freaks") give her the creeps.

She rarely tries to prevent anything from happening that seems to have to happen: when Frankie wants to take a splinter out of her foot with a kitchen knife, when Frankie smokes, when Honey needs a stimulant, when Frankie rushes out to the town, she cautions, but does not fight. ("I'm just trying to head this thing off, but I see it's no use.")

This is her wisdom: the acceptance of the pain and sorrow of life. All this is, as she puts it, a "thing known and not spoken."

Her movement is quiet, solid, strong. Her eyes look deep with a slight slanting glance—so that she may see better out of her one good eye.

And suddenly—she, too, feels the loneliness, the fear, the terror of life . . . and needs consolation from John Henry or anyone else. This pain of life is always sensed by her, but she lives on despite it. She knows the irony of life—John Henry's death—she didn't believe he was sick—a rebuke to her "practicality," to her too-sensible nature.

She ends alone—tragic, majestic, patient, waiting—while Frankie dashes out joyously to learn—some of the things Berenice knows.

This contrast in their destinies (that of Frankie and Berenice) must be clear in action at the end. They change "colors" —Frankie becomes more "extroverted" and "superficial" at the end. Berenice more quietly profound than ever.

JOHN HENRY

Spine: To learn to connect.

The pathos of the child is that it imitates the process of life as it beholds life being lived. There is mystery and comedy in this, too.

The child repeats a pattern of behavior without realizing its significance. The child has hardly any conscious tastes, appetites, or desires (they all seem automatic).

The child develops conscious appetites and ideas through imitation.

Hence it is likely to imitate bad things as well as good, it might kill or die almost as easily as live and love. The environment teaches the child through its tendency to imitate, its capacity to be formed unconsciously.

The child's imitation is a species of attachment: hence the child appears to be "loving." It loves to repeat what it sees and hears—and since most life is an effort to "connect," the child is always learning to connect and so grows to be a man.

"Me too" is the keynote. But since this is just the sign of a desire to follow or imitate a pattern without any reason or justification beyond what appears to be merely an imitative impulse—it strikes us (grown-ups) as funny.

John Henry says "how pretty" about Frankie's dress, but repeats Berenice's less flattering description; that is, he imitates

Berenice, attaching himself or reflecting her . . . so that
Frankie calls him a "double-faced Judas."

The child reflects life: it reflects connection, attachment,
but it has to learn to develop a conscious connection which it
doesn't possess at first.

The child's lack of consciousness makes much of its behavior seem meaningless and mysterious. Hence there is something sad as well as funny, and, from a conscious point of
view, oddly pathetic about the child.

The child is fragile: death is "natural" to it . . . it is always
close to death. The "realest" thing John Henry does is to
say he is sick, but because he says such things as a reflex he is
not taken seriously.

A child is like the light of a flickering candle—bright, gay,
pretty, sad, extremely sensitive to the atmosphere around it—
easy to intensify or to extinguish.

Frankie wants to get out of herself so that she can connect,
even more with the world. Berenice connects because she has
learned to live and John Henry is learning the process in the
unconscious way of a child—but he stops (dies) before he has
gone very far in the process. . . . In a word, he presents the
image of the fragility of the whole process—hence our tender
feeling toward him. How susceptible he is (the life process) to
destruction—disappearance—"the ghost in the arbor with a
little silver ring!"

The first step in connection after imitation is attachment,
and from the attachment, "love" develops, which we observe
in John Henry's consolation of Frankie and Berenice.

When the child's connection is sharply cut off, it becomes
afraid—"scarey." It has become used to the connection. The
child isn't a bit lonesome (as John Henry says) but comes running to get together—connected—with what he has become
used to.

The child "studies" to be a man. Observe the rapt look of a
concentrated child. This "study" is the essence of the child's
activity—the study and the action that follows—sometimes
slow and hesitant, sometimes sudden as if inspired.

ADDAMS (FRANKIE'S FATHER)

Spine: To keep in touch.

He can barely make it. . . . His connection is faltering, bleak. "Marriage is a sacred institution," he says, but it's a long time since he's been married. He keeps on going, but he has connection only with memories and the little mechanisms—watches—to which he has set, automatic responses.

Life is queer, a little strange or "funny" to him—he has a trace of humor. Life is sad for him because its objects are dim, sweet because he realizes no evil, sour because he's pushed into a corner and his area of nourishment is limited.

He's widowed of life. "A good provider," he works without aim. He pets life (Frankie) in passing, and wanders off into bleakness—and rest.

All that remains to him is his "white superiority." Even his porter doesn't show up to work for him. People don't pay attention to him—because he's not there for them. ("Answer me when I call.")

Handling people who are "alive" embarrasses him. He's "evasive"—constantly clearing his throat in embarrassment.

A baffled man.

JARVIS

Spine: to make the simplest connection . . . with the first thing that's nice—a girl.

He's an ordinary boy—rather unimaginative—his father's son—proper, good-natured, conventional, cautious—pleasant and inconspicuous—except to Frankie and people who admire his looks.

He smiles a lot, friendly, even sentimental, normally affectionate, but without much expression. He is comparatively mute"—awkward in expressing his feelings. Affectionate gibberish is the best he can manage in response to Frankie's adoration.

T. T.

Spine: to make as much conncetion as he can find.

Modest, resigned, soft, unhappy. He hasn't enough energy for his unhappiness to develop into resentment. He is acquiescent.

He is self-effacing, "understanding," honorable—"understanding" in a mediocre, practical way. Hence his deaconish fat. "Respected"—walking in a state of grace. He is almost "womanish" (or eunuch-like).

He would take a blow, quietly, hurt, unangry. ("I'm not particular—whichever way is convenient.")

He's even afraid—or at least shy—of being unseemly in front of Frankie. . . .

Yet he is not obsequious—honorable in a way, dignified, understanding and kindly—slightly depressed.

HENRY BROWN

Spine: to force connection—(or die).

Rejected, humiliated, his only connection is through violence, hostility (defiance) or mad escape ("snow," liquor, the protection and romance of jazz).

He is depressed and crazed by his own violence.

He's always on the verge of breaking loose or getting into a stupor of sadness—followed by an outbreak toward escape. He's repentant about hurting John Henry—for a second—tries to make up for it by playing with him, giving him money.

He has a kind of hysterical lyricism about him (his movements are dance-like in their nervousness).

A kind of terrified joy in being pursued. He takes a kind of mad pleasure in his violent connection through pistol or razor. . . .

DIRECTOR'S NOTES FOR

The Autumn Garden

by LILLIAN HELLMAN

(First presented in New York at the Coronet Theatre, March 7, 1951, by Kermit Bloomgarden.)

First impression: There is an atmosphere of unsentimentally expressed *regret* in the play. It is not the regret of a beautiful past but of a past which is vague and an immovable present. The air is still: there is not even an anticipation of a new tempest. Perhaps hopeful of one—timidly so. There is also the regret that nothing is likely to happen. . . . The dead end of the middle-class spirit.

Everybody is so "nice." That is as near as these people can get to love.

(1951—the year of the national nervous breakdown!)

The spine of the play: to "fill out" their lives.

NICK

Spine: to rub himself up into things.
Psychological gesture—one form or another of cuddling.

To get tied up, lean on, mess with, so that he can "fill out" his life, which he finds inadequate.

He pats everybody, kisses everybody, wants to be sweet to everybody . . . so that they will be nice to him . . .

He tries to embellish every situation. He likes to make matches, go to parties, where he can "cuddle."

Such people are sentimental, nostalgic. Because they imagine they were happier, "fuller" *then*—long ago—they try to recapture that lost fullness.

He *flatters:* which is a way of "rubbing up" and being "rubbed."

Hates to be bothered. Hates to be bored: nothing to "rub" into.

He loves Nina in his way, but most of all he loves her response to him. It gratifies him that he can arouse her. He plays the whore with her. She's the woman he's most used to lean on, to fulfill himself with. She can stand him longer than anyone else.

He's an "enthusiast," a perennial boy.

CONSTANCE

Spine: to realize a dream.

Psychological gesture? Carrying a tray—with love. Turning away delicately.

Only the consummation of the "dream" will fill out her life. Her dream of the beautiful life is based on childhood ideals, "notions" of the past.

She's a dignified lady—and a little girl. A hero-worshipper. She idealizes or romanticizes everyone.

She hides, like a hurt and forgiving child, unwilling to know about wicked or ugly things.

She is a secondary mother to Crossman, Nick, Sophie and the others.

She is credulous and vulnerable.

She tries to avoid truth: she lies, and being essentially good and honest, she retracts the fib.

She has more delicacy than vitality.

If she were able to love she would still love Nick.

The play's situation furnishes Constance with her last chance. She *flutters* toward it like an eager and awkward bird.

She likes music, Renoir, and all pretty things. . . . There is a certain real purity in her withal. She is one who serves. . . . She is a woman of another era. She falls into attitudes and poses that are too picturesque to be true. Still, she is sincere. She was brought up to see, think, behave that way through books, pictures and training in decorum.

CROSSMAN

Spine: to probe or "understand."

Psychological gesture: the manner in which he indicates "No, thank you" or his indifferent compliance.

He began with nothing, fell in love, failed. Hoped that love would fulfill him. But now he feels that his life has been wasted. He feels "empty." He took recourse in reading. When that proved insufficient he satisfied himself with sensation (sex) and drink.

He has no objective. But *understanding* is left to him; studying, observing, interpreting. He finds a certain vengeful satisfaction in exposing pretense, sham, foolishness—some of which he feels ruined him. In his "punishment" of others he is vicariously punishing himself. But his greater contempt is for the others: this is his "compensation," his little claim to wisdom.

He has become bitter and stoical. While he mocks Sophie, he understands and tries to help her. He is obliquely kind to those who need kindness: Griggs, Constance.

His understanding leads him to realize his failure. He is not, however, aggressive or nihilistic: he is too gentle for that. He "refuses" everything and will quietly disappear when his friends and the broken machine of his body disappear.

He resents Constance's foolishness a little as he does the maintenance of hoax or self-delusion in his community. Still, "he is doing the best he can."

Plays with a paper knife(?) A kind of scalpel or dagger. His posture is symptomatic of his refusal. But he still shows signs of emotion—for instance, when he is told that it is only his drinking which causes him to unburden his heart.

NINA

Spine: to follow Nick.

Psychological gesture: her laugh. Hurt (half-closed) eyes.

Following Nick is the only way she knows of "filling" her life. This is bitter for her because of what Nick is. She has contempt for herself but cannot help doing what she does.

She's a puritan; she's a little ashamed that her sexual urge keeps leading her back to Nick. So she punishes herself and him by her contempt. She pays "too heavily inside. . . ."

She has breeding, intelligence, yet the best she has been able to find is Nick. Therefore she laughs at herself, at Nick whom she sees through, at the paradox of the situation which deeply wounds her.

She accepts her life "manfully": her instinct tells her that Nick can't help himself, isn't responsible, is even a little pathetic and, after all, needs her protection.

She is "Boston"—therefore, according to Nick, "cold." But because she is of so proper a family she is attracted to Nick as an "artist," a bohemian with gallant manners, warmth, gaiety, boyish enthusiasm, a sense of adventure.

She knows more about art than he does but she isn't able to *do* anything. She was not trained to be anything but a "lady."

She woos him with gifts. . . . She appreciates Crossman and Griggs. She tries to save herself by contact with these nice men. After all, she is better off!

She has humor, even wit, crossed with asperity, nervousness and "trembling" . . . which she controls.

Nick is a cheat about money. He is paid for pictures he never paints, then has an affair with the lady who commissioned the picture. This is one of the real scandals and shames of her life. With all this, a certain weariness or disgust.

GRIGGS

Spine: to free himself.

Psychological gesture: he looks into space.

Free to be the man he believes himself to be, the man he promised himself to be, the man who was comfortable with himself. He has never lived his life.

An idealist: he wanted to be a serious man, the man who was his serious mother's son.

He's grieved or pained—more than shocked—by his wife's frivolity.

Very upright—disciplined—no self-pity.

With Rose: it's as if he were constantly talking to a deaf person or one who very successfully pretends to be deaf. He does not know how to master her.

He is shy, a man who cannot easily formulate the imponderable but real emotions within him.

His only companion—a fellow sufferer—is Crossman. He's kind to all the "outsiders": the young, the foreign, the abused, the defeated.

A way to freedom is to think straight and true, and though even this is no longer easy, he works at it.

He's a little stronger than Crossman because he has a goal, and he began with something real to him: a serious way of life, serious thoughts.

He's not neurotic. . . . He has a curious protective feeling in regard to his wife, for she is a victim of her own foolishness and of the environment which made her foolish.

His patience, of which he is a victim, is a heavy burden to him.

His desire for freedom is now his only passion, that and the contemplation of what this freedom might mean: thinking, studying.

When Rose is broken, he feels he has to protect her; she must be spared. He is trapped by his kindness.

Perhaps he was afraid of his freedom, for freedom is hard. It is easier to be a victim: it absolves one from responsibility.

ROSE

Spine: to play at life as a "charming" woman.

Psychological gesture: twittering, fluttering.

Life for her consists of doing all the things a charming, well-brought-up lady is brought up to do, to think, to say.

She is a lively kid who needs attention, flattery. She must "mix," fly, flirt, be the life of the party, dance, dress . . . (No wonder she has a bad heart!)

Nothing has a true meaning: only the form, the display and the energy have.

She is deserted by everyone because she has never attracted anyone on a serious level—except for her superficial sensuality: eating chocolates and drinking champagne.

As she senses her advancing age, she becomes pathetic. Poor little butterfly!

When she "flutters" she believes all is well because it has always been considered delightful. She fluttered so much she couldn't tell what was going on, not even what people thought of her. This became auto-intoxicating.

She really has no idea, because she has no capacity to understand, what Griggs really wants.

Her children don't like her any better than Griggs does; she doesn't know anything about them, except that they think her a silly nuisance.

Though seriously ill, she flirts with Nick.

She has the most old-fashioned feminine "wiles," gestures, manners—to the point of caricature. She coquettes about her "heart murmurs" as if they were an attraction. . . . If she flirts with a man, she thinks he likes her (Nick is like that too) and they—the man and she—have something in common.

She really doesn't understand her illness, but she is truly scared, like a kid who fears being left alone.

MRS. ELLIS

Spine: to fight the lie (get things straight).

Psychological gesture: a skeptical look, a rejecting look.

She says witty things, but she is not witty.

An intelligent woman who married an empty man, and was thus cheated of fulfillment. She became neurotic. She does not have either Nina's sensuality or her puritanism. She saw the emptiness of life around her, Carrie's failure, her son's inadequacies and the nullity of it all.

She resents fraud. Being old, she does not feel herself too involved. She won't stand for any sentimental messiness. This is her consolation and "revenge." She is cynical without being harsh.

She doesn't kid herself; she doesn't want to be kidded and despises those who kid themselves: they are weaklings and fools. She observes and keeps cool and clean, which is her consolation.

She is "neat" in her relation to life, patrician. Her environment, like Nina's, was empty but she was not talented enough to evade it. So she became a "loner" with social graces. She is thoughtful. She doesn't crack jokes for the sake of fun.

Her main concern now is that the young—Frederick and Sophie—be given a chance.

CARRIE

Spine: to hold onto the last thing remaining to her—her son.

Psychological gesture: an alternation between "proud carriage" and her head bent as if pleading.

A woman who has always been squelched, almost "fractured." She tries to resist, but she has no strength and always ends a victim. She needs help. She is soft and without inner resources.

She was always *correct*. And being so made her seem strong, but nothing in her was strong enough to overcome a neutral husband, a domineering mother-in-law, a weak son.

She has no real convictions or knowledge. She treats her son as if she were his governess, schoolteacher and lover. She suffers from a kind of frustrated reticence.

She probably wants her son to marry Sophie because their love isn't "romantic," a genuine attachment. For this reason she believes she can control the boy.

FREDERICK

Spine: to escape into another world. Away from mama and even grandma.

Psychological gesture: he "ducks"—broods and smiles tentatively.

A masculine and youthful counterpart of Nina, Carrie, and Mrs. Ellis, in their various struggles to free themselves from the limitations of their "old society."

But no one encourages even his talent for appreciation. He is always under pressure because he is financially dependent and emotionally immature. Sensitive though.

He likes Sophie because she exerts no pressure on him, nor is she herself under pressure. She is his "equal" but he is in trouble with her. He is attracted to Payson who is "free"— and wants to join his free world. There is hero-worship in this.

He respects his grandmother's brightness and will power. He is sorry for his mother, though dependent on her.

Europe is an "ideal" (a fantasy) with him.

Sophie treats him as his mother should have.

Like Nina, Frederick knows his own inadequacy and impotence. . . . He's rejected even by Payson.

A tender, lost character.

SOPHIE

Spine: to *do* the best she can.

The affirmative or positive in her role must be stressed to counteract the shyness which under the circumstances may be thought to be her "character."

Her action must be straightforward, clear, never cloying. More *action* than characterization.

Sophie is a "mother" to Frederick. Being a mother is not a submissive action. It is vital and purposeful.

A sense of humor is constant in a person of alert intelligence. She is never passive. She likes to laugh.

She is curious, interested, trying to learn and understand. She is never frightened or pathetic.

She'd rather be thought guileless, shy, than not. It gives her greater freedom . . . people bother her less. She will find her way—in time.

She is not a waif—she is spirited.

Her "meanness" comes from her logic, her rationality. Both these qualities are exasperating to her American guardians.

LEON

Spine: to keep out of trouble; to have fun.

His humor is based on a scorn for his white employers.

Tiger at the Gates

by JEAN GIRAUDOUX
in a translation by CHRISTOPHER FRY

(First presented by Robert L. Joseph and the Playwrights Company, in association with Henry M. Margolis, on October 3, 1955, at the Plymouth Theatre, New York. This production was first presented in London at the Apollo Theatre, June 2, 1955.)

Costumes: lightweight. Don't use too much material. Actors must be able to move freely.

Setting: provide places to sit all over stage—but no ordinary chairs.
Laundress passes on the lower (stage floor) level.
Hector's entrance on the topmost level as high as possible.
The middle level is the main playing area.

Style: The play is a passionate comedy. Passionate by virtue of the basic content. Comedy in the writing. There is a certain detachment in Giraudoux's manner: sunny, playful, witty. Behind a sly grin and an "uncaring" mode of speech, we must feel a tragic sense of life—without tears.
People are forces in this play: graphic symbols; they stand out in strong relief. Each posture, position, move, must be sharply defined.

Theme: the play is about the struggle against Destiny (the Tiger). Destiny is reality: the natural world without morality. Beautiful like the face of Helen. Pitiless, without mind or soul.

The struggle is between the idealists—Hector and Andromache—who combat Destiny and those who yield to it, gaily like Paris, stupidly like Demokos and Priam, and those who want to see only the pretty side of Destiny (Helen). Helen herself is on all sides and no side . . . except that she is magnetized by what is pretty.

War is a paroxysm of reality with two faces: the face of Helen and the backside of an ape.

The spine of the play: to struggle with the forces of chaos; to make sense of them.

HECTOR

Spine: to quell the "Tiger."

A full man; a fighter. But not a fanatic idealist.

He has begun to hate war, but not because he has no feeling for it. He is tender, but capable of rage. He is tolerant but inclined to savage disdain which becomes murderous anger: he kills Demokos.

There is integrity in him: not the integrity of the one-tracked mind. His integrity is a matter of control and the balance of opposing impulses. Profoundly serious, he has humor, irony and wisdom.

He has returned to Troy converted, a changed man. He was not always the Hector we first meet. He is a romantic who once romanticized war, but his romanticism has now been tempered by a new maturity.

A man of strong will. He is resolute through moral conviction.

He's capable of sensuality. He sees "two charming buttocks," but that's not all he sees!

He moves with sudden resolution, a hawk looking straight into the sun.

He has intimations of doom but he must fight even this. He will not resignedly accept fate. He will stand up and combat the "Tiger," even if the chances for victory are slim.

He is also a shrewd politician: as exemplified in the scene with Busiris.

ANDROMACHE

Spine: to sustain (support and aid life-forces) . . . but she needs help.

Exemplifies womanly love and loyalty. She trusts Hector. She is *giving*.

But unsure of herself in all else. Easily depressed, and out of love, moved to fear.

"I don't understand abstractions."

She sustains Hector, but needs to be sustained.

Admires Hector's idealism which is at the core of his "fighting" spirit.

She is real, not just an image of noble womanhood. . . . She admits that she'd prefer Hector a little less good!

To put it in the vulgate: Andromache is "nervous." (Helen is like an element of nature, a diamond or a bit of marble.) Andromache palpitates.

HELEN

Spine: to respond (and conform) to the physical or natural forces of life.

She is ruled by the beauty of the physical world which is not bound by morality or ethical direction. Her beauty and the beauty which attracts her has its own soulless, implacable life.

She has a kind of sweet abstractedness. . . . If she were not so serene, playful and fundamentally strong, she might be called silly or vapid.

"I leave thinking to the universe."

Though powerful, she is essentially passive.

She knows and enjoys the pleasures of others: in a sense she is *cold*. She has no pity and is equal to anything—high or low. She defends herself against those who attempt to engage her on a moral level.

PARIS

Spine: to enjoy "Destiny" (in its physical, injudicious manifestations—Helen!).

He is very "fresh." A good-humored, good-natured playboy or sportsman. He's neither deep nor passionate. An average sensual man. He doesn't like to be "possessed" by a woman: hence his feeling for the "remote" Helen.

The most physically active of the characters: leaps, springs about.

Given to boyishly "wicked" jokes. A nice chap with very few convictions. He has no idea of why Hector should want to prevent a war. He doesn't think about war. If it should break out, he will fight it and take his chances with it with little sense of its horror.

He listens distractedly to the philosophic arguments. If he participates in them, it is with a certain detached amusement.

He passes responsibility by: in fact, rejects it. It hardly exists for him.

A male flirt! He's occasionally "cute" ("I suppose you wouldn't like to take just one look at Helen").

He has little imagination. He kids Troilus about Helen. He doesn't anticipate Helen's later interest in Troilus. . . . He's bright but not very intelligent.

CASSANDRA

Spine: to expose the "fraud" (in French: *démasquer*) Destiny.

She's "on" to Destiny; in other words, she distrusts it.

She mocks. She has sensibility and intelligence. Sharply humorous, even biting. Disabused.

She's an artist (like Mary McCarthy?). A lance-like brain. Most often contemptuous. Acid.

Often cryptic: "Your wife is going to have a child." (She intimates that this is both good news and bad.)

Peering into people's faces, she grins. What is she grinning about? She sees the frailty, the fraud, the self-deception. It "amuses" her.

She taunts her brothers. She's the sister "in the middle." Not honored like Hector, not spoiled like Paris.

Is she a little "jealous" of Helen? Helen is a nuisance, and men, the idiots, are crazy about her. But that's "life." Destiny (the Tiger) is a whore.

The ending confirms her bitter prediction and she, too, must suffer the slings and arrows!

HECUBA

Spine: to unmask men (as instruments of a stupid Destiny).

We are dependent on men and men are fools. A realist, disenchanted but not rebellious.

She's not "bitter" or mean. She respects Andromache; she is tender with Polyxene. She realizes, as does Cassandra, that Destiny imposes its hoax on men. Hecuba's barbs are directed toward men's weaknesses.

A strong person. She has borne much and will bear more. No pettiness, she is not personal in her contemptuousness of men's follies. . . . Occasionally a vast hatred bursts forth from her with sibylline incisiveness as in her description of war.

She is "on the side of the angels." Cassandra no longer believes in "angels"!

She probably loved Priam, but being a man, he is foolish. Zeus forgive him. There's no fool like an old fool!

PRIAM

Spine: to defend the way things are by "ennobling" (romanticizing) them.

The "Tiger" is nothing but a splendid animal.

An old sensualist posing as a lofty, dignified lover of Beauty. (A French academician!) He commands a rhetorically passionate eloquence. He wants Helen to remain in Troy because of the "kick" and prestige involved. Her presence gives the men of his generation a renewed life. They see only Helen's pretty face; Hector sees the danger in her.

Like the Mathematician, he, too, might cry over *La Femme et La Beauté*. He is something of a lecher along with his august manner. He puts garlands over the graves of fallen soldiers.

His most sincere moment is his defense of war: voicing a conviction which is the heritage of the best days of his youth.

DEMOKOS

Spine: to fight for the romanticized Tiger.

Destiny is always benevolent: one shouldn't combat it. The official romantic and therefore reactionary. Vigorous, lusty and venomous. Sullen outbursts of heroic aestheticism. Philosophical *and* violent. He is sentimentally priapic. Like the French poets and politicians who tremble when they speak of *la patrie*.

He is part of a government which works. Such men would rather be drowned in blood than acknowledge that the world they knew—which worked so well—has to be changed.

He is a consummate orator and demagogue. The rhetorician of official patriotism.

Priam is warm: married, a father; Demokos is frustrated. He sublimates through poetry and mistresses. He's a killer at heart: the violent chauvinist. Very conceited, as are most bad poets. Something of a ham.

He's over sixty. Helen is his last tremor . . .

War furnishes him with an opportunity to inspire the nation: he will write.

ULYSSES

Spine: to face Destiny (the Tiger) as it presents itself—with grace, strength, reasonableness.

Very composed, business-like, shrewd, a realist with an eye on fate. He doesn't trust fate too far. . . . He has a sense of humor. His "anger" and calls for vengeance are dictated by his duty as a general and statesman: they are not very personal. Skeptical rather than cynical.

He's willing to gamble (occasionally) on idealism or humane considerations, though he doesn't believe they will work.

AJAX

Spine: to engage in action for its own sake. Thus, the Tiger's accomplice.

He is the willing, boisterous, almost joyous instrument of Destiny because he is by nature a bully and a troublemaker: a bulldog who is pleased with the chaos of existence: drinking, roistering, killing and laughing . . . he has a good time getting angry, getting drunk, etc.

He's baffled by Hector, then won over. He admires courage, grandeur ("guts"), "class." He laughs a lot: soldier's humor. Rough, but not really ill-natured. Born the "lieutenant" for great men: Ulysses, Hector.

A *follower:* he enacts the motions of destiny; he wants to reconcile Hector and Ulysses because both are great . . .

He tries to take Andromache but desists because he is impressed by Hector's nobility and fears Hector's sword, which he knows Hector will thrust efficiently.

MATHEMATICIAN

Spine: to complete (extend) his life.

He's a deprived man; physically weak, sex-starved. He wishes to compensate for all this. He needs a greater share in what Destiny (fate, the Tiger) has to offer: excitement, sex, even war.

When he speaks of Helen he becomes terribly excited, fanatically inspired: he weeps. When he speaks of war he uses violent epithets: which is all the violence he is capable of. He comes close to having a stroke in describing Helen. He screams the epithets—exalted!

BUSIRIS

Spine: to rationalize Destiny (therefore to falsify it).

In this way he puts himself at ease with life. Unimaginative. Stiff.

He has a tic: his nose twitches.

To be impressive, he speaks dryly. To be persuasive, he speaks unctuously. All pose. The basic motive is self-preservation.

THE TOPMAN

Spine: to assert his pride and patriotism.

In the prowess of Paris' penis he finds the symbol of his patriotic pride. It is somehow a testimony of his own strength. Very much like people who say "our whiskey is the most potent, our women the most beautiful," etc.

A baritone!

ALPIDES

Spine: to admire the world.

"Oh, the things I've seen." Naive, astonished. (His voice breaks.) He can't get over the miracle of what he has beheld from the crow's nest. He's wide-eyed, lyrical . . . a light tenor!

TROILUS

Spine: to begin living (to start the Tiger stirring).

Young desire. Growth and its pains. Passionate and shy. Ambitious and ready for renunciation! Reckless and timid. The desire for life causes the drama and the enchantment of living.

ABNEOS

Spine: to play a role in the drive of Destiny. (There is an element of hysteria in all the old men.)

Such men—fat, grotesque, senile, always offer the silliest suggestions in an officious manner, which are taken seriously because they reflect the surprising stupidity of the most intellectually backward people. They are stuffy, self-important, noisy. Gossips. When there is a sign of trouble they are the first to holler "murder" and call for a lynching.

IRIS

Spine: to charm and play-act.

She is the pretty messenger of the gods.

She is three different ladies in one. (She imitates three different feminine stage stars.)

(a) Aphrodite . . . simpering and cute.
(b) Pallas Athene . . . serious.
(c) Hera . . . *grande dame.*

POLYXENE

Spine: to cling and to give to all.

A budding Andromache. . . . She echoes love, wants to help. Imaginative.

She absorbs, listens, imitates, wishes to please. Her eyes are always on Hecuba or anyone who shows the most feeling.

Because of this she is used in the conflict by Andromache to move Helen to pity: but Helen cannot be moved. And Polyxene does not understand what she is called on to say.

The Waltz
of the Toreadors

by JEAN ANOUILH
translated by LUCIENNE HILL

(First presented by Robert Whitehead and Robert Stevens at
the Coronet Theatre, January 14, 1957.)

The spine of the play: to seek "romance" (the romantic
life), "la belle vie," prettiness, sensuousness, dreaminess, softness.

There's a mood of "regret" in this play. A smile when the
mouth is salty, the eyes moist, the heart full!
Sex and love—in confusion.
Soul and the flesh . . .
Morality and practicality . . .
The humdrum and the Dream . . .
Romance and Reality . . .

Setting: The French bourgeois home—somewhat humdrum in contrast to the lovely garden and landscape outside
(Bonnard).

The more bittersweet the regret, the more the comedy will emerge.

The audience is to enjoy the irony of confusions, the tears of our disappointments and the laughter of our folly.

THE GENERAL

Spine: he wants to "give his all"—romantic fashion.

He's a softy, a big "kid," an elderly youngster. . . . He was brought up on dreams, even in the army: the battle for *la patrie,* etc.

Naive about sex, love, etc. Bewildered and sometimes credulous, despite himself.

He likes dancing, gypsy orchestras, and tends to reject everything plain or bad or real (his children, for example). He loves a *good time.*

Even his picture of the Moroccan campaign is "operatic": replete with naked Arab girls, etc. His "culture" is academically romantic in painting, poetry, music; but his daily life is petty bourgeois in its practicality.

Because he's a kid, he's still afraid of his wife—reality harasses him. He romanticizes his women, falls in love like a moon calf of military background.

(A sentimental animal: a dog.)

He's forever wishing, longing, dreaming, regretting that life is so different from his dreams.

"There is one who never hurt me: true, I never lived with her" . . . and when all the blustering and little "adventures" are over, there is fear: "I'm alone, and I'm afraid."

When he explains the drabness of bourgeois existence he offers romantic reasons for abiding by its ritual.

MLLE. DE STE.-EUVERTE

Spine: to transfigure the world to her idea of the beautiful. A storybook romantic: she sees life as the mild romantics describe it. But there is a certain practical side to this: it leads her to what she wants, to her objective—a young man, love, marriage.

Her posture and demeanor express the single-mindedness of a person who brushes off everything that is not to her purpose. She is as "intrepid as an Amazon," a little middle-class Amazon. Hers is a *hard delicacy*: very French. She is willful, determined, decoratively romantic and entirely proper.

Almost everything she does has a practical core, following the straight line of her will.

She has a slightly solemn manner: "proud." There is a practical purity in all she does. She is, in her special way, *perfect*.

THE GENERAL'S WIFE

Spine: to possess everything: husband, household, lovers.

She was poor—on the fringes of respectability. Her mother, a dresser at the opera. Gounod held her hand. (What a dream!)

She is the fiercest of romantics, she wants all and is willing to kill herself to have it.

A vulgar woman of fantastic energy and will. Enough to bellow Wagner in a small-town theatre and to work herself up to the Paris Opera; to marry a promising officer, to acquire lovers, to hold her husband even when he has lost his appetite for her, to bring up children (teaching them economy) and to maintain a fine house.

In a sense, she is the most romantic person of the lot: she has stopped at nothing to realize her "dream" and ideal. . . . She wants to possess her husband's thoughts.

The person who desires to possess all becomes possessed: capable of anything. Such a person can make herself sick, climb down vines. Her inner energy is boundless. She becomes pure will. She is a demon of strength and imaginative projection. Since, after all, she cannot possess *anything*, she screams with the pain and frustration of her effort. Anguished, horrified and horrible, pathetic finally in the knowledge of her failure. . . . When she cries out that her heart is shrinking, it *is* shrinking!

DOCTOR BONFANT

Spine: to live (enjoy) life as it comes, as it is. (That is realistic romance. The doctor is a realist.)

Life is acceptable as it is . . .

An amused, skeptical, yet a friendly and tolerant person. He's an understanding *observer.* The action of observation is central to the characterization.

He always has a slight smile on his face.

He's patient, modest, in normal health. He's almost *tender.*

GASTON

Spine: to find (the ideal) *life.*

He's a beginner in hope. He looks forward, "dreams" of life. (He sings Italian romances in the garden where he reads the classics.)

He pants for life: undercover, in dark hallways . . .

(The General sometimes clasps his hands as does Gaston: it is a romantic gesture of innocent imploring and waiting.)

Something delicate, young, fragile, in everything he does no matter how physically virile.

He's "under wraps" through shyness. Life has hidden from him, it has been closed off. His feelings and behavior are solitary and "secret." . . . He's not effeminate.

An element of quiet surprise in everything he does.

Obedient, honest, upright—not at all stupid.

ESTELLE (THE REDHEAD)

Spine: to get what she wants from everything.

Her mother in little. Aggressive. She is the initiator.

She does the asking, she does the spying, she makes the resolutions.

A little grasper, with some of her mother's vulgarity, "sensuality" and shrewdness.

SIDONIA

Spine: to get what is morally due her.

The "bigot." The file. The shrew with *right* on her side.

EUGÉNIE (THE MAID)

Spine: to do her work so that she can live her own private life.

She's seen everything, suffered everything, knows everything, observes everything. But she understands only what relates to her job.

Her bosses bore or disgust her; her real life is somewhere else. She is like most "permanent maids": *bonnes à tout faire.*

She's not at all perturbed or excited by the accident in the house. "Maybe she wanted to kill you," she says. This interests her somewhat but does not alarm her. It would be one more mess she would have to clean up.

MADAME DUPONT-FREDAINE

Spine: to live it up.

She has a sweeping good time. A successful, much pleased woman. All the men play up to her and she has what she wants. She's queen of a small comfortable world.

FATHER AMBROSE

Spine: to please the world: to encourage everyone to like the world, God, himself and the life of the town.

A jolly little man, an accommodating man. A man pleased with small comforts as if they were great comforts.

He flatters his flock . . . treats everyone as a child. What are his little comforts? White wine, the events of the day, playing the part of the wise, all-knowing, friendly, forgiving person. . . . He's not at all stuffy. He wants to win over everyone to his or her own joy: a simple, peaceful life to his or her own measure.

THE MAID

Spine: to respond to the call of life. Innocently and readily. Life's no problem!

A Touch of the Poet

by EUGENE O'NEILL

(First presented in New York by Robert Whitehead at the Helen Hayes Theatre, December 8, 1958.)

The characters are immigrants in a new country: they want—

The spine of the play: to make a place for themselves.

This play, written as realism, is a kind of parable. Its tone is objective, sober, almost detached. There is a quality of dignified but sympathetic understanding in it. Under the rather stoic surface is a sadness, a tenderness, a warmth, even regret. The author says, "I'm sorry. But this is how it was." He's too mature for bathos, but his heart is touched. He soberly examines the "moral" of what he has recalled. It is a strong man's play. It has pity in it, but it is not soft.

CON MELODY

Spine: to retain his sense of himself, his Ego.

He has the personality he assumes. He is not a fraud but he overacts his personality because circumstances are depriving him of it. . . . The falsity, the pretense, creates the pathos of his situation: he has to exaggerate what he is. That is why he is absurd to the outside eye. When one is solitary one cries out for a reflection. Those who "reflect" him are his unaware wife, his carping, down-to-earth daughter. He is of foreign origin; his alien disposition ignores trade, labor and the democratic spirit of the times. He finds it necessary to seek his true self (the image of it) in a mirror. He wants to assure himself that he is present, that he exists as he knows himself to be.

He feels guilty. But he fights this sense of guilt: it would make him acknowledge that he is not what he would have himself be, what indeed he is. This would mean to forsake his past, his accomplishment, his being. But who can forever persist in denying the world's evidence—which is entirely against him? He therefore clings to the remnants of his past in Cregan and in the tattered rabble, the lowly Irish who were once his subordinates or "vassals." He *needs* Roche, O'Dowd and Riley—mocking and shabby ghouls though they be. They play his inferiors to cadge drinks. At least he can subdue *them.*

He is the lord of the mirror and several cowed derelicts whom he despises and who, at best, fear him.

His wife loves him. She sees him as he was and, to a degree, still is. She is the earth which bore him and above which he has tried to rise. She represents for him the old sod, the lowliness of his origins—which he has abjured. He holds on to her and looks down on her.

He is "grand" and ridiculous, a sorry, funny, pathetic character. He is finally crushed, demolished and perhaps "saved." The seed must rot before it brings forth new fruit.

What else must he retain in order to preserve his personality as he conceives it and as he wishes the world to view it?

(a) His mare. She contributes to his inner power, vibrant and bounding, physically real.

(b) His uniform: the colorful sign of his former position and abiding personality.

He must ignore his lack of money, his plain abode, his want of credit. He makes phantoms of them; when we make a phantom of reality we ourselves become phantoms. He is a phantom major.

He hates England that has forsworn him. He hates Ireland from which he has escaped in order to become "free." He only accepts America as an Idea—something poor and uncultivated now but which may in the future become worthy.

He is constantly apologizing about his drinking. But liquor helps him forget the present reality, inspires him with a renewed sense of himself and arouses him to undignified outbursts because of the contradiction. Drink is the crossfire in which he burns.

Byron has written *his* (Con's) *truth* in ringing and melancholy words: "Among them but not of them." This was and is true of him everywhere. It is the state of mind of every intelligent and rebellious *emigré*.

He barely understands the nature of his pose. (Why must he pose at all, since the pose is a metaphor for the truth? But since posing is ludicrous, he has to apologize for that too.)

His wife is his solace and his support, but she smells of the rank earth above which he wishes to rise. He loves her but cannot embrace her.

His daughter challenges him so he must scorn and correct her. Yet he is attached to her and is proud of her, for she is strong and fair. She is the future America which may ultimately redeem him. (The immigrant is frightened and shamed by the assimilated first generation and also resentful of it.)

His *gallantry* is not sexual; it is an expression of pride,

pride in the exercise of power, of grace or ornamental passion. It is an attribute of the acquired cultivation of his natural gifts.

Only his having been subject to a beating and the humiliation of it makes him *know* that he is the dust and dirt of the country, that he is riffraff, one of the rabble, comrade and companion of the Cregans, Roches, O'Dowds of the vicinity.

After his beating he trembles and shakes with the aching memory of what he was and imagined himself to be. He is in a fever as if a sword were being withdrawn from his body which cuts and tortures him in the process.

Thus he arrives at his new credo: "It's to hell with honor if you want to rise in this world."

The "world" (America) has won, has triumphed over him. What world? The coarse world without honor, glamor or any aspiration beyond gain and material satisfaction. . . . He'll no longer be lonely with his ideals and dreams.

NORA

Spine: to give (devote) herself (with its joy and sorrow).

For her, her husband is God. He's a *gentleman* . . . beautifully strong. He can do no wrong.

Her *place* is with her husband. She is weak and rheumatic when he deteriorates, spirited and well when he flourishes. ("There's no slavery in it when you love.")

Hers is the love story of the play. She plays all the actions of love, every nuance and color of it, in high and low, in smiles and tears.

She has the energy and strength that love bequeaths. The role must not become passive.

Because she's a simple and honest peasant she realizes that her husband's dreams are dreams. Yet they are dreams he needs to live; she therefore sustains them, that is, their reality.

Her drama is that she loves what she has been taught to be ashamed of loving: she has become a renegade from the

Church, her religion. She is hurt by this, but not shattered. Her love is strong within her, though she cannot altogether "justify" it. She's at a loss to explain the contradiction.

The end is tragic for her. After his defeat, she has Melody back, but he's "dead" now, a crippled man. Her victory is bitter; she will suffer it as all else, forever wondering what it all meant. A pitiful, sweet, grand and confused child of nature is what she remains. Her only conviction and task is that one must do all for love.

SARA

Spine: to win her place.

She speaks of her marriage as ". . . my chance to rise in the world and nothing will keep me from it" . . .

Also, "We'll get on in the world—for I'm no fool either."

First-generation American: between the old and the new—which way?

Proud, almost imperious. Her father's daughter . . . she has spunk, energy, courage. Willful, a fighter.

She's opposed to the old country and her father. She's going to be an *American*. But the old has its hold on her through her father; his glamor, pride, "style."

She's practical: she wants to take care of the money. Not such a fool, she says, as to be in love, but . . .

The first-generation American is always a little ashamed of and antagonistic toward parents from "the old country." So Sara with Con.

(The American woman of the pioneer period: "Oh, if I was a man with the chance he had, there wouldn't be a dream I'd not make come true.")

She thinks Harford's dreams are "crazy" because she knows what people are like.

But she's still young; she has to learn everything—her sensations are "new."

For all her boasting she's still a little in awe of, even obsequious with, Deborah.

Still, her father is grand, handsome, independent, proud and "like Napoleon," if he would only be that way truly. For that is her dream: to be *great*, strong, above the mob.

The pride, will and capacity to dream beyond their station destines the new Americans to conflict . . . conflict of similar personalities facing two different sets of conditions and needs.

The contact with love transforms her, softens her, completes her and brings her closer to her mother and to *her father*. With less resentment and self-confidence she is more prone to understand him. . . . Her dream has changed to a dream of love. (Will she become like Deborah?)

She gathered strength from her father's pride and background. When he is broken, something in her—some mainspring—is injured. She will be weaker because of her father's defeat. That is why she cries unconsolably at the end.

DEBORAH

Spine: to escape the place she has found—"transcendentally" in her self-made prison and dreams.

She has a place but she "never goes out at all but stays home in her mansion reading books, or in her garden."

She sees the world ironically with a wistful, resigned irony. . . . Life will take its course—fate is implacable—the country will follow its historical necessity.

She wanted to be a great man's delicate treasure: "*Josephine*."

Her big speech is her swan song. "I shall never again venture forth to do my duty." She has told Sara to beware of New England's puritanic idealism. It crushes whatever stands in the way of its ideals whether it be "poetic," political or material.

CREGAN

Spine: to find a place to settle.

A certain sturdiness and dependability. The honest worker. Trustworthy henchman.

He's on the loose. The worker without a steady job. He needs a base, seeks a boss, a homestead. He's not without toughness, an ability to endure tribulations—with the help of a little liquor.

He's a dependent, a supporter.

MALOY

Spine: to get along (live, work in an inferior position).

Another variation of the *Immigrant.*

He's an average mick. Gets along. Doesn't like to be patronized or bossed. He looks for the flaw in those who treat him shabbily in order to preserve his pride and ward off the taunts of his superiors—to hold his own. His malice and cunning are a defense against "oppression." But he's not a bad lad. Grateful for all favors. Responsive to Nora's kindness, to all friendliness.

He has a kind of crush on Sara and is a little afraid of her . . . which is part of her attractiveness. Because she scorns him, he would like to get back at her—but not meanly.

Shrewd and observant, as he must be to live and work in a humble job in a rather inimical world.

GADSBY

Spine: to carry out the important mission of the ruling class.

One of the settled, the assured. He has a right to his place. He is polished, decorated by the place he has come to occupy. He shines with position. He is a little apprehensive when he faces the unfamiliar roughness of the new elements that have come to New England. But he cannot but believe that his sovereignty, as part of the "establishment," will ward off all inconvenience and trouble.

He has the manner of a surgeon, sure of his craft, with the oiliness of a prosperous businessman who has the protection of his even stronger superiors. He would be really hard if his authority were all his own.

THE BOTTOM RUNG—THE TAIL OF SOCIETY— THE UNAMBITIOUS AND "WORTHLESS" IMMIGRANTS

ROCHE

Spine: to bluff his way through.

Loud-mouthed, blustering. Empty windbag. Talks as if he were important as long as he feels protected. Stupid. Envious. Rather cowardly. Fawning. He brays and prates.

O'DOWD

Spine: to squirm through.

Slippery, snivelling. A sneak. He snickers as high as he dares.

He would be a spy if he were bright, but he isn't.

He also thinks he's funny, a "sport." He cadges everything.

RILEY

Spine: to settle in a dream.

He's in "air," nowhere . . . far gone. Altogether without roots except in some distant memory. He has passed out of the real world. He dwells in a mist. His look turns toward whatever is warm, attractive, lively. But he has no hope of anything beyond his contemplation and the direction of the stimulus.

His only true expression is *a song* which he sings as if prompted by the spirit of another planet.

Heartbreak House*

by GEORGE BERNARD SHAW

(Produced by Maurice Evans and Robert L. Joseph at the Billy Rose Theatre, October 18, 1959.)

FIRST NOTES

This *crazy house* is a truth house—for adults.

There is a certain "childishness" in this play.

The play of a bunch of brilliant kids not as old as the people they impersonate—much wiser and gayer and more crackingly articulate than such people would "normally" (naturalistically!) be.

A charming, surprising *harlequinade*. (An intellectual vaudeville.)

Make them funnier—"nuttier"—than Shavian "realism" (or literalism) usually permits.

"The house is full of surprises," the Nurse says. The Cap-

* First published in the *Tulane Drama Review*, Volume V, Number 3 (T 11), Spring 1961. © 1961 by the *Tulane Drama Review*. Reprinted by permission. All rights reserved.

tain's whistle, the sudden entrances and exits are Shaw's clues to this.

Another character says, "Something odd about this house."

The style tends toward a bright-minded whackiness. A puppet show! (Shaw jokes about bowings, introductions, greetings, etc.)

"We are under the dome of heaven."—The garden outside should be very much part of the first act "interior." (Variable nonrealistic lighting.)

Sound—"a sort of splendid drumming in the air." Later air raid is compared to Beethoven. Ideally the air raid should be orchestrated—use musical instruments—on a Beethoven annunciatory theme—but not the motto of the 5th!

SECOND NOTES (ON FURTHER READING)

Shaw's characters are ideas—conceptions of people, theatrically and comically colored. The adverse criticism of certain critics who say that Shaw's characters are merely puppets spouting ideas should be made a positive element of the production style.

They may be made as puppet-like as the nature of the play's dramatic structure and the audience's taste will allow.

Mangan says he wants to get "to hell out of this house." Everyone in the play wants somehow to escape his or her condition. All are dissatisfied with it . . . it's a crazy house, driving them crazy!

All in a sense are "crazy," not true to themselves, not what they seem or pretend to be. So everyone is somehow odd, a *clown*—disguised, masked. Outside is "the wide earth, the high seas, the spacious skies"—waiting.

"In this house," says Hector, "everybody poses." "The Trick is to find the man under the pose."

This is the director's job as well:

(a) What is the pose?

(b) What is the man or woman under the pose?

MORE RANDOM NOTES (AFTER STILL FURTHER READINGS).

These English in *Heartbreak House* do not behave as English people do: an Irishman has rendered them! They are more impish, more extrovert, more devilish, devilishly *comic*.

Hesione is a "serpent"—she has mischief in her—not a "proper" lady. She's the cat who swallowed the canary, an intelligent minx. Mentally speaking she *winks*.

An element of "ballet-extravaganza" throughout—as if everyone were "high."

The audience is to enjoy: ideas as color, comedy, and "show," or intelligence as clowning.

They are all aware that they are living in a looney world, which they are expected to take seriously—but can't. As they progress they become aware of the need to act mad in order to approximate reality. To achieve their liberation—their world must be destroyed.

Some of the madness demands that they hide it—which is the greatest madness. Thus they speak of "form," of not making scenes—while they are always making scenes. (Lady Utterword.)

They want to burst the bonds of the old times—convention —"to get the hell out." Thus the comic outbursts. (Prelude to England's "angry young men.")

RANDOM NOTES CONTINUED

Shotover roars.

The world's askew (the set to begin with).

They are all flying off the handle: the "handle" being the old steady values, the desire to get the hell out of a situation which no longer supports anybody. The "handle" supplies the form—which these people no longer can grip. Lady Utterword still wants to hold on with her unseen husband Hastings Utterword. (A "wooden" handle!)

The movement of the play is not placid, polite (or Chekhovian!). It is rapid, hectic, almost "wild." (The actors are asked by Shaw to sit on tables, etc.)

Mangan "not able-bodied." Has aches and pains—presses his liver when he is irritated.

Randall—curly hair ("lovelocks"—like the fop in the film of *Kipps*).

The spine of the play: to get the hell out of this place.

This "hell" suggests some of the explosive quality desired in the playing—the element of *opéra bouffe* involved.

THE CHARACTERS

SHOTOVER
THE SAGE OF HEARTBREAK HOUSE

This "sage" has fed himself on rum, worked hard with his body, his fists, and his wits. The rugged person on whose hard work and tough life the house was built. But this sage has a mask—a Pose—as important for the actor as his wisdom—indeed more important. It is the mask of the Drinking Devil—almost the "debauchee" with his West Indian Black wife.

Bluff, gruff, hardy—also shut off from anything but his own thoughts and "ways." (Modern England was built by such men: born 1818 . . . in their prime in 1865.)

His dismissal of everything secondary comes from his urge to get at fundamental reality—to run the ship—to find the means to set the boat on its due course. This requires the "seventh degree of concentration."

To drive toward *that* goal (the seventh degree, etc.) is his spine—his prime motive or action. (To scare people into doing what he wants, or to be free of their nonsense, their blather.)

He wants to go on with his quest; his energy is great enough to do so, but at eighty-eight, he knows it's late. Therefore he's wistful too. Despite himself he has to relax into a resignation which is a sort of "happiness." This is his pathetic side.

(The clearing and cleaning up necessary to achieve the "seventh degree" will entail a certain amount of destruction —dynamite. He is prepared for that too.)

He moves with nervous energy, sudden shifts of pace, to absolute quiet or concentrated energy—as when he sits down to work on his drawing board.

I'd rather he looked like old Walt Whitman than Shaw!

ELLIE
THE NEW LIFE OR YOUTH IN HEARTBREAK HOUSE

She wants to find Port. (A goal for her life.)

The Pose is the Sweet Young Thing: the well-bred ingenue.

The real person is eager, intelligent, with a strong will and capacity to fight.

The House is bewildering, heartbreaking: all the facts she learns are upsetting. . . . She encounters hidden or masked wisdom in the Devil—the ogre Shotover. So she ends bravely in a sort of exaltation—"greater than happiness."

In the transition between these two aspects of her character she is miserable, hard, calculating.

Then she "falls in love"—differently—with life itself, in all its danger in the person or symbol of Shotover.

This is the Education of Ellie.

Shotover's dreams and ravings—his wisdom and idealism— are the most real things in the world to her—new blood.

She knows her strength (the last curtain), so she *looks forward* to another air raid . . . as toward the prospect of a new world, a fresh start!

HESIONE
HEARTBREAK HOUSE IS HER HOUSE

The Eternal Woman! (And an "actress" by nature.) She wants to make life beautiful, to keep it romantically beautiful.

She wants to get out of the house too (they all do) because she knows its madness . . . yet she likes it here—the adventure, the uncertainty, the fun . . . like an actress who understands the theatre's absurdity and deception but at the same time enjoys its warm charm.

She is loving but so intelligent that she occasionally is sharp—in the face of hypocrisy, or stuffiness.

Hushabye (the Soother!). She loves company, the "menagerie." She sees through her husband, admires and laughs at him. . . .

She is active . . . yet "lazy" . . . likes to fall asleep when unoccupied because she enjoys all agreeable sensations and experiences. She is not a particularly good housekeeper . . . not thrifty . . . not very neat (show this through business at the very outset) . . . the maid takes care of "all that."

She likes to gossip . . . so she's socially endearing. Frank, open, *Enthusiastic,* likes to tease affectionately.

She's a flirt—for fun. It is also gracious, it keeps things "interesting."

Something of the improvident Bohemian—with very little care for money.

"You are your father's daughter, Hesione." (She's got the Devil in her too.)

She has temperament and temper too—like an actress!

She is changeable—with swift alternations of mood.

LADY UTTERWORD (ADDY)
THE FINE LADY OF HORSEBACK HALL

Conventionality is her mask and protection—the sense of "form" in the "Colonel's lady" manner.

Her reality beneath the mask is a hunger for experience . . . her desire to escape the prison of her class convention. This expresses itself secretly, stealthily, unobserved . . . except in unguarded moments of hysteria.

"The first impression is one of comic silliness." She has the English "twitter."

Her "form" makes her appear more stagey than Hesione (who is real theatre!). Addy is what we call theatrical theatre of the old *very* English school (1910).

She swishes quite a bit.

Her way out of Heartbreak House is to run off to India, to the garden, to tea, to fashionable behavior.

She wants to cultivate, hold on to the "manner" which "saves" her and perhaps gives her the best of both worlds—that of feeling and that of decorum: the one utterly private, the other a "style."

A consciously picturesque *flirt* . . . but her flirtatiousness rarely goes any further than that—titillation plus elegance, and a slight touch of danger.

When all is said and done she is very practical: she sticks by her husband, Hastings—the "enduring" Englishman.

HECTOR
THE INTELLIGENT MAN WITHOUT EMPLOYMENT IN
HEARTBREAK HOUSE

He wants *to get* out—*somehow* . . . but there's no place to go. He cannot see the goal. Therefore he wants everything destroyed! He has no task. For this reason he dreams up exploits, philanders, plays "parts," dresses up (in "crazy" costumes), becomes decorative . . . even in his intelligence.

Like Ellie he's trying to find—a port, but he knows of none, foresees none.

"I am deliberately playing the fool," but not out of worthlessness, out of aimlessness.

He's a dilettante—forced to be one—yet he has the energy and intelligence to be something more.

Debonair and cool like a practical madman. A bit of a show-off. This gives him an identity. . . .

But this is his pose . . . the real man is dissatisfied, unhappy.

A pretty woman is a challenge to him: it leads to an activity of flirtation, the semblance of impressive action. He is telling the truth—or part of it—when he says he doesn't like being at-tracted—for it arouses him without leading anywhere. He is a civilized person, not a lecher. Thus he is a romantic without a cause.

He sees futility in all positions and arguments—even that of the anarchist . . . he hasn't even the confidence to feel superior to anyone.

He curses women because they are the only thing left for him to deal with . . . yet he knows they are only distractions for him.

He wants "beauty, bravery on earth." But he cannot find it around him or in him—except as a senseless activity.

The "saddest" character in the play, and he behaves like an ass and a liar . . . though he often speaks honestly and even wisely.

MANGAN
THE "STRONG MAN" OF HEARTBREAK HOUSE
("NOT A WELL MAN")

He wants to get in everywhere—and to get the hell out too.

The big "capitalist"; the sharper, the practical man, the man who counts in business and in politics. All of this is the Pose.

The real man is wistful, twisted, rather frightened and a somewhat resentful child . . . the most "cheated" or frus-trated person in the house.

He's "aggressive" . . . yet he is always caught off guard. He's sure an aggressive manner is the way to success, but he be-comes unsure when his success is challenged or his aggressive-ness doesn't impress.

Except in a very limited sphere, he's always out of his ele-ment, shaky—unhappy.

So he's always *forced* to pose—except when he believes it's particularly clever of him to tell the truth about himself.

"I don't quite understand my position here"—is the key-note. He never does—anywhere outside his office.

In the end he has a "presentiment" (of death) because he's insecure, a "worrier."

Afraid of women—gullible—an easy prey for them. Shy with Ellie, mooney with Hesione.

Like all lower-class folk who have arrived in the upper middle class he has an excessive sense of propriety—or priggishness.

He's full of unaccountable resentments (a source of comedy in this)—secret and almost ludicrous hostilities. He gets sore and vindictive in spurts. One can hardly discern the source of his irritations.

The craziness (or "unusual circumstances") of this house bursts the bubble of his pose . . . he collapses into tears, a hurt boy.

MAZZINI DUNN

THE INEFFECTUAL INTELLECTUAL IN HEARTBREAK HOUSE

To be helpful to all (in Heartbreak House) is the "spine." Mazzini has "moist eyes," always smiling—except for moments of total consternation, and even then there's a little smile. He is obliging to everybody.

He feels a bit inferior, insufficient, guilty. Thus he wants to make up for it by being helpful. He regards everyone as somehow better, cleverer, stronger than he. He admires everyone.

(From the actor's standpoint: a sweet zany.) Shy and modest because of all this. But sweet: there is nothing cringing or undignified about him. He accepts his humble position.

He loves his wife as he does Ellie but he feels indebted to them—as to everyone else.

He is credulous, gullible . . . the world is always a surprise to him; he smiles with wonder and admiration. He really doesn't understand evil.

He thinks all one has to have is the right influences and inspirations to become good, loyal, strong.

(Key lines: "How distressing! Can I do anything I wonder?" "Think of the risk those people up there are taking"—

in reference to the bombers in the air raid. "And the poor clergyman will have to get a new house.")

RANDALL

To act as if he were the one proper—immovable—person. The "imperturbable," the superb English gentleman. Ornament of all diplomatic circles.

That is the Pose. Unruffled, exquisite, the last word in smoothness. Narcissistic.

The real man: a bundle of ragged nerves, a spoiled, almost hysterical baby.

He believes himself a romantic character, so impressive in bearing that no matter what he does he must somehow appear dashing and right.

He's always play-acting till his "hat" is knocked off . . . then he screams like a helpless kid.

The most absurd of all the characters . . . the most "typically" British—in the old-fashioned comic sense. A "cultured" dandy, super-sophisticated. He will still look and be a kid at sixty-five.

His nerves will always show through his *sang-froid*.

His eyelids flutter . . . a bit effeminate.

He has no real passions or convictions. Therefore he needs his adoration for Lady Utterword. All his convictions have been absorbed in his pose—which is his class pattern.

BILLY DUNN

He reverses all values in *Heartbreak House.*

To get out, make out—anyway he can.

Shaw's intention with this character is to illustrate the total topsyturvydom of Heartbreak House. A sense of guilt hovers over Heartbreak House. Its inhabitants no longer believe in the old justice. The criminal no longer believes in his crime: it's just another way of earning a living.

Because of all this Dunn behaves like a clown—now contrite, now shrewd, now crooked, now pious, now immoral, now joking: for all these poses serve him. (A "ham" actor.)

The real man is the poor bloke who couldn't make it either in Heartbreak House or in Horseback Hall, and therefore preys on both—preferably on the former, since he would simply be given a tanning in the latter.

He ends in a terrified attempt to escape—in vain.

NURSE GUINESS
THE LEVELER

To wait it out—with a minimum of worry.

She's an "anarchist"—she doesn't care because she does get along.

"Quite unconcerned," says Shaw. She's quietly brazen.

A CONCLUDING STATEMENT*

Sitting at the back of the auditorium at a Washington performance of *Heartbreak House,* I was delighted to hear a spectator whisper to his neighbor, "Shaw certainly wrote wonderful gags." Why "delighted," why not dismayed? Shaw a gag writer: blasphemy! But I *was* delighted because the spontaneous remark in ordinary American meant that the person who had made it was glad to be attending a "laugh show."

Everyone nowadays refers glibly to Shavian wit. But in relation to *Heartbreak House*—not well known because infrequently performed—there is a tendency to become solemn. Shaw himself is largely responsible for this, first, because he called his play a Fantasia in the Russian Manner on English Themes, and, second, because in his Preface he cited Chekhov's plays as models.

In directing the play the first thing I told the actors was

* Published in the Souvenir Program sold in the theatre a few days after the opening.

that both the phrase "Russian manner" and the name Chekhov were to be disregarded in connection with *Heartbreak House:* they were altogether misleading. True, the name *Heartbreak House* signifies in Shaw's words "cultured, leisured Europe before the [First World] War" and Chekhov's plays deal with the educated middle class of the late nineteenth century. It is also true that in Russia Chekhov's plays —despite their melancholy—are construed as comedies, but there most of the resemblance between *Heartbreak House* and Chekhov ends.

The only other parallel between the work of the two playwrights is that Chekhov's world was destroyed by the Revolution of 1917 and the folk in *Heartbreak House* drifted into the First World War and if not destroyed were terribly shaken. Also the emphasis in this Shaw play—as in those of Chekhov—is not on the plot but on character and atmosphere.

What makes *Heartbreak House* utterly different from Chekhov is its unique style. Shaw's play is extravagant, full of capering humor which verges on the farcical. One of the characters refers to the environment he finds himself in as "a crazy house" in which one's mind "might as well be a football." The fact that this "crazy house" is also a truth house— a sort of distorting mirror which exaggerates the features of the people who enter it gives the play its human and social relevance but it does not distract from the topsy-turvy fun that my Washington playgoer enjoyed so much.

Years ago when there was still some resistance to Shaw—as we all know the greatest playwrights of our time encountered resistance as they came on the scene—certain critics complained that Shaw's characters were not people but puppets. There is no need to deny this. Shaw's characters *are* puppets— unnatural only in the sense that they reveal the truth about themselves more directly, more pointedly, more eloquently, more wittily than people in life are able to.

The director's task then was to combine the "fun" aspect of

the play—its arch frivolousness—with its basic intent. The setting had not only to disclose a place but make a comment—
smilingly suggestive of the author's mood. The clothes had
to be costumes. The characterizations had to be tipped from
realism to a kind of gay picturesqueness. Gravity had to be
avoided, except as fleeting reminders that we were still dealing with a truth about life—our lives. This slight duality—a
sort of "gayed up" seriousness, part game, part prophecy—is
only a reflection of the text itself which begins as a comedy of
mad manners and ends with an air raid by an enemy never
named or even hinted at throughout the course of the play.

What was Shaw's purpose and why did he write *Heartbreak
House* in this peculiar way? The play exemplifies a typical
Shavian "trick." *Heartbreak House* is all carefree talk and
horseplay—apparently devoid of dark portent; then it bursts
for a moment into a scene of shock and ends ironically on a
note of almost languid peace. "Nothing will happen," one of
the house guests says. Something does happen and something
more fatal may yet happen—expected, almost hoped for, by
certain of the characters.

These "charming people, most advanced, unprejudiced,
frank, humane, unconventional, free-thinking and everything
that is delightful," are content to drift. No matter what inner
qualms they may have, no matter what emptiness or discon-
tent they occasionally experience, they have settled for the
happiness of dreams and daily pastimes. For all his sharp teasing, Shaw is tolerant of them. Only, says he, in earnest jest,
if you go on like this without "navigation"—that is, without
plan, purpose and preparative action—your ship will "strike
and sink and split."

The thought or warning which informs the play—stated in
a frolic of entertaining word and postures—is wholly appro-
priate to our day and our theatre. Though the people of
Heartbreak House are English, it is not merely a play about
a certain class or a certain country. Time has turned it into a
play about practically all of us, everywhere.

Incident at Vichy*

by ARTHUR MILLER

(First presented by the Repertory Theatre of Lincoln Center at the ANTA Washington Square Theatre, New York City, on December 3, 1964.)

An Impression of My First Reading of the Script (July 11th, 1964):

The Play: A medallion or emblem engraved on metal or stone. When the curtain rises (there is no curtain at the ANTA Washington Square Theatre) two pauses: one in which the characters remain immobile—arrayed as if in a "memorial tablet" or "frieze" in commemoration of the dead. Then they move as living characters—slowly. There is a long wait of anxiety. They are in a hell of expectancy, uneasiness, bewilderment, wonder.

Business? The Prince gives the boy's ring to Leduc. (This business and an accompanying line were not in the original

* First published in the *Tulane Drama Review*, Volume IX, Number 4 (T 28), Summer 1965. © 1965 by the *Tulane Drama Review*. Reprinted by permission. All rights reserved.

script. I suggested it to Miller who added the line and business at rehearsal.)

The Old Jew is a "chorus"—his behavior is a spiritual pantomime. He's praying . . . he's waiting, he despairs, he pleads for mercy (of God). His gestures and attitudes are an unconscious running commentary on what is being said.

The others (in their silence) must run the gamut of indifference, self-absorption, fear, horror, a desire to interrupt, to object, to stop the conversation, to watch what is going on in the office behind them, etc.

August 12th: Conversation with Boris Aronson about the setting. It must seem constructed of metal and stone. Its locale not too specific. (Originally it was called "a police station." Changed by Miller to "a place of detention.") The fact that the play presumably takes place in Vichy is not important. A first sketch rejected as rather too decorative—though macabre. Something hard, mysterious, "Kafka-like" desired. A "no-man's land" enclosure.

Casting. Bob Whitehead suggests Joseph Wiseman as the Actor, David Stewart as the (Communist) Worker. I prefer Wiseman as Leduc the Psychoanalyst, Stewart as the Actor. An actor outside the Permanent Company suggested for the Prince. I prefer David Wayne. All my casting unanimously accepted by Whitehead, Kazan and Miller.

Early Notes (Before Setting Down Character Description):
The Prince [Von Berg] is distracted, hesitant, uncertain as if slightly "gaga." He is puzzled. Diffident. Then deeply troubled.

The characters have been detained. Confined. "Imprisoned." Why? They do not know. They question: why? why? why? The first action is to learn, discover the reason. They are worried and confused, and they "hope"—a concomitant of anxiety.

How explain their detention?

Because they are Jews? Is the Business Man a Jew? Is the Gypsy a Jew? Is the Prince a Jew?

And if they are Jews, does that mean they must die? Why? What can save them?

Believing in the Working Class Revolution? Belief in Art? Belief in God?

Or must they fight?

All this resolves itself to "What's to be done?" Is there no hope? What? What? What?

The answer is to take responsibility. The "revolt" of responsibility without any guarantee except the belief that each must help the other.

This suggests that the spine of the play has to do with the anguished (bewildered) quest: an attempt to discover the answer to the question, the meaning of and "remedy," for *evil*—which consists, Leduc (the Doctor) says, in "the fear and hatred of the 'other.' "

Apropos of this Leduc asks, "Is there a reasonable explanation of your sitting here? But you are sitting here, aren't you?"

The Actor exclaims, "But an atrocity like that (burning Jews) is beyond belief." To which the reply is, "That is exactly the point."

All (except the Gestapo "Professor," the Police) *ask questions*. The Police and the Gestapo have the answers—through their superiors. Even the self-torturing Major asks a question: Why is he allowing himself to do what he is doing? He asks, "Why do you deserve to live more than I do?

How many ways are there to "act" tension, anguish?

Begin rehearsals quickly, with simple and clear actions, not fully expressed. Do not attempt "big emotions" at first.

They stand up when it is impossible to remain seated.

"Does anybody know *anything*?" This is the key to the spine and mood of the play. (The play might be called "The

Waiting Room." They are waiting for an answer to a question to which there is no "answer."

The spine of the play: To find the answer (to the "trap" = evil), the way out of the dilemma in which they are imprisoned.

VON BERG (THE PRINCE)

Spine: to learn (*see*) the situation fully for the first time.

He *doesn't know the answer.* He doesn't even know the question. He's vague, confused. He has lived apart from the central reality.

Life has passed him by; he's out of the mainstream. Hence his diffidence, sense of frustration, which brings him close to tears. Very gentle and polite.

"Bewildered." His first question is a clue: Excuse me. Have you all been arrested for being Jewish?" And his second remark: "I'm terribly sorry. *I had no idea.*" Very shaken by the discovery.

Long silences of "confusion." He's trying to puzzle it all out . . . he's intuitive (romantic) rather than intellectual. Almost "sweet," naive. ("I am Viennese.")

He's modest: the nobleman is a forgotten man, a relic. "Vulgarity" is the supreme sin. It bespeaks coarseness, lack of feeling.

He considers things very carefully, speaks diffidently unless intuitively certain. He's always apologizing.

His final action is explained only by the fact that he is a man of feeling, not of calculation. His is the pure impetus of the truly moved person, the basic impulse of love. Even in the Major's office he is not yet aware of what he will do a minute later.

He wants to believe the best = he hopes for amelioration. That is why it takes him so long to realize the worst.

He asks the cardinal question of the play and of our time: "But what is left if one gives up one's ideals?"

He grieves for the world . . . his final gesture is not intended by him to *prove* anything: it is a spontaneous burst of his innermost self.

Psychologic gestures:

(*a*) A timid and pained movement of hand to inquire or learn.

(*b*) Lowering of head in pain or shame.

(*c*) A suddenly fierce resolve and affirmation.

LEDUC

Spine: to see it through to the end . . . intellectually and physically.

His is an *active* mind. It seeks to find answers which work. It is a "fighting" mind. It is a firm, unhysterical mind, courageous, with the will to accomplish an end.

Reason is a weapon to be handled with care, caution, and respect. It can liberate. There is the thrust of a blade in this man's spirit but it is controlled by his humanism. He has passion but it is not indiscriminate; it is held in check by his professional training and the discipline which that entails.

Hence he is willing to fight, to kill, if that is the only way out. He tries to understand, to plan. Remember: he was a soldier, an officer.

He is inclined to "pessimism," through a scientific or objective recognition of the facts. But—less consciously—he desires a "mitigation" of the facts. He is more moralist than he realizes. (Perhaps this is his "Jewishness.") Though reason (rationalism) prevents him from hoping excessively. He is "appalled" by Von Berg's action, though he has admitted to the Major that he would be ready to escape alone.

"Come on, we can do something" is fundamental to his character.

"I am being as impersonal as I know how to be." It is not easy but the impulse *to understand* is constantly present.

His "scientific" assurances place him against a blank wall which even he cannot bear or altogether accept. Hence his tension, his ultimate bafflement. He is less "released" than Von Berg. (Von Berg's inexplicable, unreasoned action is more meaningful and more valuable finally than Leduc's knowledge and confirmed data. Leduc may learn something his reason could not reveal to him.)

When Leduc tells Von Berg that man is full of hate of the other, this "dreadful truth" is a form of self-crucifixion . . . a desire to put some terrible blame on himself.

Psychologic gesture: control; the desire to point out . . . with a thrusting finger of examination and diagnosis; then, grasping his head to lessen the agony of his own contradictory pulls.

LEBEAU (THE PAINTER)

Spine: to ask the question.

With all this, bespeaks of fear, anxiety, hope, confusion, and final fatigue.

An innocent. He feels "guilty" somehow—because he is innocent. (His "escape"—coffee!)

The average man of sensibility. Knows he can't understand—but thoroughly honest about it. (The artist!) He is certainly frightened because he has no answer: in this respect he is the most "normal" person of the lot. ("You wouldn't have any idea what's going on, would you?") He's hungry, nervous, he wishes he were somewhere else, he is almost ready to die of tiredness. It's all torment, but not "pessimism." He's simply a feeling person of our time.

The surprise, the indignity, the madness of having his nose measured!

He's in sympathy with almost everybody who is "nice." Observe how he speaks to the Gypsy.

Likes to talk, to "philosophize." He is the artist without many fixed ideas, only feelings and the heritage of a liberal culture.

"What kind of crew is this? The animosity!" This is the natural man (or artist) who resents or is offended by "closed" people—the Business Man *et al.*

Alternates between trembling fear and sweet hope . . . "nervous" hope.

"Good papers." Oh, the little things that can give one courage, a sense of stability. *Repetition* of self-assurance.

No realist he. He can only paint what he imagines. He has a need to be with others, to feel himself with others, but the others, being more "practical," hold back.

Psychologic gesture: arms apart, questioning the world. Then dropping them in discouragement.

BAYARD (THE WORKER—ELECTRICIAN)

Spine: to stand by and save himself by his answer or social conviction.

His conviction—the triumph of socialism—keeps him erect, sustains, fortifies him. (His costume, typical of the French worker, should have some of the "stiffness" of armor!) He has earned his answer by a life of work and struggle.

He's watchful, alert, ever "on the ready." He's learned how to take care of himself, fight if need be.

He's helpful: to Lebeau for example. Wishes to cooperate, work with others. He's not impulsive; he's strong, contained. Somewhat "didactic" in the leftist manner. Not entirely without humor. But downright!

(Use of French popular gestures.)

There is vigor (quiet or explosive) in all his utterances.

Psychologic gesture: shoulders set, jaw tight, clenched upright fist.

MONCEAU (THE ACTOR)

Spine: to live by the ideal of his cultural environment, his "public." He's a bourgeois idealist: as an artist I serve the public, my country, humanity. This is my justification and my support.

A certain dignified hauteur. A certain *histrionic* "simplicity." A conscious pose of modesty.

Still there is *le geste, panache,* the courage and pride of the stage. Dresses conservatively offstage with only a hint of the theatrically self-conscious. There is here the mixture of the

academic (French Establishment) and the discreetly Bohemian. He's tense withal.

It is the bourgeois in him which assumes the "sensible"
attitude in everything. But like so many actors of this kind,
he is not altogether secure, though usually in an optimistic
frame of mind. He vacillates and may at times be superstitious. . . . Still he clings to his ideal to the end.

He has eloquence, a forensic ability both French and theatrical.

Psychologic gesture: he stands at attention with a tendency
to throw his head backward employing graceful gestures
(*noblesse*).

THE MAJOR

Spine: to carry out orders.

But he has been wounded and he is no longer sure of his
ability or desire to carry out orders. But what else is there for
him to do?

So he is "caught" too . . . sickened by the compulsion to follow orders. Still he tries not to listen to the voices of his
doubt or guilt. He fights them off as symptoms of weakness.
He almost hates himself for suffering from these symptoms
and hates those who provoke them in him. He would like to
prove that he has no cause to harbor any doubt.

He hates to talk to the prisoners, tries to avoid them. Tries,
because of his ambivalence, to "appease" Leduc, and failing
that, to subdue him as the embodiment of his guilt. For a man
with his job he suffers the fatal weakness of feeling!

He's at the breaking point. He wants to calm himself with
drink, which only stimulates the pain of his various wounds.
When he fires the gun, it is a signal to himself and the others:
Schluss! Shut up, you Jews; shut up, my soul! Get on with the
job: we're all under orders anyway.

Like many Germans, he is a semi-disciplined or controlled
hysteric.

He's "tempted" to break ranks, to defy the Professor. This
is the specific and immediate cause of his tension. The debate

with himself is carried on through his confrontations with the Professor, Leduc, even with the Old Jew!

After his scene with Leduc he resumes the procedure of examination, savagely confident that he will now be able to follow the Gestapo orders. He very nearly "glories" in the fact that he shall succeed in doing so.

Psychologic gesture: stands with clenched teeth, tight fist, trying to carry on with power; determined eye, and yet he is never wholly secure.

THE PROFESSOR

Spine: to carry out or perform the answer.

The Enemy ("evil") is anyone or anything standing in the way of the Third Reich. He functions through will, science and force.

(He dresses very correctly. Like a "polished" university bureaucrat.)

He is *absolute.* His certainty makes him dangerous, quietly fierce. He's in command.

Psychologic gesture: cold imperious eyes (he wears glasses); straight-backed, efficiently spare in gesture and movement.

THE WAITER

Spine: to worm out of trouble.

The most defenseless of all the characters. Timid, always "friendly," obsequious, terrified by his humble position. (He feels superior to the Gypsy only.) He makes friends through *café* and *croissants.*

Perhaps he is an emigré from Poland . . . previously terrified there. Now he hates "irregularity." He finds comfort only in the quiet nest of the bistro or café where he works. He *leans* on people, looking to the strong for protection (his native-born French boss, the important customers including the Major). He tries to smile his way out of trouble. Always seeking to be reassured by authority. A "schnook."

He's the only one who tries to flee in terror and is seen to be beaten. The only one thoroughly cowed. (He's naturally very pale.)

Psychologic gesture: smiling and crouching away as if ready for flight, that is, when he's not leaning on someone for protection; looks as if he were always prepared for a slap; compensates by always trying to ingratiate himself.

MARCHAND (THE BUSINESS MAN)

Spine: to do important work. To be in the center of activity. (Should be rather comic in effect.)

He is annoyed, indignant at his being detained. He's carrying on the business of the world, of France in the moment of its need.

He puts people "down" because he is right. Condescension is natural to him. He knows the answers.

Obsequious in a "reputable" manner to authority. He's "above" the situation. He sounds as if he were giving orders reasonably yet with a touch of indignation.

(The French bourgeois knows how to fix and correct everything. He always complains about the government and the powers that be.)

Psychologic gesture: impatience; sits on edge of chair; pushy in his desire to get on; he throws his weight around; waddles with impatience, walks rapidly.

POLICE CAPTAIN

Spine: to get even.

Vengeful because of hurts—real and imagined—suffered all his life. People have been getting away with murder: now men of my sort have a chance to get rid of all the vermin—wipe them out.

The knowing smile of a mean twirp. Squints, grins with malice and "shrewdness." He is at once "sneaky" and obsequious in regard to the Germans.

Cutting voice.

Psychologic gesture: a malicious smirk on his face like a

man about to play a dirty trick or discover something which will justify his pleasure in punishment; walks with noiseless tread.

GYPSY

Spine: to disregard it all.

He's used to being arrested. He's a vagrant. Indifferent. He's waiting for—what? He's disconnected from the others, from their problems.

He's sure he'll get out of the jam somehow . . . hardly concerned. The others are all "strangers," "outsiders." They are hostile forces of nature to be avoided, not to be fought with. One must deal with them as best one can.

He doesn't laugh; he grins. Not a grin of amusement but rather a protective coloring. It may look idiotic or sinister. A mechanical response. "If it were possible I'd like to cut your guts out"—is his secret thought.

His voice whines a bit on "No steal." "Fix." The "whine" is not an expression of sorrow but rather a plea or an assurance made for the thousandth time.

Psychologic gesture: he abstracts himself from his environment, generally turned away from the others.

BOY

Spine: to take care of his mother.

The son of Polish Jewish parents. He's been in trouble most of his life. Worked hard, concerned only with protecting his mother. (Father died in 1932).

Intelligent, aware, sensitive. Quietly trying to survive. Taut, attentive and spunky. His main idea: "How can I get the money to my mother if I fail to get out?" His courage is an extension of the love for his mother. That is why he attempts to "jail break."

Psychologic gesture: he's bent over in the pose of "The Thinker," turned toward the corridor door—*the way out.* (The Gypsy is turned away in the opposite direction: he has no intention of escaping. The boy is straining toward the only point of egress.)

FERRAND (THE CAFÉ BOSS)

Spine: To get along.

In an incomprehensible world which he has long given up questioning or understanding. He is all "adjustment."

Trying to please the customers, the powers that be, always scurrying and in a sweat.

Weeps with fright, with sorrow, with impotence: inability to help, fear of becoming "involved."

Psychologic gesture: the hurry and bustle of service.

DETECTIVES

Spine: to ape the Captain.

Without an opinion. They have no business with an opinion. They are the "mutes" of the world, those who stand by and do not interfere with superior force.

THE OLD JEW

Spine: to endure *in faith.*

He has been in hiding. He is dragged onto stage. He is neither hero nor victim. He has become "resigned" since he has no weapon against evil except faith, which is something between himself and the Almighty. He does not fret over trouble. He is inured to pain to the point of death. He is above fear, he will not break under torture. For him, endurance itself is meaningful. He is aware of the "atmosphere" around him. He prays . . . he remembers, he sighs in sorrow, he pleads (with God) that he may come to understand, he falls in a faint. He "resists" in his spirit.

He is not the "abject" Jew though he may be the eternal wanderer" or the eternally pursued. Sorrowful or exalted he may be but not "little," martyred but never degraded. His eye accuses his tormentor.

Long Day's Journey into Night

by EUGENE O'NEILL

(Directed with an American company for the Kumo Theatre, Tokyo, 1965.)

FIRST IMPRESSIONS

Guilt—a keynote
↓
Apprehension—suspense   The characters are
↓   sustained by no faith
More guilt
↓
Self-accusation

The eyes of each character are on the other.
Foghorn—a desolate sound of aloneness.
Loneliness—everyone is alone with his or her own secret and guilt.

The play is a self-examination, a search into oneself and

into others. Through understanding to find forgiveness, relief, the connection of love which may overcome loneliness.

Long Day's Journey (self-examination) into Night (the darkness of the self). The journey to self-discovery. The search for the true self which has somehow been lost.

Mary: "If I could only find the faith I lost so I could pray again!"

Later, "What is it I'm looking for? I know it's something I've lost."

The spine of the play: to probe within oneself for the lost "something."

TYRONE

Spine: to maintain his "fatherhood"—the tradition (the crumbling grandeur).

He is a *positive* character: he wants to sustain the structure of his home and family, above all, his wife whom he still loves. If she were well, he thinks, all would be normal. There would be no suffering, no crises. He hopes and hopes—so that that he may not see the failure of his whole life, his part in that failure, his guilt.

He still clings to his religion: his faith in the theatre, his world. (He takes pride at never having missed a performance.) His gods are Shakespeare and Edwin Booth. . . .

But the tradition has been shattered in the struggle for existence in the dark days of America's Gilded Age. . . . Tyrone is "redeemed" by the discovery of the past in his son.

Tyrone's heartiness is something more than a sign of physical health. It is part of the fortitude in his *struggle* with poverty, his *struggle* to educate himself, to lose his brogue, to learn Shakespeare, to become a stage star. (The theatre is his religion.) But he has betrayed his religion through his fear of poverty. He wants land, which means security to him ("the farm"). He seeks roots, lost in the departure from Ireland and in the effort to grow new roots in the new and different American "soil."

It is hard for him to admit the least fault or guilt in himself. He can't even admit that he snores, that he drinks too much, that he is greedy. He does not, at first, understand his faults as a consequence of his background and situation. He must maintain his self-respect to be a father, a god, a leader, a man.

(American children of immigrants rarely understand their fathers. They are always disappointed in them. They do not appreciate the hardships of their fathers' struggle as immigrants or as "pioneers": *Desire Under the Elms, A Touch of the Poet*.)

"Socialism," for Tyrone, means destruction of the tradition. His sons blaspheme against the theatre, Shakespeare, etc.

He shuns "Wall Street"—the forces, which without his realizing it, have conspired to ruin him. He doesn't understand his life—or his country. Hence, his constant self-contradiction, his absurdity.

He's a good man, a soft man. He always yields to his better nature, to sentiment and affection. Like most actors, he is susceptible to compliments. He's an "old-time" actor: life was composed of work on the stage, stage lore, companionable drinking, dreams of glory, celebration of success.

MARY

Spine: to find her bearings, her "home," to seek them (for they have somehow been lost).

Her bearings? Her religious faith, her peace of mind, her beauty, her womanliness, which have been abused by the neglect of a man who has *his* bearings in the theatre and its people.

She feels the loss as a guilt. Is she to blame? She justifies herself, rationalizes, but she still feels guilty, inadequate to her ideal.

"You haven't a nerve in you," she tells Tyrone. She admires this and resents it. She sees this as a strength which has hurt her. . . . He is insensitive (unaware) of what he has done to her. It makes him a "preacher," in his own way, a "fanatic," intent on maintaining the respectability of the family and his position. She's a "romantic," he a "classic" personality. The "classic" person cannot comprehend faltering or weakness. The "romantic" cannot forgive the unreality (rigidity) of the "straight line": its unbending determination and sense of direction. That sort of character seems inhuman. Still, it is awesome in its justness, its power. That is why Mary defends Tyrone against the boys' accusations: you must *respect* him.

She is all contradiction, because she struggles against things she does not fully understand, as the loss of her ideals, the causes of her illness, the fact that she finds "excuses" for her sickness.

She would be "lost," even if she were not addicted to drugs. The theatre, which sustains Tyrone, means little to her. She has "lost" her children who have their own and new problems—besides their horror of her illness. They have lost her protection; she has nothing to protect them with. They are caught between their father and mother, neither of them capable of giving them what they require: moral, spiritual support.

Tyrone wants a home, a solid home; he didn't have one as a boy. But his only home is the theatre and the bars he goes to —which are an extension of the theatre. That is why he has never created a home for Mary, a home in which the mother is the center, the queen. She is an appendage. He is a "guest" in the house; she merely the caretaker. This is one reason for her loneliness.

Isn't there some defiance in her addiction to dope? She not only escapes through it but she punishes the others through it for their "neglect," their lack of understanding. "We can't forget," she says. She means: I am condemned, I am guilty, there's no hope for me. I'm bad and I must continue to be bad because you have made me so. You have left me no other course.

There is *childishness* in her, innocence. She has not grown up to mature understanding, to any degree of impersonal objectivity. Her wisdom is unconscious, intuitive.

The more pressure put on her, the greater her pain, the greater amount of dope she takes.

Her resignation and "acceptance" of Tyrone's faults is like an accusation to him. It increases his sense of guilt and his resistance to it. . . . What keeps her going, the last vestige of stamina, is her husband's love and need of her, his fidelity. That is why she still loves him—despite everything.

The wedding gown is the symbol of what she has lost; her innocent, trusting, confident past.

EDMUND

Spine: to discover or understand the truth (thus to help).

He is the strongest of the four. "I'm trying to help. Because it is wrong for you to forget. The right way is to remember."

After his father's long confession he says, "I'm glad you told me. I know you a lot better now."

He's *independent.* . . . He went away to sea, to discover, to learn. . . . He's more just than anyone else. He slaps Jamie for being cruel. When he hurts his mother it is to help her by making her face the truth which may save her.

He is without self-pity. He feels the need to find some saving truth. All of O'Neill's quest for transcendence is in Edmund's description of his mystic experience at sea: he even speaks of God—*meaning.*

JAMIE

Spine: to free himself from guilt.

To do this he finds it necessary to denounce the fraud in others, to sneer at life's double-cross: this to him consists of his mother's loss of innocence (her vice), and his brother, who came between his mother and himself. He confesses the evil in himself as a way of alleviating the burden of his guilt.

He's the guiltiest in his own eyes. Can't free himself. Must blot himself out. He despises himself for everything. No pride in himself, a loser to himself.

The sneering and denunciation of everything (including the stage) is a way of proving that he is *not* as guilty as he feels, that he is *justified* in his cynicism.

He humiliates himself through sex with the most unattractive whore.

"If she'd [his mother] beaten the game, I could too." He wants to pass out with his brother: to accomplish either a double redemption or a double suicide.

"Caught her in the act with a hypo." As if she had *"deceived"* him.

He loves Edmund—a kind of compensation—for Edmund is clean, healthy in his spirit. But Jamie is also jealous of him. For if his brother is good, then he is not, is wrong about everything. Yet he wants to absolve himself of this guilt—jealousy of his brother. Hence his confession: his one positive act.

The actor should perhaps think of Mary as his sweetheart and all the others as people guilty of her "downfall."

DIRECTOR'S NOTES FOR

Uncle Vanya

by ANTON CHEKHOV
translated by ALEX SZOGYI

(Produced at the Mark Taper Forum, Los Angeles, California,
August 13, 1969.)

IMPRESSIONS

There is a peculiar turbulence in the air, a constant nervousness, everyone is impatient with the other, impatient with
himself. There is self-contemplation which ends in annoyance
with the other. "No exit."

"I am dissatisfied with life like you, Uncle Vanya, and we
are both growing peevish" . . . "I have no light in the distance."

Yet there's an underlying warmth, kissing. The intimacy of
it all. Truly Christian.

They all talk about what they want to do and always fail to
do what they wish.

Still there is a great reverence for life, a faith in life just as
it is, though so terribly sad.

They all speak from the unconscious. . . . The deepest feelings are somehow entangled in the most nondescript, insignificant remarks and things.

The people are a queer lot—eccentric.

This play cannot be acted through the lines. A skein of emotional impulses must be woven. A web of odd sentiments which have only the "logic" of feeling. Even the violence—the shooting—is ordinary!

Act One—The landscape, the outside "world."

Act Two—Domestic (night).

Act Three—Conference.

Act Four—"Buried: the grave." "Peace" and quiet! We shall endure.

The spine of the play: to make life better, find a way to be happy.

They are not satisfied with life; therefore they are grumblers—

"I want to live, I want success," the Professor says.

"How will we live through the winter . . ." (the years!)

"I don't like this house; it's some kind of labyrinth . . . one can't find one's way in it . . . nobody can find anybody."

"What do I do with myself? What do I do?"

"Give me something to comfort me!"

"If I could only live out the remaining years of my life in some new way."

"They, those of the future, may perhaps find the way to be happy but we—."

VANYA

Spine: to find some way—some positive way—to live through the suffocation of his life.

A man of delicate sensibility. He is intelligent: a would-be artist of continental stamp. (He wears a "fancy tie"—"bohemian.") He's moral. Has a sense of justice. Self-observant. What, then, is his "weakness"? Self-sacrificing, overidealistic. He lacks aggressiveness, ego. No self-confidence. ("I'll shut up and say I'm sorry.")

"I know my chances for a little reciprocation [from Yelena] are almost nil. . . ." (Astrov does try to have an affair with her. Vanya defeats himself.) His idealism consists of too much consideration and regard for the other person. "Help me make peace with myself."

Everything in him is tentative—he's never certain . . . he cannot push through.

The symbolic (and actual) symbol of his defeat is the Professor who represents mediocrity in power, and selfishness.

His tentativeness comes from too great an awareness of the other person's situation: "That may be . . . that may very well be . . . everything may just very well be."

He drinks because "it makes you think you're alive. . . ." He still yearns to get on. Hence the violence and the ineffectuality of his most active gesture—the shooting. And the other effort: his attempt to woo Yelena.

Yet he's shocked by pessimism: Yelena's thoughts about the world going to pot are "distasteful" to him. . . . He advises her to be adventurous, "jump in head first."

When he has fired at the Professor he cries out, "What am I doing! What am I doing?"

End: there's nothing left but to go on as before, "to work!"

ASTROV

Spine: to do what he has to—despite everything.

When called away—his visit interrupted—he says, "What can I do? I have to go."

He accepts what Vanya isn't able to: he's more down-to-earth. He sees through his own contradictions. This makes him ironic. His perceptions are negative, his actions are positive: he accepts life as it is.

He's an objective idealist, less abstract in his thinking than Vanya. He hopes for amelioration, even if only in two hundred years! "We'll have played some part in this." His soul is filled with pride when he sees a birch tree growing from the seed he planted. Then, dismisses it all with apparent cynicism.

He has no hope for himself as an *individual*. "My personal life . . . there's nothing good about it."

"I work—and I keep getting beaten down by fate, but *I don't stop*." (This is the essence of his spine.)

He doesn't love anyone (except the old Nurse) but he responds to beauty and he suffers guilt at the death of a patient.

YELENA

Spine: to obey and to justify her obedience—as the only thing she can do. (Her spine is weak in relation to the play's spine, almost negative.)

She is shy. . . . She is the worst failure: she is beautiful, a potentially passionate woman. Yet she's repressed herself—she's not strong enough to act, to dare. Raised in gentility without courage. Everything is potential in her, nothing realized. She's languid because she doesn't hope to accomplish anything.

She has given up. "Wait, in five or six years, I'll be old too."

She can't stand scenes, ugly situations, violence. "Several times I've been on the verge of tears. . . ." She wants peace (quiet). Everything to be accepted without squabbling. She is an honest, good person, meaning no harm.

When she speaks about Astrov she becomes lyric; we realize that she's a feeling person. She's not a bore, but *effaced*.

Once she's expressed herself, she has an impulse to play the piano, but because her husband says "no," she obeys and desists.

Faced with Vanya or Astrov, she always tries to escape. . . . All she is capable of, except for one kiss, is to take Astrov's pencil as a reminder!

SONYA

Spine: to serve everyone with love.

She is constantly attentive to every little need of the people around her.

She scolds and corrects those who behave foolishly or selfishly: this, too, is service, for she hopes they may improve. A sturdy person, a worker.

She is open, intelligent, tender and *smiling. Resolute* withal, not just "nice." She's on to her father and treats him as he should be treated for his own and everyone else's good. Yet she protects him from Vanya's hostility.

She's happy when she can declare herself, when she can express her feelings as with Astrov and later with Yelena. She cries with happiness when she's opened herself to someone in friendship or affection.

She always wishes to hope, to live in hope.

THE PROFESSOR

Spine: to improve things for himself.

He's unfortunate: he believes in his superiority, in the importance of being a professor, especially a professor of art . . . but he is not famous, he is unloved, he hasn't enough money, he is getting old and he has gout!

So he insists on having everyone take care of him, serve him. He tries to preserve his superior attitude. Vanya is a nonentity to him, the doctor knows nothing, his wife is too young. He wants everyone to appreciate his cleverness: he acts like visiting royalty. But he's sure that he behaves with largesse and that he harbors charitable feelings toward everyone.

His manner of dress shows that he takes care of himself.

Even his illness is more important than the ordinary person's complaint because Turgenev also suffered from it.

He summons his family to a conference with regal imperiousness. His joke about the "Inspector General" is that of a superior being clowning before his inferiors.

He can't face any real resistance. He retreats from a quarrel. He's a coward in the face of life.

He leaves as he came, not having learned anything—except that Vanya is impossible and that the others should work (which they do, while he only prates about it).

TELYEGIN ("WAFFLES")

Spine: to keep himself attached to these people (the family).

He's inspired by something other and more than mind—the guitar expresses him. He's sad and happy in his "uselessness."

He knows the meaning of bliss . . . which is simply to be alive next to good people on the land and in the house his family owned.

He upholds or exemplifies the old (basic) morality. He feels close to Marina, always sits beside her. This establishes his social position, his "throne."

He doesn't think he's *seen*: he's inconspicuous. "If you deign to take notice, I have dinner with you every day." (But Sonya says, "Telyegin is our helper, our right hand.")

He follows people like a little dog: the attachment of a faithful dog.

He kisses Vanya when he sees Vanya's upset. . . . "I can't stand it," he says when Vanya becomes violent through frustration.

The Marina-Telyegin relationship is embodied in Act Four when they are winding the wool together. (His *attachment*.)

"Hey you *sponge*." But said as an insult, it gives him "a bitter feeling."

"Yes, my friend" to Astrov. Everyone is his friend, he's everyone's friend. Note the first stage direction: "Telyegin plays his guitar quietly."

MARINA

Spine: to help everyone (including animals!) to live.

The part must not be played stolidly. She has a sly humor, forbearance and saltiness. She's the "earth."

She calls the Professor "my little fellow." She is tender with him, treats him like a child. All these "children" have to be scolded sometimes, but above all, understood and loved.

When Sonya is frightened and heartbroken she seeks comfort in Marina.

She uses the word "Christian." It means a good, well-ordered, decent way of life. "We're all sponges on God."

She knows and appreciates that "all of you work hard."

"May the Lord forgive us all" are her concluding words—as she keeps knitting a stocking.

MARIA (MAMAN)

Spine: to side with learned authority: there is dignity and safety in that.

She enters with a book. We see her last with a book.

(I see her as thin, boney. A blue-stocking, old-fashioned Russian style. Wears a pince-nez with a ribbon.)

Complacent amidst woe. She's satisfied, nothing touches her. A "liberal" pillar of society.

Her essential character is expressed when she scolds Vanya, "*Jean,* don't contradict Alexander. Truly he knows better than we do what is right and what is wrong."

A psychological gesture: she beats her hand on the arm of a chair in reproof of Vanya, "listen to Alexander."

At the final curtain: "Maria writes notes in the margin" of a book.

THE WORKMAN (THE DOWNTRODDEN)

Spine: to do (depressed but without complaint).

There is a certain dignity in his deference to the doctor and the others. . . .

Part IV

Actions	Adjustments	Activities
To advise	Strongly, urgently.	
To hear the results	Perhaps he has already become convinced of his wife's guilt and is now ready to take the fatal step.	

The Waltz of the Toreadors*

by JEAN ANOUILH

Act I, Scene 2

DOCTOR: Then you must make haste, General. One good
honest explanation. Cut to the quick before gan-
grene sets in. Hurt if you must but do it without flinching. And then start again afresh.
Crossing the threshold of that door seems like
flying to the moon, but in fact all it requires is
this one step.
(GHISLAINE *appears at the door*)

GHISLAINE: I can't stand it! I must know!

---

* Adapted by permission of Coward, McCann, & Geohagen from *The Waltz
of the Toreadors,* by Jean Anouilh. Copyright © 1953 by Jean Anouilh and
Lucienne Hill.

Actions	Adjustments	Activities
To fight off being rushed	This is the nervousness of the man on the verge of doing something he wants to do but fears.	
To fight for her due (her spine)	Impatient! A real Woman.	
	More reasoned urgency—harassed.	
	Powerful (with heart)	Urgent
	becoming tearful—	fast tempo
	Exasperated!	
	Icily tearful (insulted) Harassed! Women are nuts —so unreasonable ("I adore you"— nervous reassurance)	This stops her! (She stands rigid) Swinging his head and body.

GENERAL: (*Slightly on edge*) Dammit all, Ghislaine, you've
                waited seventeen years, surely you can contain
                yourself for an extra ten minutes!

GHISLAINE: No I can't, not even for ten minutes.

GENERAL: I must have time enough to make her confess,
                and inform her of my irrevocable decision. She
                is an invalid, dammit. I owe her consideration.
                Don't *you* be cruel, too.

GHISLAINE: I bore her cruelty and respected her love so
                long as I believed her faithful to you. Now I
                know that she dared to betray you I shall know
                no pity, Leon, and no patience. Either way,
                should you be capable of hesitating still, I have
                a little revolver with a mother of pearl handle
                which you may remember, here in my reticule.
                I shall end this life within the hour, without
                ever having known more of love than your vain
                promises, Leon.

GENERAL: Give me strength! All I ask is a moment to set
                my life in order. Go back into the morning
                room and be patient. There are some magazines
                on the table.

GHISLAINE: Magazines! Like at the dentist's! You have
                wounded me for the first time, my dear.

GENERAL: My beloved! Who said anything about a den-
                tist? Anyhow, you aren't the one who is going to
                have the tooth out. *I adore you!* Just one mo-
                ment.
                (*He pushes her gently but firmly back into the
                morning room*)

Actions	Adjustments	Activities
	A rapid suggestion (under pressure)	He's holding his head in agitated confusion.
To remind him	Stands his ground —as a way of urging the General on.	
	Stops. Convinced.	Turns to go. Stops for a second —he goes very quickly (count of three or four).
To tell alarming news	that he has hardly been able to grasp. Also alarmed! Stronger—discovery of an amazing feat. He's about *to deny* the possibility.	
Frantic!		Rapidly
		a count of one or two.

Time is getting on. Suppose you spoke to her first, Doctor?

DOCTOR: That might prove a little awkward considering those letters. Suppose she falls into my arms? There'll be no end of explaining to do then.

GENERAL: That's true. Stay here though will you, and if I cry out "Help" come in.
(*He goes into his wife's room, and rushes out again almost at once, distractedly waving a letter*)
Doctor, she's not in her room!

DOCTOR: What! Is there another way out?
GENERAL: Through the window, by hanging on to the wisteria.

DOCTOR: In her condition—
GENERAL: She left this letter on the table.—"I heard everything. Men are all cowards. Whatever they may have said to you, Leon, I have never loved anyone but you. I can walk when I want to. I am going. You will never hear of me again." Good God! Does she mean she wants *to kill herself?*
DOCTOR: (*Looking at his watch*) The railroad crossing! She spoke of it! It's two minutes to, the train goes through at five past!
GENERAL: The pond! You go one way—I'll go the other!

Actions	*Adjustments*	*Activities*
		The General downstage—the Doctor through rear door.
To "discover"	A desperate secret! A desperate resolve. *Almost* grand—then very quiet, quick, intense.	
		Tearfully. With little half-dry sobs or gulps.
	Sighing— "Disgusted" (with a little tearfulness) A moment to decide—with her hand on her mouth.	

(They both rush out. GHISLAINE *comes in almost at once)*

GHISLAINE: I too heard everything. *You love her still,* Leon! Only one way out.
(She sits at the desk and begins to write rapidly, calm but dabbing away a tear through her veil) (Murmuring)
Leon, here is my last letter to you—
(Her voice trails away, she continues to write. GASTON, *the secretary, is heard outside the window, singing his Italian love song. The ditty continues throughout the writing of the letter. When she has finished,* GHISLAINE *leaves it on the General's desk in a prominent position)*
There. On his papers. That's all. It's the simplest thing in the world.
(She rises unhurriedly, picks up her reticule, draws out the revolver with the mother of pearl handle, presses it to her heart, and pulls the trigger. Nothing happens. She looks at the gun in surprise, pulls out a catch, pushes another, blows into the barrel and fires again. Still nothing. Sighing)
Seventeen years you too have been waiting.
(She throws away the gun, looks at her fobwatch and mutters)

Too late for the train. The pond!
(She runs to the door, but changes her mind)
No. Not in the same place as her, for Heaven's sake!
(She darts a quick look round the room)
The window! With a little luck . . .
(She takes a run at it, swings her legs over the

Actions	Adjustments	Activities
To find out	Startled—but not too much so.	
To complain	Dismay! and almost annoyance.	
Not too excited.		
	Surprised! Life is a surprise! Servant girl's annoyance. (Inefficiency of the "master" rather than fright is expressed.)	
To try to do something	He's very worried . . .	
	A young boy's excitement. Practical! Strong!	
To examine and fix	All tremulous— worried for her— for himself. At sixes and sevens—worried.	
To get consoled— solace	"It helps me"—a bit sensuously Very nervous.	

balcony and drops. The singing ends abruptly in a loud hiccup. The stage is empty for a moment, then GASTON *enters carrying a senseless* GHISLAINE, *closely followed by the* MAID)

MAID:	Goodness gracious sir, whatever's the matter? You hiccupped fit to raise the dead!
GASTON:	I was rocking quietly in the hammock when this lady comes tumbling down on my head.
MAID:	Well fancy that! Maybe she wanted to kill you?
GASTON:	Herself more likely. Besides I don't know her from Adam. She's fainted.
MAID:	And the Doctor just this minute left. The man as good as lives here half the time, and the one day we have a suicide he's out!

GASTON:	(*Slapping Ghislaine's face*) For God's sake go and fetch something.
MAID:	What?
GASTON:	Well *I* don't know—ointment, smelling salts— iodine. . . . Anything.
MAID:	I'll make her a good strong cup of coffee. (*She goes*)
GASTON:	No blood, anyway. (*He feels her all over*) No bones broken, apparently. No bumps. Madame! Madame!
GHISLAINE:	(*Weakly*) Mademoiselle.
GASTON:	Mademoiselle—I beg your pardon. Are you feeling better?
GHISLAINE:	(*Murmuring*) Leave your hands where they are, Leon.
GASTON:	(*Turning away in embarrassment*) Excuse me, but you are making a mistake.

Actions	*Adjustments*	*Activities*
	Stronger.	
To become aware of what is really happening	After this quiet— trying to straighten it out with himself and for others.	He flutters his hands as if he hadn't realized what he had been doing.
To gush out her desires	Hysteria! Sweet hysteria! A nervous outpouring of her thoughts and feelings . . . a mixture of staccato sobs (like pre-orgasm) coquettry included.	—fluttery
	To himself (but almost turned out to audience with a kind of frightened apologetic smile turns back for the kiss)	
		Her arm goes round his neck in a big swing
		she's a determined girl . . .

GHISLAINE: (*Crying out*) Leave your hands Leon—all over me—or I feel I shall swoon again—your hands quickly!—I'm going—

GASTON: (*Looking in panic at his hands*) My hands? Oh dear, I can't very well let her faint away again. Not that it's at all unpleasant, and I am such a lonely young man. Besides I'll mention it when I go to confession.

GHISLAINE: Oh how good it is! You are touching me at last, Leon! You thought me strong—and I was strong —I had to be, but oh how long they were all those nights on my own! Before I met you I was alone too, but I never knew it. It was on the morrow of the Saumur Ball that my bed suddenly seemed wide—that next night and all the nights for seventeen years. And all the wicked thoughts—you don't know! I shall never tell you. I struggled alone. No one was to touch me until you finally came. Your arms are strong and gentle your hands, gentler even than at the Saumur ball. Kiss me, now that you know I am going to die. *What are you waiting for, Leon my death!*

GASTON: The lady is obviously making a mistake, but seeing that she may be going to die—(*He kisses her*)

GHISLAINE: (*Has the time to sigh*) At last! (*A long kiss*) (*Enter the* GENERAL, *carrying his unconscious* WIFE *in his arms. He stands rooted to the spot at the sight which confronts him*)

Actions	Adjustments	Activities
		Music—overture —fanfare, and then sensuous, grave music.
To invite	With pleasurable eagerness and curiosity	
To refuse	With trepidation —almost sullenness	
	A little sharply	

Tiger at the Gates*

by JEAN GIRAUDOUX

Act II, Scene 1

> *A palace enclosure. At each corner a view of the sea. In the middle a monument, the Gates of War. They are wide open.*
> *(Helen. The young* TROILUS)

HELEN:	You, you, hey! You down there! Yes, it's you I'm calling. Come here.
TROILUS:	No.
HELEN:	What is your name?
TROILUS:	Troilus.
HELEN:	Come here.
TROILUS:	No.

Actions	Adjustments	Activities
To flirt	Wheedling—coaxing—with satisfaction	Troilus: need not play with childish timidity. The adolescence shows through the passionate virility.
To "hide"	A little *assertive* Teasing . . . (as if it were naughty) To give up As to a child—dog —man!	
	Half "angry" More commanding—archly	
To "take"	An outburst (yet shy—fifteen) Coquetting	
	Telling him!	
	Sharp Stronger Passionately (grown-up)	
To study	A delectable, interesting creature	

HELEN:	Come here, Troilus! (TROILUS *draws near*) That's the way. You obey when you're called by your name: you are still very like a puppy. It's rather beguiling. Do you know you have made me call out to a man for the first time in my life. You will pay for that. What's the matter? Are you trembling?
TROILUS:	No, I'm not.
HELEN:	You tremble, Troilus.
TROILUS:	Yes, I do.
HELEN:	Why are you always just behind me? If I walk with my back to the sun and suddenly stop, the head of your shadow stubs itself against my heel. Tell me what you want.
TROILUS:	I don't want anything.
HELEN:	Tell me what you want, Troilus!
TROILUS:	Everything! I want everything!
HELEN:	You want everything. The moon?
TROILUS:	Everything! Everything and more!
HELEN:	You're beginning to talk like a real man already; *you want to kiss me!*
TROILUS:	No!
HELEN:	You want to kiss me, isn't that it, Troilus?
TROILUS:	I would kill myself directly afterwards!
HELEN:	Come nearer. How old are you?
TROILUS:	Sixteen. Alas!
HELEN:	Bravo that alas. Have you kissed girls of your own age?
TROILUS:	I hate them.
HELEN:	(*Yes!*) But have you kissed them?

Actions	Adjustments	Activities
To talk about himself	There is a certain masculine egotism in this.	
To tantalize	Staunchly Play with him	Holds on to his hand—she wants to pull away (twists around him—circles)
		He pulls away—retreats—almost ready to beat himself or her.
To have fun (make fun) To have fun too	Very graciously—into his eyes Blithe energy—almost gaiety Playfully	Music ends
	Mock-seriously	

TROILUS: Well, yes, you're bound to kiss them, you kiss them all. I would give my life not to have kissed any of them.

HELEN: You seem prepared to get rid of quite a number of lives. Why haven't you said to me frankly: Helen, I want to kiss you! I don't see anything wrong in your kissing me. Kiss me.

TROILUS: Never.

HELEN: And then, when the day came to an end, you would have come quietly to where I was sitting on the battlements watching the sun go down over the islands, and you would have turned my head towards you with your hands—from golden it would have become dark, only shadow now, you would hardly have been able to see me— and you would have kissed me, and I should have been very happy. Why this is Troilus, I should have said to myself: young Troilus is kissing me! Kiss me.

TROILUS: Never.

HELEN: I see. You think, once you have kissed me, you would hate me?

TROILUS: Oh! (*Older*) Men have all the luck, knowing how to say what they want to!

HELEN: You say it well enough.
(*Enter* PARIS)

PARIS: Take care Helen, Troilus is a dangerous fellow.

HELEN: On the contrary. He wants to kiss me.

PARIS: Troilus, you know that if you kiss Helen, I shall kill you?

Actions	Adjustments	Activities
	Teasing—serious	(The boy is ready to kiss—kill or jump over the parapet)
	Tossing it all off —the game is done	
To put him up to a prank	With delighted energy	
To assert himself	But now melancholy self-awareness—reverse egotism Egging him on	
To provoke (arouse)	Big—(but "down") Excited teasing, playful challenge With a shocked reaction—pleasant and disturbing A kind of sensuous and grave provocation (provoking to Paris and perhaps to Troilus)	Touches his mouth

HELEN: Dying means nothing to him; no matter how often.

PARIS: What's the matter with him? Is he crouching to spring? Is he going to take a leap at you? He's too nice a boy. Kiss Helen, Troilus. I'll let you.

HELEN: If you can make up his mind to it you're cleverer than I am.

(TROILUS *who was about to hurl himself on* HELEN *immediately draws back*)

PARIS: Listen, Troilus! A committee of our revered elders is coming to shut the Gates of War. Kiss Helen in front of them; it will make you famous. You want to be famous, don't you, later on in life?

TROILUS: No. I want nobody to have heard of me.

PARIS: You don't want to be famous? You don't want to be rich and powerful?

TROILUS: No. Poor. Ugly.

PARIS: Let me finish! So that you can have all the women you want.

TROILUS: I don't want any, none at all, none.

PARIS: Here come the senators! Now you can choose: either you kiss Helen in front of them, or I shall kiss her in front of you. Would you rather I did it? All right! Look! . . . Why, this was a new version of kiss you gave me, Helen. What was it?

HELEN: The kiss I had ready for Troilus.

Actions	Adjustments	Activities
To make it part of the game		Troilus is leaving—stops when Helen addresses him—and then goes.
	More provocation	
	Calling— surprised—eager —"amorous"	
To become aware		
To seize an opportunity	Also his sort of flirtation	He rushes in eagerly—as if to "catch" her and stop her from leaving.
To stop this	Annoyed—and an element of jealousy (Troilus, etc.)	
To oblige	She likes to respond to every flattery His concentration is part of a sexuality "Coquettishly," "poetically"	
	A little let down —dry—flat	

PARIS: You don't know what you're missing, my boy! Are you leaving us? Goodbye, then.

HELEN: We shall kiss one another, Troilus. I'll answer for that.
(TROILUS *goes*)
Troilus!

PARIS: (*Slightly unnerved*) You called rather too loudly, Helen.
(*Enter* DEMOKOS)

DEMOKOS: Helen, one moment! Look me full in the face. I've got here in my hand a magnificent bird which I'm going to set free. Are you looking? Here it is. Smooth back your hair, and smile a beautiful smile.

PARIS: I don't see how the bird will fly any better if Helen smooths her hair and gives a beautiful smile.

HELEN: It can't do me any harm, anyway.

DEMOKOS: Don't move. One! Two! Three! There! It's all over, you can go now.

HELEN: Where was the bird?
DEMOKOS: It's a bird who knows how to make himself invisible.
HELEN: Ask him next time to tell you how he does it.

Mlle. Colombe

by JEAN ANOUILH

(Produced by Robert L. Joseph and Jay Julien; opened at the Longacre Theatre, January 6, 1954.)

November 2, 1953

Dear Boris:

On re-reading the script of our play, I was struck by the fact that many of the characters act like *clowns* and then I realized that in the commedia dell'arte sense they are all clowns. *Julien* is a "Pierrot"—*Colombe* is a "Columbine"—and the rest are "Pantalones" and "Dottores," etc. The play is, as the commedia dell'arte plays so often are, a kind of tragic farce and pure theatre. It is, in fact, a sort of serious *circus*.

This leads me to believe that the play should be made as colorful as possible in costume and setting, in turn romantically gay and romantically sad. It must be heightened to a thoroughgoing theatrical picturesqueness. The shabby element, which also exists as part of the atmosphere, may be minimized in behalf of the picturesqueness. We should see

the theatre with the eyes of Colombe, who thinks of it as a fulfillment of everything she desires. If we see the theatre too
realistically, we would be seeing it through Julien's eyes and
that is not desirable.

The color should not be garish, but rather *light* and
tasteful in the French manner. In *Colombe,* the theatre is the
world, the world which Anouilh loves and despises at the same
time because it is a place of beautiful illusion and terrible
cynicism, in contrast to Julien's inner world which is asceti-
cally pure and bleak. I want the set to be the most glamorous
of many seasons. I intend to heighten makeups, color of hair
and characterizations in line with this feeling I have about the
play.

Perhaps what I say here is more useful to the costume designer than to you, but I think you ought to know how I
sense the atmosphere of the play. One thing is sure, I am not
going to have a realistic production.

Love,
Harold

The Creation of the World and Other Business

by ARTHUR MILLER

(To be produced by Robert Whitehead; early fall, 1972.)

October 11, 1971

Dear Boris:

The Creation of the World and Other Business is a philosophic comedy or a comedy with philosophy. It is even more philosophy than comedy if we understand "comedy" not as rib-tickling jokes but as a special way of presenting vital matter.

The reason I insist on the "philosophical" aspect in this play is not intellectual but *theatrical*. I explain later on.

Though it is not strictly necessary for the purpose of this letter which is to guide you in my concept of the play (also Miller's), I shall summarize the play's philosophy in the simplest terms.

The *dramatic struggle* in the play—what the text calls the

"issue"—is what *principle* or *power* shall rule the world or who and what force must dominate in the world.

There are two principles: God, in every sense, the Father: powerful, benevolent, warm, hearty and sometimes so perplexed and confused by what he has created—the Family of Man—that he makes terrible mistakes and is rarely altogether sure he has done the right thing by his Family and his own intention. He is, in short, like every father and also like every great Artist—passionate, powerful, exalted and never sure his own work is as good as he wishes or thinks it is—and therefore he is in need of both praise *and* criticism.

Physically he is massive, commanding, sometimes unctuous, quick-tempered, irate and given to changing his mind—variable. He is also as cute as a bear, playful and "sensuous" like a man in love with his large brood of troublesome kids. He is *Love*—which is also variable and can be turned to fierceness and tremendous mischief. Love is not "sweetness and light," it's the surge of all creative force which sometimes deviates toward destructiveness but always aims at tenderness, harmony and passionate coherence. The author is on his side not because God is always "right," but because without him there is *Nothing*. It is he who created Life and the author is for an acceptance of life even in its ferocity. Man (who is in God's image) also has this desire, need, passion for the creative life force.

Lucifer is Reason, the corrector of God's possible errors in logic. Lucifer is the Awakener who sees the Father's and the Artist's errors and believes that he is "smarter" than Him—which he is—even more persuasive, because more logical—pure intelligence, in fact. Without the Awakener to challenge God and thus Man we should all stagnate. He is witty (whereas God is only kind, warm, or angry), he is keenly perceptive, lithe, handsome, with an electric mind. He knows his "weakness" (dryness of heart) but he believes he is right because he can *prove* it. He is in all of us, as is God, and his reason often triumphs or seems to because he is much more plausible than God, who at times is all "mixed up," as are Fathers and Artists.

I see Lucifer as slender (God is heavy), quick of mind and limb, a veritable *dancer* in body and spirit, a ham actor, a clown, a flirt, a lady's man, a killer of utmost fascination. God is a bass, Lucifer a tenor. God is ponderous, slow-moving, Lucifer quicksilver and varicolored—as the fireflies in the play who twinkle in the night as Lucifer's charming helpers.

Adam and Eve, Cain and Abel, are the pawns and instruments at the mercy of the two mighty forces which rule the *World*. Adam, good-looking, healthy, between thirty-five and forty, is the good ordinary man, who sides with the Establishment. He is *obedient* above all to God's will, knowing it is good—even if he hasn't the intelligence to understand Him. His heart is on God's side. He is moved by emotions more than thought—for this reason he suspects Lucifer and loves God, who like him is all *feeling*. He favors God's order. He has a good heart and partakes of God's *fatherliness*. He belongs to and with God—but he is of this earth. There is nothing "mystic" about him, but he is both superstitious and trusting.

Eve is the ingenue (Act I), she is the tormented one (Act II), she is the Mother who despite everything perpetuates the race and for which whatever we think of her frailty we must bless her—if we believe in the acceptance of God which is the Acceptance of Life—horror and all!) . . . She is attracted by Lucifer because he *is* attractive and brilliant, she is changeable and is also with God as she is with that other father, her husband Adam, and above all, despite pain, she wants *to give birth* to the race. She is the Earth Mother—she who bears us and bears with us. She so loves life that she will let her children play with her and even make love to her. For she lives through her children.

She should be between twenty-eight and forty: not "beautiful" (Hollywood style) but truly womanly. Hers is the glory and the anguish of life.

Cain is forever seeking righteousness and fearful of his own potential corruption. He is the average good man who suspects that he is no good at all. He is always eager to *"make good"* and wants assurance of it from some power that is above suspicion. He wants life to be fair to him, to be just and respectful of his good deeds and to reward him. When he is not rewarded, he sees no reason to believe in anything. But this, too, torments him. Therefore he *needs* religion: it is his only support. He needs God though God "betray" him.

He will go into the world, ever smiling as a man of the world, but gnawed by a sense of his own unworthiness, for he knows that he has killed and may kill again. He is forever torn between Heaven and Hell, God and Lucifer—he is what most of us are. . . . The actor who plays the part should have some of this Dostoevskian torment and "twistedness" in him: lean, a little devilish, as if he were related to Lucifer. He is inwardly restless and violent.

Abel is the pure, simple soul, loving, innocent, credulous and willing to accept everything at its face value—he doesn't speak of God or need him for he is without guile or guilt. He plays with his mother but he will not mount her with fierce desire as Cain does. He only wishes to love and to be *loved*. The desire to be *loved*, to win approval, is his "weakness"—which leads him to trouble.

THE PRODUCTION

I said this is a philosophical comedy. Which means that whatever else we accomplish, the *Words* and *Sense* of the play are more important than the Spectacle. If the *Words* aren't clear, striking, ringing, or if they are interfered with by any other stage element, the play as *meaning* will fail.

Therefore we must consider how to make the speakers stand out above everything else. The setting and background must be beautifully *Simple*. (When the world was created, it was bare. There wasn't very much there!) No matter what mechanical complexities are involved, to the spectator, the audience, the stage must look simple—even to the point of "bareness." We must forget the *Setting*, once we have admired and felt its tone. The setting should not express the play but serve as a background for it as well as a "machine or podium for the actors."

Therefore: (a) It should be or represent what the Germans call an *Erdball*, the globe, a *circle*, the WORLD itself. This circle should be made the inner frame behind which the action takes place and in front of which, if possible or desirable, Lucifer may step out of God's reach and soliloquize. But everything is contained within the *Circle* which is the World and which has the perfection and completion of circularity—no matter what terror occurs within it.

(b) The sky is important. It should be limpid, blue or cream white with occasional shots of red when storm and strife are indicated. All the colors, including that of the grass, should be on the lighter side of their vibrations, almost pastel. Delicate and very often transparent so that bushes, trees (as sparingly used as possible) may be employed as masking and when desired (as in Act III when Abel's bloody body is discovered) make visible what is behind it.

(c) Places to sit and lie down are boulders, rocks, stone protuberances—but not too many. Clear space must be provided on the forestage—most of the boulders upstage a bit—so that characters can move freely or dance: there are two real dances in the play: "God's waltz" with Eve and its distortion by Lucifer with Eve, Cain and Abel.

(d) The upper—heavenly level—should be circular too—a lateral half-moon going from its center upstage to downstage right and left. It must carry the throne for God and lesser seats—not chairs or thrones—for the angels (six or seven of them). Since God and Lucifer hold forth there, the upper level must be solid enough to support *nine* actors. This platform used only in Act I; first scene should either be lowered from the "flys" or rise from below. It must go out of sight in Act I, Scene 2.

(e) The Total Effect and Style is *Magical.* Thus God and Lucifer never enter or exit but appear and disappear—materialize or dematerialize mysteriously. God does walk off with the Family in Act III and comes in normally. Lucifer should sometimes seem to shoot up from below suddenly. God descends from above. This is also true when the Angels come down or return to Heaven. (Remember: Eve says Lucifer has come out of the mist.)

(f) Speaking of Magic: the electrician, the Light Designer or a person who is a magic specialist must know how to make fire sparks or smoke come out of blows, delivered by Lucifer and the Heavenly Creatures—just as the winds, animal noises and whatever not are created electronically.

(g) *Nakedness:* The simplest solution would be thin tights over naked bodies. On these may be drawn "leaves" (or nature spots) so that the tights look like the filmy waters of the lakes and the leaves which float or are shadowed on them. Adam's penis may be dimly perceived under the tights, which should also be true of Eve's breasts and pubic hair, or they may be shadowed over by one of the painted leaves.

I wouldn't want the "costume" for nakedness to be too clever or "original." Let us get as close to real nakedness as possible without competing with *Oh! Calcutta!*: embarrassing neither to actors nor to audience. The tights should be easy to slip off and be replaced by the large fig leaf between I and II.

(h) There is a tree of knowledge on stage with *an apple* (or two). But the script speaks of figs and pomegranates. Would these be on less conspicuous bushes or trees?

(i) The change from 1 and 1 (I hope it can be made in *one* minute) should be mostly a change of white or silvery blue light to sombre hues. The tree of knowledge can be rolled off with only scrubby bushes and rocks remaining. Perhaps the green grass of the ground cloth can through lighting lose its hue and seem ashen, dusty.

(j) A costume note: Lucifer when he first appears is in electric or steel blue—a *Radiance.*

General notes:

Let's not worry about too much *realism*.

Don't try to express everything in the play *scenically*: it will complicate matters and get in the way of the *all* important Words which express all the play's nuances. We are only there to help project them. The play is a dramatic debate—it is a *literary* play, essentially: the *writer's* play. The play's "Hebraic" quality is in the language. It will be in the intoning of some of the prayers, invocations, etc. It can be expressed, too, in the rough simplicity or rudeness of the *costumes* and props (such as the "throne" in Heaven).

Makeup, too, should highlight certain features: the handsomeness, Lucifer's wicked wit, the devil's torment in Cain, the gravity and awesomeness of God's body and *eye,* etc.

The lighting should be the most elaborate and complex of all the scenic elements. The *watchword* is *Simplicity*—plenty of *Air* on stage. *Gentle* colors.

Except for the Altar, rocks for reclining and other properties essential to Action, we must make it seem that there is really not much "scenery" at all—otherwise willy-nilly we shall move into the "musical" or "operatic" area. The sky can become "angry," "bloodshot," etc. But the effect, I repeat, must always return to a certain lightly tinted calm, an evaporating, a disappearing, a beautifully fading calm: the *Heavens* always return to serenity. Life goes on . . .

A raked stage is desirable. The last disappearance of God and Lucifer on either side of the stage will be helped by this— and they should "go out" magically, too—so to speak, forever.

None of this is easy: but it must never occur to the audience that it was difficult, that our solutions are complex and hazardous.

Good luck,
Harold

P.S.: We must try to make the play a two-act play. One minute after Scene 1; fifteen minutes between Scene 2 and Act III. Make very few changes between 2 and 3. If you want a deeper tonality for the ground cloth (earth) in the now Act II (formerly Act III), O.K., but your worry about the change of tone between the Beginning and the End is not altogether well-founded. The play is beautifully *unified*. There is as much seriousness as comedy in Act I—though it is not as strongly marked as at the end. The play is also—like the *world*—and the framework of the set—*circular*. It keeps coming back to its single theme: *who and what shall rule the world*. It is finally *Man* who is always closer to God's Love than to Lucifer's Reason—and that is why the world will roll on in perpetuity unless Reason (the Atom Bomb and other brilliant devices of reason) blow us all to Hell—which neither I nor Miller nor the play really believes to be our Destiny!

P.P.S.: The specific physical actions, pieces of business, are clearly marked in the text and may be followed literally. I need not repeat them. If any special idea occurs to me which affects you, I'll let you know.

Index